HERE WE GO AGAIN!

A candid autobiography

of the life and times

of a

WW2 RAF Veteran

and

Entrepreneur

By

George Pritchard

Co-Author - Penny Stevens

TABLE OF CONTENTS

Dedication

This autobiography is a tribute to all of my family, friends and colleagues over the years, and to all those past comrades, some of whom were sadly lost in the act of a senseless war........

Foreword by co-author Penny Stevens

As co-author of this book for my father, George, I have immensely enjoyed recording all the stories and anecdotes from his lifetime to this present day in 2022. Most of these aspects of his life he has shared with us, his children, over the Sunday dinner table, where we have listened in fascination to all the antics he got up to as a boy, during the war, his time in active service in the RAF and his working life. He has a way of re-telling stories to bring them alive and make us laugh till our sides are splitting. Of course, for us as children back then, they were embellished time and time again.

As we grew into adulthood, my siblings and I have often urged him to set his chronicles and anecdotes to paper in the form of a book for others to enjoy. He has always had an amazing memory for names, dates, incidents and detail and, of course, an amazing ability to 'tell' the story. Plus, the fact that he definitely had nine lives!

As time has gone on and my father, still working, I might add, has now reached his ninety-ninth year. I have found more time, since my recent retirement, to visit my father, and we have spent many a happy day chatting about life back then. Armed with a handy mobile phone to record all that he said, afternoons would pass by in a flash, and I would go home to type up the day's recordings onto my computer. With all the problems of the Covid19 pandemic affecting our regular get-togethers, my father would often send me chapters that he had typed up on his iPad for me to edit and add as another chapter in his life story. What had started out as a short booklet for the family to enjoy, has eventually led to the makings of quite a substantial book. We have tried to place the anecdotes in this book in sequential order and with some accuracy regarding dates, but there may be a few accounts where my father's memory of the date is not so accurate.

One particular story that stands out in my mind from my childhood, is that of the Hindenburg, a German air ship that eventually met it's Waterloo in the USA in 1937. This was his version of the story told to us as children.....

Dad tells of a time when he was young, just before the war in June 1936, when he and his brother, Charlie, were sitting playing in their shorts and T-shirts, like most 12-year-old boys did in those times, kicking at the dust or hedging some plan to occupy their time on that day. Suddenly, they felt the world around them darkening as a great shadow enveloped them from above. As they looked upwards, they saw, to their disbelief, a great sausage-shaped dark and ominous shape. They were scared! They had heard stories about these great airships from their mother related to the Great War. They had heard the people inside them talked about as 'wicked' people; 'nasty' people (Nazis). Like all young boys, they wanted to save their beloved country from any wickedness, and it was down to them to develop a great plan. They ran into the house and hedged their devious plan. They came out brandishing their catapults, feeling like the heroes in their comics. They followed the great airship along the streets of Thornton Heath in South London on that sunny day in June, firing small pebbles at this monstrosity.

"It's a hit!" they shouted with glee, as the last pebble found its target and the monstrosity burst with a loud 'bang' and gradually deflated, somewhat like a burst balloon, whizzing across the sky backwards and forwards. The boys watched in awe as the monstrosity got smaller and smaller, dancing across the sky, eventually landing in a nearby field. They looked at each other in horror! Oh no! they were for it now. On arriving back home, they nonchalantly wandered into the house, whistling in unison, to hide their Catapults away from the prying eyes of their mother and younger brother.

"I do hope you boys have not been up to any mischief?" says mum, wiping her hands on her pinny.

"Us? No!" two guilty-looking faces grin at her.

The story then continues in many different ways, from police experts searching for a British spy plotting the downfall of the airship, to veterans from the Great War seeking a personal vendetta. No-one suspected those two innocent boys!!

I believed this story for many years. Ha!

The belief we have in our parents!

Now approaching his hundredth birthday, he has decided to write his autobiography. The autobiography, in its entirety, is either written by my father on his computer or recorded on a mobile phone, and then transcribed by me over a period spanning five years. He is now 98 years old as we finish the book. It may not necessarily all be in chronological order, but it's as near as we can make it.

Covid 19 has meant that for the past two years, he has seen very few people through his door and was not able to go out or use the car, a situation which he (along with the rest of the nation) has found very frustrating, but hopefully, we look forward to better times as we move through 2022. He still works, is still active and independent and has only recently stopped driving.

His story is one that I think will touch the hearts of many and tells of the many facets of wartime Britain, and its impact on his life and the lives of others. It will tell the story of an intelligent and positive-thinking individual, who has truly succeeded in life due to his positive outlook, his tenacity and single-minded determination. Many of the things he has done in his working life have had a tremendous impact on the lives of many individuals, including saving many lives through his inventions in the medical field and beyond.

We sincerely hope that you will enjoy reading it.

Penny Stevens (nee Pritchard) daughter of George Pritchard

July 2022

Preface by the Author George Pritchard

My four children have always listened most attentively to my telling of stories and the adventures from my youth, my wartime in Britain as an RAF pilot, and my working life. Many afternoons of laughter have been shared by my wife, Florence, and I, as we reminisced with our children and their families over the years.

My children, and grandchildren, have always urged me to put pen to paper so that they, and others, can enjoy my many tales of joy, sadness, exhilarating and near-death experiences; the lessons I have learnt and the many skills I have acquired as I journeyed through my life.

And I haven't finished yet!

George Pritchard

Acknowledgements

I would like to express my sincere thanks to my daughter, Penny, for all her hard work in helping me to get my story onto paper.

Thank you also to all my family and friends I have met on this journey who have encouraged me to create this book.

First, A Bit of Family History

My maternal grandfather, Bill Crockett, was married and living in Glasgow until around 1900, when my mother, Annie, was born. He brought his whole family to live in London, where there were more jobs. He had been working as the foreman in the maintenance team on the trams in Glasgow. On one particular day, it was the birthday of one of the 'gang', so they all decided to go to the pub for a quick round of 'half' a beer each. Unfortunately, they didn't only stop at one half and, after a few halves, they had been gone for over an hour and returned to work, some 'a bit worse for wear'.

The superintendent was there waiting for them on their return and was not looking too happy, "You are supposed to be setting an example and keeping these people in order, but you are worse than any of them," he said to my grandfather.

"Well, it was a birthday, and we were celebrating, and I couldn't get them back once we were in there," my grandfather explained good-humouredly. The superintendent was having none of it and fired him on the spot.

Jobs were hard to get then, and he knew he wouldn't get another job with the bus company; or, indeed, any other bus company in Glasgow. He was out of work and had a family of hungry mouths to feed; a wife, three sons, and a baby daughter (my mother, Annie). After some deliberation, he decided to uproot the whole family and head to London. He had been reliably informed that London Transport, then called Thomas

Tillings, was looking for trolley bus drivers and maintenance workers to employ. He decided that he would first go and secure a job and a place to live, and then send for the family.

In those days, Scottish engineers had a reputation of being the best, probably because of all the ship building, so he was interviewed and instantly offered the job as a foreman. He found a house for the family to live in at 8 Burlington Road, Thornton Heath, which was handy for him, being close to the tram stop to get him quickly to work. He approached his boss after a week, asking if he could have a shift for that week to allow him time to go to Glasgow and get the family. The boss was very understanding and told him to take his time and that he could have two days off to do this. The family packed up their things, sold most of the furniture, and headed south to London via train and tram, bags in every spare hand, arriving in their newly acquired, empty house in London. They then set about trying to find second-hand furniture in the next week to furnish the house and make it more habitable. Many years later, once my grandparents had passed away, that same house was rented out to a Welsh family, their daughter was called Dorothy. She became a great friend of ours, and through her, I met Florence, my wife. Dorothy had been her school penfriend, and when she came down to London, Florence had lodged with Dorothy's family.

What a coincidental set of events which led us to meet!

I was named George Wellesley Pritchard and was born in Croydon on 25th January 1924 to parents George Wellesley

Pritchard (senior) and Annie Crocket, who had been married the year before. In the 1920's they lived in two rooms in my grandfather's house in South Norwood, where I slept in a cot. My younger brother, Charlie, slept in the bed with my parents, and my younger sister, Phyllis, slept in a drawer in the wardrobe. Then, in 1930, we moved to a private house in Purley Way, Croydon, near the airport, which we rented for 7 shillings a week (quite a lot of money then). My father didn't like paying so much, as it was nearly a weekly wage for many people. A little later on, my parents had two more sons, Peter and Edward. For us, it was great living near the airport, as we would see famous people like Amy Johnson, Jim Mollison etc., as they travelled to and from the airport. Charlie, my brother, and I were old enough to be in the forces during WW2. Phyllis and Peter were too young, though Phyllis did serve in the land army for a while, and the youngest, Edward, died before the war from Diphtheria, aged 3.

Later in the war, Charlie signed up and served in the Fleet Air Arm on an aircraft carrier called the Courageous. He was sent to operate from Ceylon in the Pacific War fighting the Japanese. They were joined by the Americans and regularly attacked by Kamikaze pilots. Sadly he was only 44 when he died from throat cancer due to smoking.

George, Charlie and their father, George senior

PART 1 – LIFE BEGINS

The highs, the lows

the withs and withouts

1. Early years & Schooldays – 1924-1938

I really wanted to be part of an aircrew in order to get my revenge on the enemy for what they did to all my lovely friends, both men and women, who were killed at the cardboard box factory, where I worked, when it was bombed. Those were my feelings in 1940. Feelings that made me feel very patriotic towards my country.

I always had a love of flying machines, and some of my earliest memories were of times as a lad when I would spend hour upon hour, finding out about the physics and mechanics of flight in building my own model aircraft, destroying my mother's best tablecloth with glue and cuts in the meantime!

So, where did these two passions in my life lead me? Perhaps it would be best to start with my earliest memories and to tell the story of ME.

....

One of my earliest memories is with my brother and parents when I was two years old. I remember my father telling me off because I was rattling the cot. Another is of sitting at the window on a snowy day, seeing my uncle Vic coming towards the house and of me shouting to my mum, "Uncle Vic's here!"

I also distinctly remember sitting on the stairs in the afternoon waiting for my grandfather to come in because he always brought me sweets. Fond memories, indeed!

We lived in a three-bedroom house, so my sister had the box room, my two brothers and I had the middle room, and the baby, Edward, slept in my parents' bed with them.

For me, school was always an experience! And one that I enjoyed, most of the time. I started school in 1929 at the age of five at Boston Road School in Croydon, London. In readiness for my first day at school, my mother had managed to get some good clothes for me to start school in, second-hand, of course, but perfectly serviceable, nevertheless. Times were hard, and we often had to share clothes or make use of worn hand-me-downs. It was such a memorable day for me. I very much remember looking forward to meeting new children and sitting in a classroom learning with a respected teacher, the kind that you will remember all your life. But things didn't quite go according to plan! During playtime, when I was innocently looking forward to kicking a ball around and making new friends, some older boys set upon me, probably because I was new and dressed relatively smartly compared to them. You see, I was wearing a tie! And this was just too smart in their eyes. After a few pushes, kicks and the odd punch, I eventually ended up being rescued by a teacher, with my cuts and bruises being patched up before sending me off home at the end of the day. I returned home in a rather dishevelled state, with torn clothes and a lovely black eye to boot.

Needless to say, my father was really not impressed when he saw me arrive home. It was then that he decided to give me boxing lessons and instructions on how to properly defend myself in all circumstances. My father enjoyed participating in the sport himself and would often attend matches in the local boxing ring, participating himself at times. Therein began my interest and another life-long passion in boxing. This was the best thing he ever could have done for me and, indeed, it has got me out of many a tough and tricky situation throughout my life (and into more than I ought to mention!).

I had many interests and hobbies; making model aeroplanes was one hobby that continued throughout my childhood. I was also into every kind of sport, running, football, boxing, everything. I joined the school boxing club (it was a popular sport in those days) and played football with the local lads and at school.

When I was five years of age, the family moved to Purley Way, near Croydon. This was right near Croydon Airport, a main airport in those days. Throughout my childhood, I was transfixed by the planes I saw on a day-to-day basis, not half a mile from my home. I saw the 'flying flea', a tiny aeroplane, Amy Johnson as she left for and returned from her famous flights, Jim Mollison and so forth.

As I grew up a little, I used to visit the aerodrome alone, where there was a huge field where it was possible to fly model aircraft; the members of Croydon Model Aircraft Club would often fly their model planes there too. I have mentioned this passion for all flying aircraft, so I set about the task of designing and making my own model aircraft, which really did fly rather well. I would save up the pennies and buy balsa wood to carve and make into the bodies of the aircraft, and would use paper glued over a framework for the wings; I even carved the propeller. Any scrap item found in the garden or the street, would have a use at some time or another. One day I arrived at the field with my latest design and prepared to wind up the elastic in order to send her off. One of the men from the Model Flying Club came over to me and showed an interest in my model.

"What's that?" he asked, "That's a weird-looking thing. Where did you get that model from?" he asked me.

"I made it myself," came the reply, of course!

"Oh, I've not seen a kit in that style before," he replied.

I told him that it wasn't a kit, it was my own design that I had made on my own from scrap. He found it hard to believe me.

"Ohhh! That will never fly though, young man," he laughed. I proved him wrong on that count. I wound it up with a hand drill, set the tail rudder and the ailerons so that it would fly in a circle, held it high, then let go, and it flew perfectly around in a large circle, landing purposely at my feet again. The man's jaw nearly hit the ground.

"Are you going to join our club?" he asked.

"I haven't got the money," I replied. He congratulated me on my model and then embarrassedly went back to playing with his own plane. They found it hard to understand that I was capable of making a model.

Later, I moved on to secondary school at The Kingsley School, which was even rougher. It was tough too. In those days, the boys and girls were separated into different buildings, having separate playgrounds as well. The only thing we saw of the girls was when they were jumping up to shoot into the net in netball. Boys came to school without shoes or maybe just plimsolls in the coldest of weather. There was no lunch provided, just a free government issue of a tiny bottle of milk to fill our bellies during the morning break. For school, I had to wear my mother's old cut-down shoes, which were excruciatingly crippling on my feet. Boys wearing girls' tops and their sisters' shoes was the norm, so no one made fun of your attire here, to my relief. However, my new-born skills in boxing meant that I was able to survive against all comers at the school, and so I soon joined the school boxing team. Boxing was a very popular pastime and sport in those days. It was also often the way that playground and street altercations were resolved, generally looked upon and approved of by school staff watching from a discrete distance.

There was one teacher, a rather small man, who some of the other boys bullied relentlessly. They were very big boys and were too much to handle for this rather frail, small, ineffective man. On one particular day, they held him out of the first-floor window and dropped him to the ground below. It's a wonder they didn't kill him! Poor fellow, I did feel sorry for him – it was a rough school. Boys who couldn't fight with their fists and stand their corner were bullied, and they really suffered.

Being a fairly bright boy, or so I was often told, I did well enough in the boxing ring and also in all my school subjects, but I was not 'chosen' to sit the eleven-plus exam. You see, in those days, it was the prerogative of the class teacher to select those pupils who were deemed 'good' enough to take the eleven-plus examinations for them to attend grammar school. However, they were not always necessarily chosen on the merit of their academic competence, but sometimes on whether they were 'liked' by their teacher or not, as the case may be. I was NOT considered 'good enough' because my teacher at the time did not really like me; I was NOT a teacher's pet. It was all my father's fault, really.

My trouble with the Teachers (who were all male figures) was due to a caning I had received for a very minor misdemeanour. In those days, a caning was given as a reprimand for many minor and major offences. My class teacher gave this caning to me, amounting to six bleeding cuts across the palm of my hand. And it really hurt! I felt that this punishment was rather excessive for simply blowing a raspberry to another boy during lessons (actually, he had started it). In those days, you didn't go home telling tales on the teacher for fear of another caning and your parent saying that you obviously deserved it. So, on arrival at home, I endeavoured to hide my hands from the prying eyes of my father for fear of further retribution. But not much got passed his beady eyes, and he soon noticed me holding my hands under my arms. On inspection of the wounds, he stared at me and asked me the name of my teacher and class.

Now, my father was a figure to be reckoned with, and one did not tell fibs because he could see right through a lie. Obviously, I had to tell him, but I spent a very restless night wondering why he needed to know and what he was going to do about it. The next morning, I hoped he had forgotten the incident, and I headed cheerily off to school. The afternoon came, and we were all working diligently in the classroom, heads down, when I happened to look out of the window and saw a very familiar figure marching across the playground. My stomach lurched! Suddenly, my father burst into the classroom, called me out to the front to stand with him and the teacher, and said to me, "Show him your hands." The teacher, I could see, was quite rattled and told my father to "get out of here!" My father did no more than punch the teacher very hard, and, to my horror, he fell to the floor right in front of me, accompanied by the loud cheers of all the boys in the class. I was mortified! The headmaster soon arrived and said he was calling the Police but, when shown my scarred hands, swiftly apologised and hurried my father out of the school. From then onwards, I was picked on by all the school's teachers, and there was definitely no eleven plus for me!

There were many sad times in the school classroom in those days. You would start the year with about 20 or so children in September, and by the time the end of the year came around, there would probably only be about 15 children left, evidenced by the empty seats. Children would die from polio, tuberculosis, diphtheria, and other diseases that have virtually been eradicated in the UK nowadays. It was part of life in those days. Even my siblings were hospitalised with diphtheria, but luckily most of them survived; I lost one brother aged 3. I was quite lucky as I didn't seem to get any of those life-threatening diseases.

It was very difficult for my father to get sufficient work at that time in his mid-thirties, and he barely earned one shilling a day. Before the war, we really didn't have much food at all. They were lean times, and it was really tough. Sugar sandwiches were a very common meal if there was nothing else, which was quite the norm, sometimes jam and butter on the bread if we were lucky. None of us liked margarine at all; we wouldn't eat it, so my mother had to get butter, which of course, would run out early in the week as supplies were limited, so then we'd have no butter on our bread. The baker would bring the bread van around – it was a horse and cart, and he would sell bread, jam, butter and sugar. My mother would get two loaves most of the time and, if she could afford it, some jam. Because the baker knew my mother, she could get it from him on account, which she settled at the end of each month, if she could. The baker was very good, and he always knew that he would get paid, eventually. We loved loganberry jam, which my grandmother often used to make; it was our favourite. Sometimes we would have tapioca or rice as it was only about one penny for each of these staple foods, which were sold in very large bags.

We were always hungry. We would have a slice of bread and butter for breakfast, jam if there was some, and that would have to last us until the evening. There was no school lunch or packed lunch in those days, so we would get home from school, and we might get a small baked potato each, or bread and sugar (which was very cheap at the time). No wonder everyone had rotten teeth!

Later on, when my father started to get a bit of money, things got a bit better in the food department. We would then occasionally have a little meat, sausages or liver, the cheap meats, except at the weekend. At the weekend, my father would be there for Sunday dinner, so my mother would often send me to get the meat from the butcher. She would give me a shilling (old money) on a Saturday to go to the market at around 9 pm in the hope of getting a joint of meat for the family's Sunday dinner, as Saturday night is when the butcher would usually auction off any leftover meat. The means of refrigeration was not very good in those days, so Butchers did not keep much meat over the weekend. My mother would give me instructions to not get a lamb breast as it was too fatty, and to make sure that it was a lean and meaty joint of meat. Mum always hoped that one day I might get an 'H' bone of beef rather than small pieces of cheaper cuts of beef or lamb that was our usual fare.

The butcher had come to know me quite well over time and was often kindly in providing for our growing family. I was there every Saturday, money in hand, looking for the best cut of meat I could find, usually lamb or beef if I could. I always had to wait very patiently as it would be towards the end of the auction that the best bargains were to be had. One day, the butcher was particularly generous and made my mum an extremely happy lady. It was one Saturday, whilst I was standing at the front of the crowd, shilling in hand in my pocket, big, doe eyes looking upwards expectantly, that the butcher asked ME what I wanted and how much money I had. I think he felt sorry for me because when I told him in the barest of whispers that I had a shilling and threepence, and my mum wanted that joint of beef (pointing only to the biggest and best).

"Oh! does she now?" he said, laughing. But he immediately put one up for auction, and in spite of many raised hands offering far more money, he sold it to me. Now that joint of beef could probably have fetched him ten times what I had in my hand! My jaw dropped, and then a toothy smile spread across my face. I couldn't believe my luck and raced home in the gaslight at the fastest pace, clutching the valuable, wrapped joint to my chest as if it were a precious baby.

My mother could not believe what I had acquired when I arrived home at 10.30 pm. She then eyed me suspiciously and said, "You haven't stolen it have you?" I told her vehemently that the butcher knew me from my weekly appearances and had been kind enough to favour me. I was an honest boy, and stealing was not in my nature. I think deep down, mum knew that too; she just couldn't believe what I had managed to get.

Dad was particularly pleased as he went into the garden to dig up some horseradish to accompany the beef along with vegetables from grandad's allotment garden, mum's roast potatoes and gravy, and maybe a little rice and jam to follow. Heaven! Needless to say, we all tucked into a hearty Sunday dinner, and I was the hero of the hour! The bone would then be used to make a hearty stew and soup for the next few days. I'm sure that beef tasted better in those days, or maybe it's just that we didn't often get the chance to have such a lovely meal.

When we were not at school, my brother, Charlie, and I, aged about 11 and 12 at the time, would go up to the street market and walk along the pavement behind each of the fruit and vegetable stalls looking for damaged fruit that had been thrown into an old box behind the stall because it could not be sold. We would then 'recycle' it. We were generally 'good' boys and would never steal. One day there were some lovely oranges sitting in a box on the ground, which we assumed were for the bin. Lovely, we thought! We picked them up and then were caught red-handed, and the police were called. We were arrested by the police because the oranges were designated for the stall and were not damaged goods. We were taken to the police station. On questioning, we avoided telling them our correct address, instead giving them a false address. We were scared to tell them because we knew our father would give us a belting if he found out. The police were wise to this, and in the end, we had to tell them. Later, there was a knock on our front door, which was answered by our very shocked mother when she saw her two eldest boys and a policeman standing there; thank goodness our father wasn't home at the time. Mum didn't tell, and our father never did find out! Thank you, mother. So that put paid to us ever doing that again, cutting off a good source of food.

It was 1937, and I distinctly remember my brother, Charlie, and I, sitting on the curb in the street outside our grandmother's house in Thornton, Heath, because our mother was in the hospital. It was a lovely sunny day, and we were passing the time, playing in the dirt. All of a sudden, the brilliant daylight became really dark as a great big shadow loomed over us from above with a roaring noise, which really frightened us. We both looked up, and there was an almighty great airship, the Hindenburg, flying over us with six very large engines roaring away. We had heard all the stories of the Zeppelin air raids during the first world war, so we ran into our grandmothers, thinking the world was going to end at that moment.

"There's a great big Zeppelin overhead, Gran, we think it's going to bomb us!" we shouted in unison. Gran laughed.

The Zeppelin moored up at a mooring tower, probably at Crystal Palace, where it would let people on and off for their journey. Once we had realised that it was harmless to us, we could appreciate its beauty and was quite a sight to see, quite a sedate form of transport in those days. The trouble was they were full of hydrogen gas which was very volatile. We heard that not long afterwards, on May 6th 1937, it tragically caught fire, and many passengers and crew were killed. The Americans discovered that helium was a better gas as it was not so explosive, though they did not share their ability to make helium gas with the British or the Germans at that time.

Charlie and I developed a love of 'scrumping' in order to make up for not being able to go to the street market anymore. There was a private school nearby, The Ruskin School, and they had a lovely large orchard on their grounds, easily accessible via a high fence, which we had no problem negotiating. It was a very posh school. We would climb the trees and fill our shirts and pockets to bulging point with beautiful pears, plums and apples to take home. Our father would come home from work to see, on the table, a row of lovely pieces of fruit laid out for him. "Where did you boys get these lovely pears from?" he would say.

"We went scrumping, dad," we would answer.

"Oh, that's alright then," would come the answer. Scrumping – a childhood ritual in those days. Where are all those lovely orchards now?

We didn't really get much at Christmas as there was never any money for presents. But my mother would do her best and tuck a few things in socks, such as sweets, a biscuit, and little packets of this and that. My grandparents would also give us fruit and a few nuts. One year my father must have had some money come in from the horse races or somewhere. He bought us all a small present, but he got me a little 'cinema' toy with a

Charlie Chaplin tape that you would put in, switch it on (it had batteries in it), and it would play a bit of 35mm film onto the wall or a sheet. I loved it, and I was fascinated with it, playing with it all the time in my bedroom. I had it for a week, and then, on returning from school one day, I found that it was missing. I looked everywhere for it. Eventually, I asked my mother if she had seen it anywhere, thinking that we must have had burglars or something, to which she answered that my father had taken it back to the shop to get it mended.

"But there was nothing wrong with it!" I replied, starting to get anxious now.

"Oh, yes," she said, "He thought there was something wrong with it. It will be back soon, maybe in a week."

I found out a week later that what he had done was taken it back to the shop, saying there was something wrong with it, and got his money back. I never saw that lovely toy again; I was gutted, and it really upset me.

We would often be seen sitting on the curb surrounded by muddy puddles and horse muck with nothing much to do, other than getting out from under the adults' feet. We had a very tough upbringing, but it put me in good stead for when I joined the RAF.

When I was thirteen, my brothers and my sister all had contracted diphtheria and had to spend some weeks in hospital. Sadly, our youngest brother, Edward, died, aged just three years old, from diphtheria and pneumonia. This was, of course, an awful time for all of us. It was very common in those days to lose a young child. I was lucky enough never to have had any of these nasty illnesses, and to be honest, I don't really remember ever having been ill apart from maybe mumps.

After Xmas, in 1938, just before my fourteenth birthday, I left school. Following the Christmas holiday period, I went to the job exchange to look for work as I felt that times were hard for my mother, and I wanted to help provide for our family as best I could as my father was a bit stingy. I found employment at a firm of electricians called Buxton and Longley as an apprentice. My wage would then help my mother to make ends meet and to be able to afford to put some more food on the table for the family.

I had mentioned that I have always had this passion for aircraft and all things to do with flying, so when I was fourteen or fifteen, I joined the Air Cadets, which later became called the Air Training Corps. I had a uniform, and I really looked smart dressed up in it, ready to go to a meeting. We used to have lectures and talks on aeroplanes. The man who was running it was an ex-WW1 pilot, and he used to tell us all the stories about the camaraderie that went on in those days when flying the Sopwith Camels with the Germans and their Fokkers (Fokwulf's) and shooting them up. There were many interesting stories to keep us all keen to learn about flying. He would teach us about aeronautics, navigation and all sorts of things about aeroplanes. Then we would practice marching up and down the parade ground and saluting, turning in formation and so on. I was in the Air Cadets until I was sixteen or seventeen, and then I lost the will to attend because one of the fella's who ran it was 'interested' in young men, and I didn't want him paying attention to me, so sadly, I left. I had met Florence by that time and was hard at work, so I had other things to occupy my time and interests.

I sometimes did washing-up for my mother and various other little chores that needed doing. One day I had worked a long, hard week as an electrician, and it was on a very late Saturday evening that I returned home from work, utterly exhausted. My mother had dinner waiting for me on the table; the rest of the family had all just eaten. Then, at the end of my meal, I thanked her and told my parents that I was exhausted and going to bed. I was just about to excuse myself, when my father told me to go and do the washing-up. I was not sure why it had to be me – all my other siblings were perfectly capable and hadn't been hard at work all day, but I couldn't argue. I probably swore at him under my breath, but I would do anything to help my mother, so, despite my tiredness, I did it; otherwise, I would have been clobbered!

We knew the war was coming. As soon as war was imminent, the government supplied every household with an Anderson shelter. It was a Sunday, and my father, Charlie and I set about digging the first hole in our grandparents' garden, arriving armed with spades and forks.

"You're not bloody digging up my lawn and garden!" warned my grandfather, who had always been very proud of his garden.

"When the German bombs come in, you'll be glad to be in there," countered my father. Grandad really couldn't believe that his garden would get hit – he was reckoning on the air force holding back the German planes and chasing them off, like they did to the Zeppelins in WW1.

"It's the law, you've got to have it," said my father, in his 'I'm having no nonsense' tone of voice. So, we set about digging a great hole in his lawn; there were tears in his eyes as it was his pride and joy, it was like a billiard table. It was quite heavy work, digging down about four feet, but we managed to complete it in good time and erected the Anderson shelter, with even a passing nod of satisfaction from my father on our abilities that day. On the following Monday, my father told my brother and me to start digging the shelter for our garden.

"You were keen on digging great holes as kids, so now I'm letting you dig a really big one, so get going! I will mark it out for you and come back later to see how you're getting on." And with that, he retreated to the house. Charlie and I knew what we were doing by now. So we began the digging, finishing fairly quickly before our father came out to inspect our progress, smiling and acknowledging our achievement, whilst giving us a bit of a help to complete the task. We bolted it all together, put sandbags around it, and that was it, done. Good job as my mother and my siblings, Phyllis and Peter, spent nearly every night in it in 1940 and 1941 during the Blitz, and a bit of 1943 when the fly-bombs came over. It was fitted out with bunks, beds, blankets and shelves, and even had some water, tins of food, biscuits and tea-making paraphernalia. My brother, Peter, used to get very screwed up with all the bombing at night. He was only about six or seven years old at the time. Phyllis just shrugged it off; it didn't seem to worry her much at all. During the fly-bombs, my mother, Peter and Phyllis went up North to stay for almost a year in Ashington, Northumberland, with Florence's family, where they were safe away from most of the relentless bombing.

We got along well as siblings. We all used to fight amongst one another from time to time, as do all siblings, but if any of us were being bullied or picked on, then we would all be down upon the perpetrators immediately; such was our close bond with each other. Phyllis, the only girl amongst four boys, could handle herself really well. She would clout anyone who stepped out of line. In early 1944 she joined the land army, working on farms with animals and planting out fields. She loved it and had some great fun with all the other girls on the farm. She could stand up for herself, and others, amongst any bullying types on the farm too. Peter was too young to serve during the war, but after the war, conscription was mandatory, and he volunteered to join the RAF Regiment, serving in the fighting against the communists in the Troodos Mountains in Greece. The Regiment was a very hard-hitting band of troops who had a very tough time in the mountains for near on two years. He didn't talk much about it on his return.

2. My First Job – As an Electrician - 1938

It is 1938, and I was by now working for an electrical installer as an electrician's mate with a weekly pay packet of 16 shillings for a forty-eight-hour week, plus one week's holiday per year. The company was run by two men, Buxton and Longley. Longley was a really nice fellow who ran the business and electrical shop. Buxton ran all the outside contracts. The work was hard with very long hours. The electrician and I would arrive at the company's yard at 7.30 am and load the large, wheeled cart with lots of equipment to enable us to install electricity in a house, completely converting it from gas lighting to an electrical lighting system and installing the ring main. We then had to pull the cart for around a mile or so to the designated house.

After a discussion with the housewife, or the man of the house, about the work we were going to do, we began our task. This involved moving furniture and lifting the linoleum, which was always difficult as it had a tendency to tear easily; they were never very happy about that. We then lifted the necessary floorboards and I, being rather scrawny and small at that age, went underneath the floor, in the small space that there usually was between the wooden floor and the mud or concrete, among the spider's webs with the electrical conduit to just below the point where the three-pin socket was planned to be fitted above the floorboard level. This happened with every room, including the loft area. We allowed ourselves a ten-minute break for a cup of water and a chunk of bread at midday. Then we continued on until the cable was laid, the sockets and light switches mounted, the distribution board installed, and the job was finished, which was usually around 6 pm, though some jobs went on much later as they had to be finished on the day. On many occasions, the boss of the Company, Mr Buxton, who was a right bully, would arrive around 5 pm and shout at us to get a move on, unfairly threatening the electrician I was working under with the sack if he could not complete the task in a timely way. On finishing the refit and testing the installation, we had to pack all our equipment back on the cart, tidy up after us and head back the mile or so to the yard, where we had to unpack everything and lock up. The poor fellow was exhausted and always feeling rather stressed and miserable after one of Buxton's visits, as he had five young children and a wife at home who all needed feeding and a roof over their heads on the meagre wage he was paid. I would arrive home absolutely exhausted to eat a meal and go straight off to bed. Such was my introduction to the world of work!

I continued to work as a trainee electrician for some months until one day, my electrician partner did not turn up for work as he was ill. I just stood in the yard waiting for him. I didn't have a key to the equipment yard; otherwise, I would have loaded up the cart in readiness; I knew by now what equipment we needed to take with us. Eventually, the Boss came into the yard to tell me that my partner had reported in ill, so I could go into the retail shop and attend to any customers' needs, but that

I had to call for the storekeeper to deal with any money being paid. I quite liked working in the shop as it was an easy day and entailed no hard work, so, with great gusto, I set about dusting all of the stock of radios, electric clocks, toasters etc.

In stock, there was one of the recently invented Baird television sets that shone a cathode ray tube onto a rotating mirror reflected onto another glass mirror in its lid, so we watched the image in the mirror. It was a huge floor-standing cabinet and very heavy. I learned how to operate it while I was working in the shop. In those early days, television only had two hours a day of programmes, which were in the afternoon. So, one day, I had what I thought was a brilliant idea to encourage business. I moved everything around in the shop, set out a dozen chairs and invited people in to watch this latest invention. It wasn't long before the shop was full of the young and the curious, all watching their first viewing of television. I was convinced the Boss would be really proud of me! Suddenly, the Boss arrived to check on my progress. He was definitely NOT amused when he saw all the people languishing on his chairs and threw all of the customers out. Then later, realising that some of the 'audience' had taken the opportunity to steal some of the shop's stock – electric clocks, razors, irons, all sorts of things that could be fitted under a coat, he took his anger out on me. I was NOT in his good books and found that I was not going to be given that promotion I'd been dreaming about or allowed in the shop anymore. I was then given the task of stripping some old, lead-covered cable instead. So, feeling a bit downhearted, as I was only trying to help to boost business, I did as I was told, and sat in the yard with a mountain of cable and a pair of cutters. Once each piece of cable was stripped, I put all of the lead in a bucket and wrapped the cable up neatly, thinking the cable was what was needed. When finished, I decided to do my bit for the environment and help out my boss, so I sold the lead to the local scrap metal dealer, very pleased with myself for taking the initiative to recycle unwanted materials. When the Boss reappeared, he took a look at what I had done and nearly had a fit when he realised that I had saved the cable and not the valuable lead that was on the outside of the cable.

"That money for the lead was to go to the firm's annual outing!" he shouted, going really red in the face. I wasn't to know, so I duly handed over to him the money I had earned from the sale of the lead. Obviously, the scrap merchant had been delighted when he received his goods for so little cost and the money had not been anywhere near enough. Needless to say, he sacked me!

PART 2 – LIFE IN THE FAST LANE

War begins-

The highs, the lows, at altitude and at ground level

3. Working for Acme, 1938-1941

My next job, aged 16, was at the Acme Corrugated Paper & Box factory that was on the perimeter of Croydon Airport in Purley Way (Acme Manufacturing Corrugated Containers at the rear of British NSF and next to Bourjois Paris). The workforce there were a great crowd, many of them young 18 to 20-year-olds, with some older workers in their 30s. We had great laughs all day long; we all got on so well. I was trained to use a huge corrugating machine, and after a few lessons on its operation, I worked on it proficiently. I must say that working there was the happiest time in my working life. It was run in just such a way that ensured that everyone was happy and content; there was always a wonderful atmosphere, with many young women and young men all in good spirits, singing songs and telling jokes and just getting along with each other. Everyone was so friendly, and we were well looked after by the factory managers. This kind of atmosphere seemed to create good work ethics, and I am sure the factory received a greater output as a consequence. I just couldn't get there quick enough in the mornings!

Many months passed, and I was always eager to try to work a few extra hours to earn a few more shillings, but I was never allowed to as, at sixteen years of age, I was still too young. It didn't stop me from asking, just in case. On this one fateful day, 15th August 1940, I was sent home at 5 pm as usual, as I was under 18 years old and not allowed to work overtime. War had been declared, and the company I worked for had been making boxes for ammunition and such like for the Government, hence the opportunity for overtime for most of the workers.

So, I rode home on my bike, wishing myself just that bit older so that I could earn a little more to help my mother out at home. On arriving home, I found my mother and father having tea in the garden, and I joined them. Whilst we were sitting there, we saw a large number of twin-engine aircraft flying overhead, and it looked like parachutists were dropping out of them. We very quickly realised that they were bombs – evidenced by the loud bangs and resulting fires in the distance. They were over Croydon Airport, only about a mile and a half away from us, dropping bombs on the Airport. Then the RAF Hurricanes, based at Kenley, managed to get quickly airborne and arrived on the scene to begin shooting them down and give chase. We had to almost laugh at the amusing sight of one of our little Lysander reconnaissance planes being chased round and round the water tower by a German Messerschmitt. Fortunately, he wasn't caught. We heard later that many of the German Aircraft, which was what we had seen, did not survive this air raid. However, they left a trail of destruction behind them, very close to home.

Concerned for my place of work and all of the friends I had made there, I ran and jumped on my bike and headed back to the Acme factory. When I arrived, to my horror, there was smoke, flames and the pungent smell of burning corpses, a smell one never forgets. A policeman stopped me, not allowing anyone through the cordon across the road. I told him that I had come to check on my place of work and colleagues. It was then that I learned from the policeman at the barrier that the factory was no more and many of the people in it and the adjacent factories were killed. I just couldn't believe that not 30 minutes ago we were all singing and laughing together and now they were all dead. When I explained that I worked there to the policeman, he said, "Well, sadly, you won't work here anymore, son, go home and remember how lucky you are that you were not here this evening. Try to remember your friends as they were and forget about what has happened here today."

I left in tears for my poor workmates, all killed, all young people with their whole life in front of them, like me, some of whom were girls I knew who worked in the Bourjois perfume factory next door (which had also been requisitioned by the government to do war work making creams and such like for the forces). All gone. The factories of those times often had glass roofs which would have caused devastation with an exploding bomb causing shards of glass to maim and kill anybody in its way. I was so sad, hurt, and angry but understood how lucky I was that it wasn't me being mourned by my parents. The job I loved so much was no more. My friends were no more. It was then that I made up my mind that I was going to seek revenge for the loss of my lovely friends and workmates; I was going to join up into one of the armed forces and seek justice, and we needed to do this before we were 18.

When it was reported after the event, it so happened that Nine Hurricanes from No. 111 Sqd were scrambled 30 minutes before the attack on that day and were therefore able to intercept the bombers before they had a chance to line up their targets. This interruption meant that the bombers dropped the majority of their bombs outside the aerodrome, causing casualties amongst the civilian population. Seven enemy planes were shot down that day, which was a costly exercise for the Luftwaffe, especially due to the fact that the target the bombers were aiming for was probably RAF Kenley. During the bombing, Croydon had received a lot of damage - large potholes over the airfield, a direct hit on the armoury, the officers' mess reduced to rubble, to name but a few incidents. Other factories hit were Redwing Aircraft and British NSF. Five airmen from 111 Sqd and one airman from Station Headquarters died in the attack. But it was the civilian population that bore the brunt of the bombs dropping outside the aerodrome, with a total of 80 civilians dead. Four airmen, one officer, two civilian telephone operators, and 185 civilians were injured.

My friend Scotty and I set off soon afterwards to the London docks to join the merchant navy. On the dock side, we were told that we had to join something like a union or federation before we could apply to join the merchant navy. We were sent along to an office in the dock area where we could do this, but fortunately for us, the office was closed. So we returned home and started planning our next move. Scotty went off to join the navy whilst I waited until I was old enough to join the RAF. I just needed to reach the age of 17¼.

At the time, there were plenty of jobs going as more and more companies were commandeered by the government to make materials and gear for the war effort and more and more men were heading off to war. I did very quickly manage to find another job in Powers' Accounting and Tabulating Company (known fondly as the 'Acc and Tab"), operating a milling machine in a factory that made shells and bombs for the war effort, but it was not anything like the great job I had in the cardboard box factory. This new job was fairly close to home via an alleyway off our street and a quick jump over the wall, a run across the cemetery and a leap over another wall to the factory. This saved me a lot of time walking the long way around; the only problem was the gardener in the cemetery who would chase me off every time he saw me.

On one particular rather hot day, I was only wearing plimsolls and, as I leapt over the wall, I landed on a broken glass bottle that went through my foot. I felt a little pain, but, of course, I was being chased again, so I had no time to check my foot. But when I got into work, I noticed a trail of dark liquid on the black floor behind me, which I thought was oil leaking out of the machine. It was my blood from my foot, which I had to go and get sorted out, the nurse pulling quite large pieces of glass out of my foot. It was many years later before the final piece of glass worked its way to the surface and eventually came out of my foot.

In 1938 and 1939, before the war started, the government began to call up all the reserves. Britain only had a small army at the time, but we did have quite a lot of Territorial Army bases. My Uncle Cyril, who was just a few years older than me, got called up as he was in the Territorials and I remember going down to Mitcham Barracks to see him off. There were thousands of recruits there putting on uniforms, getting issued with rifles and climbing on the backs of lorries ready to go off to France before the war got started, and all the onlookers were waving them off and cheering. It was a great atmosphere but was a clear warning about things soon to come.

Across the country, we also all got kitted out by the government with gas masks – all sizes to fit adults and children of different ages. Everyone was issued with one in a box that had to be carried everywhere. They were horrible to wear, really claustrophobic, and we all found it difficult to breathe in there, but I expect if we had been involved in a gas attack, we would have been most grateful for it. Luckily, we never had cause to use it.

Then there was the 'Phoney War', where all the troops went over to France and just sat around and waited for things to happen, but nothing happened immediately, so it seemed, but all the time, Hitler's armies were sneaking around the back of us. Whoever was watching the enemy movements for us was not really paying much attention at the time! We used to call them useless 'blimps'.

It was 11 am on Sunday 3rd, September 1939, when Neville Chamberlain announced the outbreak of war on the radio because Germany had invaded Poland, going against the treaty, so we had no option but to declare war on Germany, and then they declared war on us. I was fifteen years old. We were at war.

Britain was preparing troops and sending them across to France to join their troops in readiness for the expected invasion.

To start with, the Germans didn't appear to do very much as regards our troops for a while. Instead, they carried on with their war in Poland, then strutting about in Czechoslovakia and Austria that they had taken over; they thought they could take the world, it seemed. They would have done so if it had not been for Britain. We had a very strong Navy, so, therefore, held our own against them at sea. We 'licked' them at the Battle of Britain, so we then had air supremacy as well. We had all kinds of tricks and gadgets up our sleeves to prevent an invasion.

.....And so the war started in earnest.

4. Meeting Florence 1940

Florence was a lovely little girl of fifteen, with long, dark, red, wavy hair and a great sense of fun. She had started to work at 14 years old in a brick works near her home making bricks. It was hard work and it made her hands raw with overwork, working in all weather and stacking piles of bricks. It was hard work so she left there and her sister, Nellie had got a job in service in Hull and was doing well; she was fed and had accommodation and seemed to like where she worked. So Florence applied for a similar job through an agency as an assistant cook near Newbury for The Reckits family.

It was a long way to travel. She had tickets to travel to Kings Cross, whereupon she had to stand on the platform, hold a newspaper with a red ribbon tied around it, and a man would come and pick her up and take her to Newbury. An ugly-looking chauffeur came and told her to get in the car and he took her down to Newbury. The housekeeper met her on arrival and told her that she would start at 6 am and finish at 6 pm or later (it was more often 10 pm before she had finished for the day). She would help cook, organise, wash up, prepare food, etc, on very little pay.

One of the girls there that Florence had befriended had found a better job at Eton School and had told her that it was far better pay and a much better job. The cook she worked under was a bit of a tyrant, was rude to her and treated her badly so she had nothing to lose by changing jobs. She wrote to the girlfriend at Eton to say she was interested in a job there and asked her if there were any jobs available at the moment. The girl asked her boss, who said yes, there was a position vacant for her to start. She arrived at Eton to start the job.

After a week or so, the people from the Reckits place wrote to her via her home to claim their money back. In those days, often a worker had to pay back through their wages any costs that they had incurred upon arrival, such as train fair plus their board and lodging. This meant that out of her wages, the money would be extracted weekly until debts were paid. This left very little pay in her pocket. Florence had not worked for them for very long so there was still a debt owed. This worried her but she did write to them saying that she had been overworked, not treated very well and had no money with which to pay them back. She heard no more from them, fortunately.

My friend, Dorothy, had told my mate, Scotty, and me that she had a pen friend coming down from the north of England to stay with her for a while and she was meeting her at West Croydon Station the next afternoon. Little was I to know that through this friend, I was to meet the girl of my dreams, who I was eventually to marry.

Scotty and I had planned to sneakily go and follow her but without her seeing us. When Dorothy had met her friend, they came out of the Station and boarded the trolley bus and we got on after them, heading upstairs, surprising them and finally introducing ourselves. It was a complete surprise to Dorothy when she realised that we had been following her, but they took it in good humour, and we had a good laugh about it as we saw them home, making a date for the next day with them.

She fitted right in with us and we all made a great foursome of friends in those fairly carefree days. I loved her Geordie accent and we would often rib her about it, but she took it in her stride and would pay us back with comments about us southerners. The following week Dorothy told me that Florence had decided to stay on in London to help out in the war effort and was starting work at the factory where we worked, the Acc & Tab. And, sure enough, on Monday morning, there she was, working just feet away from me on a capstan lathe. I was euphoric! This led to many future dates and bike rides into the country as a foursome together. I had to borrow a bike for her from another pal and we would often meet in the local milk bar during the weekdays to have milk shakes and listen to the Juke Box. We also went to the pictures, all of us together, sometimes in the West End of London.

Dorothy eventually met a new boyfriend who we did not like, but whom she eventually married. That left Scotty and me taking Florence everywhere with us to the point where the three of us got up to all sorts of mischief.

One morning at work, the three of us sneakily disappeared out of the back of the factory and went to Scotty's house for some cocoa and he played us a tune on his Trombone. We were there for half an hour then went back to the factory, hoping that no one would miss us. When we climbed back over the wall, the Foreman was waiting for us. We were really in trouble now! We had to go before the factory manager for a serious misdemeanour. He told us that had it not been for our youth, and the fact that it was wartime, we would be sacked! Sadly, he chose to suspend us from work for three days without pay. Scotty and I accepted this and were relieved that we had not been sacked, but Florence could not live without money as she had rent and food to pay for. She was really upset with us and said that we were trouble and that she did not want to be with us anymore. We were greatly saddened by this and felt really guilty for not thinking about the consequences of our actions, so we jointly raised the money she needed and gave it to her friend, Dorothy, to give to her.

Upon return to work, we behaved ourselves and, after some days as we all worked close by to each other, we 'made up' and were pals again. Sometime later, Scotty and I arranged to take Florence up to the West End in London for a treat to see the latest film. We went by train from Croydon to Victoria and had a really great time looking around London and thoroughly enjoyed the film, though I cannot remember what the film was. During the film, I could see that Scotty had become really struck on Florence. We both liked her, and our good friendship began to suffer as we then had an argument about who should put his arm around her in the cinema. On the way back home, in Victoria Station, Scotty told me to "Clear off!" as he protested that Florence was HIS girl. Mostly out of cussedness, I told him no, we were all together, so we would both take her home. At this point, he flew into a violent rage, saying that she would have to choose between us as he could not be going around with her anymore with me in tow. Florence and I both laughed at him with this outpouring and bad temper, so he then attacked me on the Station platform. Regretfully I had to knock him down, then to top it all for him, Florence said that he was silly and that it was me she wanted, much to my surprise. Scotty disappeared off in a huff, and I, rather embarrassedly (but proudly), took her arm and escorted her home, thinking all the time of my luck; I could hardly believe it. We made a date for us to go out together the coming week. I then thought, on my way home, that perhaps I should have kissed her; I knew nothing about girls and it must have been after a couple more dates that I built up the courage to ask her if she would mind if I kissed her goodnight. I never thought then that I would kiss her goodnight for the rest of my life, and although she is with us no longer, I still do that every night.

There was fighting in the sky by day and bombing every night, but we worked through it and fortunately for us, and everyone else we worked alongside, the factory avoided most of the bombing during that time.

We had a lovely time together and got very close, having such a lot of carefree fun in those few months until the war really got started. Then the Blitz began and changed our youth and, what should have been, the best years of our lives forever. I knew that soon I would have to join up or be conscripted so we made the best of our time together. I saved up as hard as I could and then asked her that if I went away, would she wait for me, as I wanted to give her an engagement ring. To my joy, she said yes, she would. On the following Saturday, we went around a few jewellery shops looking for a nice ring. We found the one that she loved in a shop in Tooting and, after buying it and performing the 'ceremony' by going down on one knee, I put it on her finger. She would be mine. I was euphoric!

Recently, amongst her effects, I found the receipt for the ring that she had kept for these past seventy years!

At the end of 1940, things were going badly in the war for Britain. I had reached the age of seventeen and I knew that I was eligible to sign up for joining the Royal Air Force. This I did in secret as I didn't want my mother and father to find out, I knew they would not allow me to join up until I was conscripted, but I had a different agenda. I went to the recruitment office in Croydon and saw the recruiting sergeant, whereupon I signed up, my papers were sent off and I waited. As I was underage, I could not be called up until I was seventeen and a quarter, so it was March 1941 before I received the call with railway warrants to go to Weston-Super-Mare for assessment, which was the furthest I had ever been before on my own, to sign on as Volunteer Reserve in the RAF as aircrew.

I received all the tests and physical checks, which I passed, and told them that I knew lots about aircraft already and wanted to be a pilot.

"I'm sorry, son," said the sergeant attending to me, "You're still too young to come in as a pilot. You can come in as aircrew and then we'll decide what you're going to do." I agreed, knowing that I could still apply for pilot training once I reached the right age of eighteen.

At the time, if you were still in employment in a factory doing war work at 18 years of age, then you had to stay there throughout the war and couldn't join the forces. I didn't have to worry about that, as three months later, I received a message with another rail warrant to report to Padgate, in Lancashire, to take up the training for a Wireless Operator Air Gunner. The lifespan of a Wireless Operator Air Gunner then was about six weeks! It still didn't deter me.

My parents hadn't met Florence at that time, so I thought it was time to let them meet. We arranged to all go to a local pub whereupon I introduced Florence as my girlfriend, telling my parents that I was serious about her and that she would be my wife one day and would they look after her whilst I was away during the war.

The day came for me to leave for my training in the RAF. It was so hard to leave Florence, as we had become very attached. My father and mother took us to the Station at Kings Cross by car, as I had to get the late train to Padgate. Leaving home during a particularly nasty air raid, we eventually got onto the platform. The train was delayed, as during an air raid, it could be seen by the raiding Germans and would be attacked, due to the light emanating from its glowing fire in the engine compartment. So, it was past midnight before it left.

Here we go!

It was so sad to leave them all standing there on the platform, and I worried about them all getting back to Croydon safely through the all-night air raid. They knew that life expectancy in the RAF was just six weeks at that time for Aircrew, so they were probably feeling as anxious as I was. Maybe more. It must have been so hard for my parents, let alone Florence, to stand and wave goodbye, knowing what the chances were that I would not be coming home again. I don't think I could cope with that kind of situation with my sons, but my father was quite a hard man, and they were very different times.

It was three months before I got my next leave which was for five days. Florence was then in Ashington, Northumberland, looking after her younger brothers for her father, as her mother had walked out and left them all, taking Florence's sister, Doreen, with her. I spent my whole leave in Ashington with her and met all of her friends and relatives, including her Father and brothers.

After six weeks away, her mother returned, so Florence was able to return to Croydon and work, saying that she had recovered from a long illness, as it was then illegal to leave war work for any other reason. I didn't see her again for another nine months, but we wrote to each other most days; she always kept my letters.

Florence got on very well with my family, particularly my mother and sister, so, for safety reasons, I got her to go and live at my home with them, which turned out very well for us.

For me, leave was very scarce, and we spent very little time together over the next four years whilst I was away serving my country in the war. When I did get leave, there seemed to be more and more air raids on each occasion, and I had some very close escapes from getting killed.

Once the fly-bombs started, Florence cleared off to Ashington, Northumberland, as it had become intolerable then. She took my youngest siblings, Peter and Phyllis, and my mother with her returning to her home in the North, where it was safer from the relentless bombing. Sadly, my mother had to leave the pet dog behind, who didn't fair very well when alone in the house. There was only my father at home, and he was at work for long hours during the day, so the poor thing had to be put down due to suffering from the effects of the relentless bombing.

Hard times, very dangerous times! Unless you experience it yourself, you just can't imagine what it was like.

5. The Blitz and the bombing of London – 1940-1941

Life was really hard in London during the war and particularly during the Blitz. Following the Battle of Britain, the Blitz (non-stop bombardment by bombs both day and night) ran continuously from September 7th, 1941, for eight months, and at one concentrated spate for 56 days out of 57. During the Blitz, 450,000 bombs rained down on British soil and more than 40,000 civilians were killed by Luftwaffe bombing during the war, almost half of them in the capital, where more than a million houses were destroyed or damaged.

You could literally taste the dust in the air from all the bombing of buildings. There was often no electricity, no water and no gas. Chaos was all around, yet life went on; people got up, went to work and school, where possible, and the great clear-up continued relentlessly.

There was no way that you could phone anyone to find out if loved ones were alright during the Blitz; no one had a phone in those days or maybe only one person on the street. Our neighbour had a phone for a while, but he soon gave it up as he kept getting calls coming in for the inhabitants on the street at all hours. Sometimes he would ignore the calls, but he had a phone because he was a builder and needed it for his work. My father wouldn't have a phone, "Costs too much money," he would say. Stingy devil!

Here are a few true stories from that time during the Blitz and bombing of London, 1940-41

.....A close shave.....

During this time, I somehow managed to make it home to see my girlfriend, Florence. She was having a hard time with working night shifts nearly every night throughout the German bombing campaign. It was her choice to work at night as she hated the air-raid shelters and preferred to work through the worst of the air-raids. Although she was very afraid, she still worked relentlessly at her ammunition-making machine through it all; that was real courage, something she never lacked, particularly as that type of factory would have been a major target for the Luftwaffe.

One Saturday afternoon, on a forty-eight-hour pass to visit my home, my mother and Florence had gone out shopping together and had left me at home in Limpsfield Ave in Croydon, whilst I had a rest. At about 3 pm in the afternoon, I heard the sound of German aeroplane engines, by now a very familiar sound. Picking up my father's binoculars, I went out into the garden and looked up into the grey sky. It was difficult to get a clear view with all the buildings surrounding us, so I then climbed onto my father's garage, which was at the bottom of the garden, to get a better view, when suddenly, there it was, a German Junkers 88 bomber circling the area at about 800 feet up in the air. I felt sure that he had seen me because, at that very moment, it began to release its bombs. I saw the first bomb coming down directly at me, just like a tennis ball being thrown up to catch. Jumping off the eight feet from the garage on to the garden, I dived flat, holding my head and clenching every muscle in my body for the inevitable impact, thinking this was my life's end. There was a terrific bang that remained ringing in my ears as I was covered in earth and bricks. A two-foot piece of bomb shrapnel landed with a thud and buried itself into the earth just inches from my face. My reaction was to put my hand on its jagged edge in order to retrieve it, thinking that it would make a great souvenir to add to my collection, only to find that it was, of course, red hot and gave me such a bad burn on my fingers. Fortunately for me, the bomb landed on the soft earth in the next-door neighbour's garden next to the garage, before exploding and, rather than destroying buildings, only left a deep hole just eighteen feet from where I had thrown myself. If it had landed a fraction of a second later, that would have hit the garage and there would have been far more damage, and I would not have been here to tell the tale. A really close shave for me!

The second of the bombs dropped, and unfortunately hit and demolished the house on the opposite side of the street, killing the male neighbour and his ten-month-old baby as they were sleeping. He had apparently been on night work and was looking after the baby while his wife was out shopping. The third and fourth bombs landed in front of the factory building where Florence worked, killing two more people and injuring many others, damaging the facade of the building. The Factory was the probable bombing target as it was doing essential war work, making ammunition and fighting equipment. I was so glad Florence was not in the Factory at that moment during the day as she was a night worker. A near escape! Running over to the now demolished house opposite, I looked to see whether I could be of any help. I was able to turn off the leaking gas supply to prevent any further fire there from spreading to surrounding houses.

.....The Milkman's Horse...

On my return to our house, the milkman arrived to collect the weekly milk money that my mother had left on the hall table for him. He was badly shaken, having just witnessed the devastation in the street, and said that he would have been killed but for his horse. Usually, the horse knew his milk round and would know when to stay put and when to walk on to the next delivery. It was completely out of character for him to deviate from the milk round. But on this day, the horse had inexplicably left him behind and continued, at quite a pace, on to the next street and around the corner. The milkman had turned from collecting his money on the doorstep to find his horse and the cart gone, much to his consternation. He had then run up the street to locate the whereabouts of his horse. Just as he had rounded the corner, one of the bombs had landed exactly at the house where he had just been standing. Never in ten years had his horse gone off on its own without him! It was as if he had known of the imminent danger. We then discussed the 'sixth-sense' that occurred with some aircrew and the premonition of death, which was probably far stronger in animals, and maybe this is what had happened to the horse. There were a couple of windows blown out in our house at the front and back with glass everywhere. The ladies arrived back to a scene of destruction with me covered in mud and dust and smouldering houses and gaps where houses were missing in the street. We had to board up the windows, something that we did more than once during the Blitz.

How lucky was I – again! That was so close.

.....And the one about rescuing the old lady......

One night with a colander on my head for protection, my father and I went out to help a neighbour, whose house had been hit by a bomb, before the fire engines arrived. The top half and side of the house were all exposed and the top floor to the bedroom was at a dangerously sloping angle with lino on the floor, adding to the hazard. An elderly lady was in the bed, which looked like it would soon start to slide down the linoleum slope towards us and over the edge of the floor to the ground below. She didn't dare to move and was calling out for help. We could see that the floor was about to give way very soon, so, being a lightweight, my father helped me to climb up onto the sloping floor to help the lady down. Being young and fit, I managed to crawl to this elderly lady who was covered in plaster and dust. She was unhurt and eager to get out of the bed and I distinctly remember that she was wearing a long, white, embroidered nightdress with plaster clinging to her long, grey hair. She was still sitting up in bed and, remarkably was unhurt.

"Hello boys," she said, "Look what they've done to my house, what a mess!" We told her that we were going to get her out and that we had to move soon as the floor was very unstable and likely to give way at any minute.

"I can't go just yet; I've got to find my teeth first!" came the reply. The teeth were in a glass beside her bed on a small table, which was by now full of plaster, so she hooked her fingers into the glass and fished out her teeth and duly put them in place in her mouth. "Ok, I'm ready now," she shouted. Once her teeth were in place, we started the process of getting her down. We decided that it would be best if she slid down the slope of the floor, holding her nightdress tight around her, I would guide her down and my dad would catch her at the bottom. This we did and safely slid her off the upstairs floor into the waiting arms of my father, who then carried her to a waiting ARP vehicle, which was full of the wounded and displaced from elsewhere on the street. The lady, who was in her eighties, was duly wrapped in a blanket to keep her warm. Just as we moved away to go to the next bombed house to see if we could help, hers finally collapsed with a crash and cloud of dust. We would have been killed had we not got out as quickly as we did! Lucky again!

.....And the one about the parachute bomb

Once we left there, my father and I walked up the road and by this time, an air raid was in full swing. Suddenly there were machine gun bullets falling like hail in the street coming from the aircraft overhead. We dodged in and out of doorways to the corner of the street where there were quite a few people standing due to their being a problem in Dunhevid Road. There was a large, green parachute caught up in a tree, swinging, on the end of which was a large sea-mine (bomb) that was about 8 ft long and 3 ft wide. One would normally scratch one's head in wondering what on Earth this type of bomb, normally meant for dropping in the sea, was doing dropped on a city. We could only surmise that the pilot had run out of land bombs and decided that he had nothing to lose and everything to gain in dropping this monstrosity. If it had exploded, it would have blown up the whole row of houses near to where it had lodged itself and caused undoubted devastation and injury to many more inhabitants of this street. One of the policemen who turned up went off to get someone who knew what they were doing when dealing with unexploded bombs of this nature. He ran off up the street, blowing his whistle to alert everyone as to the danger in the vicinity. Meanwhile, someone else ran down the road to a house, where the owner was known to have a phone, to commandeer further help. Within about ten minutes, a group of Navy personnel appeared with an officer who then proceeded to clear the area of all the spectators to within 100 yards. The officer and one other Navy official then went to defuse the bomb in situ, it taking them about 15 minutes to do so. The hanging bomb was then left for the army to come and take away as soon as they could get on the scene.

.....And then the Gasometer incident

As we made our way towards home, there was one almighty bang and we saw that the gasometer had received a direct hit, lighting up the whole area with an eerie yellow ball of flame from igniting the gas. Next to our street and the gasometer was a cemetery and the explosion had unearthed many of the inhabitants of the cemetery; coffins and bodies in various states of decay, which were now all over the street and surrounding area. It was incredibly eerie, like something out of a horror novel! Croydon was, unfortunately in the direct path of the German planes heading towards London, so it was always getting hit en route.

You've never seen such bloody chaos!

....Returning to base

Sometimes, if I was on leave, I was able to accompany Florence on her walk to work in the ammunition factory, the Acc & Tab, walking and dodging craters on the road, in the dark with bombs falling all around. She worked on a lathe making bomb shells and other similar items. She was such a brave girl as she continued working throughout the bombings; she didn't like it in the air raid shelters. She'd rather work and keep occupied and carry on making the bullets and ammunition. I remember one night escorting my mother to the air raid shelter and then Florence to the factory gates and saw her into her place of work, with bombs falling around everywhere. I ran back up the road dodging it all and jumped on a bus going up to

Paddington via Streatham and Kennington. I had to return to the aerodrome as my short leave was over.

The buses were still running, so I headed to the end of my road to get the 59 bus towards Kennington Oval and hoped to then dive down into the tube network where trains were still running, despite all the people using the underground at a bomb shelter. Just before the bus arrived at Kennington Oval, there was an almighty explosion ahead where another bus in front was hit directly by a bomb. The bus only had about eight people on it, but as it was hit by the bomb from the back, the explosion made it rise up into the air and land on top of a building up-side-down; it didn't look like there would be any survivors. Almost instantaneously, another bomb hit an air-raid shelter nearby and, I heard later, killed lots of people there. It was a nasty thing to see the bombs going off and people being killed so close by, bricks and mortar, and sometimes bits of bodies everywhere all over the roads. The bus driver had to steer around piles of debris, cursing as he went as the odd brick would catch the underside of the vehicle, all the time hoping that it wouldn't be his bus that would be hit. There was nothing we could do to help amongst the carnage as there seemed to be no survivors on the bus in front. Our bus driver looked nervous, but he carried on and, once I had got off the bus, I went down into the underground to catch a tube train. You had to step over all the folks down there as they were sheltering and sleeping during the air raid. Babies were screaming in their mothers' arms, and kids were running about playing games, seemingly oblivious to the perils above ground, and their parents were shouting at them to get away from the edge of the platform as another train was coming in. From there I got onto the tube and travelled to Paddington and then to find a steam train to a remote station near to the airfield base I was stationed.

On arrival at Paddington, the bombs still falling, I was able to find a train to get me as near as possible to the airfield. During any bombing, it was difficult for steam trains to run a service at night as the glow from the engine fires could be easily spotted by enemy planes – we would be a sitting target. So, on this night, the train driver had to wait under the cover of Paddington station until there was a lull in the bombing before he dared to head off out of London. Once out of the city, any bombing eased and then ceased, and we could continue our journey in relative safety.

During the Blitz, we began to be able to hear the difference between the normal bombs and the flying bombs (doodle bugs) falling by the sounds that they made. On this one day, we thought, "Thank God for that!" as the bombs seemed to have stopped coming, then the next thing we knew, out of nowhere, a huge explosion and then the noise of it coming afterwards! Later in the war, the Germans would fire a V2 rocket up into high altitude, it was travelling so fast you couldn't hear it until sometimes after it had arrived, due to being faster than the speed of sound. It was an odd phenomenon with a huge explosion, you could hear it as it passed through the sound barrier.

Anti-aircraft guns mounted on lorries would continually move through the streets, firing at the Bombers above. This sort of episode went on until Britain had built better defences against these continuous, nightly attacks. My mother and younger brothers and sister would spend night after night in the Anderson shelter, which they hated (my brother, Peter, remained petrified of spiders throughout his life). My father and I invariably would sleep on an old couch which was sitting in the garden. With these continuous onslaughts being every night at this time, one would be amazed at what one could sleep through.

One morning, whilst on leave, my father and I got up and stood at the back door and, during the course of the morning, counted 90 fly bombs coming over and landing bombs all over London. Croydon was on the direct flight path from Germany to London, so we saw it all. Our planes would be diving down on them at high speeds and getting their short, stubby wings underneath the flying bombs and tipping them over to change their course and spiral to the ground over areas that were less populated like parks and fields, etc. It was such a dangerous manoeuvre for them but necessary in order to protect as many civilians and property as they could. I was on leave, so the next day I had to get back to London in order to get a train back to the camp. I got to Piccadilly Circus, where I was busy buying a newspaper for my onward journey, when I heard one of these flying bombs right overhead then it landed in the next street.

Fortunately, there was a row of houses between us and the bomb, so it had little impact upon Piccadilly Circus.

Churchill said, “You’ll sew the seed and you’ll reap the corn.”

There was a kind of unwritten law that you didn’t bomb the general civilian population during a war, but the Germans did a bit of it from the Zeppelins during WW1 and then went all out, bombing towns and cities in WW2. The RAF avoided bombing cities and towns where possible; they bombed railways, factories, aerodromes, forts and military installations, until later in the war. The Germans were hoping that the relentless bombing campaign would have a great psychological impact on the British people and make the general population want to give up, but it actually made the British people, in general, more determined. The stress of the war did result in many anxiety attacks, eating disorders, fatigue, weeping, miscarriages, and other physical and mental ailments, but society did not collapse; families, friends and neighbours were always there for each other to support those in need. The incidents of suicides and drunkenness declined, and London recorded only a couple of cases of "bomb neurosis" per week in the first three months of the bombing, which was quite unexpected as far as the government groups were concerned. The relentless bombing had far-reaching effects on the inhabitants of Britain; it did destroy lives, homes and communities, but, despite the many ‘near-death’ experiences that many faced daily, most people were stoic, self-effacing and patriotic. That's what we were like in those days.

When we thought we were going to get invaded in 1942, I was at an airfield on guard, and we were told that the German paratroopers were probably coming and that we should 'kill as many as we could before they got you'. Every person in this country was ready to fight to the end. Churchill had said, "In fighting back, if you've got to go, then take one with you."

That put the Germans off. Everyone would do anything for anyone else. It was wonderful how close we all were to each other in wartime

Florence and I always wrote to each other whenever we could. She kept all the letters she received from me. They tell about all the places that I was stationed for that moment in time (and there were very many), some of which I cannot remember at all and some I was not allowed to divulge.

So ......Here we go!

6. Initial RAF Training - 1941

Weston-Super-Mare

I passed all the entrance tests into the RAF during a visit to Weston-Super-Mare, Somerset, where aircrew applicants were medically checked and mentally tested for suitability to join the RAF. I was to become a Wireless Operator/Air Gunner, initially. It was a desperate time; we never knew from one day to the next whether we would be alive the next day, and the possibility of invasion was the expected outcome. Everyone was prepared to fight to the death.

Padgate, Preston, Lancashire

Arriving in Padgate in the early hours of the morning, March 1941, I was surprised to find some RAF personnel waiting with a lorry to collect about ten of us who had eventually arrived on the London train. All of us climbed aboard with our cases and were taken to the Training Camp. We were given a blanket and a straw-filled pillow and led off to a large room full of beds. The beds were just four boards attached to a piece of 3x3 pine wood, with no mattress or bottom cover, so very uncomfortable. I quickly became fairly used to the hardships we raw recruits suffered in those early

George at 17

days of training, but some lads got into a bad state, particularly those that came from more wealthy, comfortable backgrounds. I was already toughened up to all the hardships we would be facing, unlike some of the other 'inmates', who had been brought up with plenty, with home comforts and who were not used to lack of food, the cold and the difficulties. Or having to fight their corner. Many of these lads went down with diseases, colds and flu. I had been hardened up as a child and was used to these tough conditions, so for me it was quite normal. I hardly ever became ill, and I certainly enjoyed my three regular meals a day.

Food in the mess varied. When I first joined up, we were given basic but good food, such as, stewed steak, potatoes and cabbage, or bacon and cabbage. But as the war progressed, food was more scarce, so there was less choice and less food at times. Travelling through Belgium and Holland towards the end of the war, we would get corned beef in batter for breakfast, corned beef hash or stew for lunch, with turnips and all sorts of vegetables and then corned beef and pickles for supper. We did get a bit fed up with corned beef, so much so that I couldn't eat it for many years after the war. Every day, seven days a week, month after month. Of course, in the sergeants' mess then, there was slightly better food, and in the officers' mess, the food was better still. The cooks were a bit more up-market as you were promoted through the ranks.

In my unit, the instructor was Billy Shankly, who, after the war, became the very famous Liverpool football team manager in later years. He was very hard but fair on us all, and we benefitted greatly from the physical fitness that resulted from his training regime. After six weeks, we were sent to Blackpool for further training as Aircrew. It was tough going from dawn until mid-evening, pushed as we were into the very cold sea in the dark and then told to run to the swimming baths and jump into more cold water. The warm showers that followed were such a great relief!

George back row 4th from right

There were some rough lads who joined up, lads who were keen to find someone to bully. Lads, like me, who had been through tough times and rough schools, fared somewhat better than those who had received a more gentle upbringing. Funnily enough, many of the inmates were afraid of 'Crafty Cockneys', as they used to call us. I was in one billet, a boarding house in Palletine Road in Blackpool, doing my initial training, where the lads were a bit older than me. The man who owned the house was not a very pleasant man at all. He dodged out of signing up for the forces by volunteering for the Auxiliary Fire Brigade, to which he turned up only about twice a week. His wife was so mean. They used to get the butter ration for all the guys who were billeted there but would never give us so much as a scrap of it. Instead, we were given margarine (which none of us liked), and they kept the butter for themselves. I complained, telling them that I didn't eat margarine, and besides, those were our rations, and we should be getting them. They wouldn't give it to me so I told them I would complain. All the other lads were listening in and tried to show they were on the side of the landlord and landlady, because if she liked you, you would get much more food. The landlord then started to goad the other lads into giving me a clout, which they all tried to do, lining up to give me a beating for stirring up trouble. The landlord told us to sort it out in the back yard.

"Come on then lads," I said, "Let's settle it once and for all – you can all come at me one at a time." So, there's me in the middle of the yard, surrounded by all these big lads. The first one to come at me was the biggest guy, a Scots guy. I was much smaller than him, so I probably looked like such a push-over to him. He didn't know that I had spent a lot of my time fighting in the playground, in the street, or in the boxing ring. His fists were up, and we were both ready. He gave one try at a punch, missed me, and I got him right on the nose with mine, blood everywhere. He didn't want to know after that. The next one was Welsh, whose father was a sea captain he told me (not sure why he told me), and he said he would 'sort me out'. He threw a few punches which missed, then I hit him in the 'bread-basket', right in the solar plexus. He doubled over and was very sick, poor thing.

"Next!" They all backed off then, offering some excuse. The man who ran the billet was goading them all on to get me; he didn't like me for some reason. "Perhaps you want to have a go?" I asked him.

"I don't want to fight you," he said, "because if I was seen as attacking the recruits, I could lose my business of billeting. They all reluctantly traipsed back into the house.

The next thing I knew was that they, the landlord and landlady, had lodged a complaint about me, and whilst I was on parade, I was called out to go and see one of the officers.

"You've been fighting and causing problems at your billet, haven't you?" asked the officer. I agreed and explained my situation to the officer. "Well," he said, "I am moving you to another billet; it won't be as nice, you are to move your belongings and move out today. Here is the address. Remember, it's your fault." And with that, I was dismissed to go and sort out my lodgings. I was fortunate that I was not reprimanded further. I headed off to this pretty little cottage and was on my own with a lovely elderly couple, who couldn't do enough for me. The man was not too well, he had varicose veins which used to burst, with blood all over the place. I wasn't squeamish, so I would do what I could to help them. They provided a super, warm bedroom with a very comfortable, old, feather bed. The food was fabulous, and loads of it. I was really spoiled, and they were great company when I was there; I was treated like family. I really had fallen on my feet. The course was about twelve weeks, so I stayed there until I went off to the gunnery classes. I was actually sorry to say goodbye.

One particular evening in Preston, I was standing, waiting to go into the cinema to see a film, all on my own, with two girls in front of me in this long queue. Suddenly, along came four men who knew these two girls and decided to push in in front of me.

"Hey!" I shouted, "Either you move to the back and take them with you or get to the back of me!" They started messing about and the next thing I knew was we were all fighting and then I found myself in mid-air with two great big military police who slung me in jail for fighting. I'll never forget that. My mum had that day sent me a parcel with some Eccles cakes that she had made, and I just happened to have two of them in my pocket which I was going to eat in the cinema. She used to make them out of puff pastry, so of course, being famished, I sat in my cell eating these with bits of puff pastry left lying all over the cell floor. The officer came in, looked at the floor, and shouted, "What's that on the floor? Who did that? Was it you?"

"No Sir," I replied, thinking that I didn't want to be in yet more trouble, "People like me come in here and expect it to be clean. I've been thrown in here into a dirty cell. I'm going to report it!" So, there was a big argument about who did it and who was cleaning it up. Someone was very soon sent in there to clean it up! And it wasn't me! I was confined to barracks for seven days, with three days in the guard house. I never did get to see the film – I was 'inside'. Peeling potatoes was a bit of a chore. I only had a small knife with which to peel a great pile of potatoes every day for the mess.

It wasn't too bad, though, as you couldn't do anything apart from read a book and wait for someone to bring you your next meal. A most relaxing few days!

We studied morse code, the theory of flight, radio operation and many other subjects for a further eight weeks before our selection for the role we were to take on as part of the aircrew. The morse code really got on your brain and you'd go around making noises, such as "der, der, der, dut, dut, der", everywhere in your head! Then they asked for volunteers for what was known as SPAGS, which was Special Purpose Air Gunners on dive bombers, so I volunteered. I was fed up with hanging about. Then I had to go to St Johns wood for a visual test in order to start my flying training.

7. Gunnery Training – At Last! - 1942

St. John's Wood

I completed the gunnery course at an airfield near Scarborough (RAF Catfoss, I think), and then there was a panic; they required volunteers as special purpose air gunners for some new aircraft they'd bought from America, Vengeance aircraft. They were going to use them as dive bombers. Well, of course, I was eager to volunteer so that I could get some action at last. The training was done, we passed, then the officer in charge of us said, "You five, you've passed; you can get yourselves down to London to have your night vision test".

I was then posted to St. Johns Wood in London for Aircrew in Training to be tested for night vision capability. I realised that the base where I stayed for the tests, wasn't too far by bus from Croydon. Our neighbour in the flats was Joe Loss and his band. So, unbeknown to the officers in the building, I would sneak out through a window, over a wall covered in barbed wire, down to St. John's Wood tube station, on to Kennington, then on to the nearest bus stop and catch a number 59 to Croydon to visit Florence and my mother. I didn't have long of an evening to visit them, arriving just in time to have a quick chat and escort Florence to her night work in the ammunitions factory, a quick cup of tea and catch up with my mother, before catching the No. 59 and a tube back to St. John's Wood and sneaking back in through the window, undiscovered. I would have been in serious trouble had I been caught!

At that time, it was a very cold and damp winter and I had contracted a severe dose of Flu, complete with severe headache, runny nose and eyes and a 'fuzzy' head. On arrival at the testing area, I asked the sergeant if I could wait a few days until my Flu symptoms had cleared up, as I was sure that I would fail the test with my streaming eyes. Unfortunately, he would not entertain this idea and insisted that I do the test there and then. I had to go into a room that had a gadget where I was to sit with a braille board and a pencil and had to write down what I saw. There was a screen with a pointer that moved around on the screen and clicked each time, and then some very faintly luminous figures would appear; Maltese cross, circle, church steeple, etc., and I had to feel the line on the board and write down what it was that I had seen. It was very dark in the room. I really couldn't see the shapes with a runny nose and streaming eyes. Anyway, I did what I could, and when I came out, they told me that I had failed. I was devastated! Trying to plead my case, I explained that I was heavy with cold and flu symptoms and asked if I could take it again. As the test was deemed memorable, a retest could not be taken for at least three to six months hence and that was the rule. They explained that I would have to do something else in the meantime.

I was gutted!

RAF Henlow & Cheddington

Faced with this delay to my intended plan to become a pilot, I was given the option by an officer to do some further training in another field. As I already had experience, I elected to take an Electrician's course in order to repair the electrics of the planes and was posted to RAF Henlow, where I completed the 16-week course with a distinction. Because of doing so well, I was then posted to Chippenham in order to do the second, 12-week, higher-level part of the course, the Group 2 course at Melksham. I passed it with a distinction in every part except one and therefore achieved a Credit. I was then posted firstly, for two or three weeks, to Cheddington, looking after aeroplane electrical equipment, taking generators apart, servicing them, then putting them back together again, etc., then on to an American Base at Bovingdon, Hertfordshire.

Moving on – here we go again!

RAF Bovingdon

My role there was to support the Americans on the electrics of the aircraft, on what had previously been an RAF base.

I was surprised to find that I was there with just two other British RAF personnel at the base. Life there was hilarious with the crazy Americans. There was, however, at that time, much race discrimination on the base, with black Americans having separate quarters and dining facilities. I would often be found talking to the black Americans and consequently got into trouble for taking no notice of the separate dining and eating with them; the black personnel told me that it was best for them if I did not eat with them, as it made even greater trouble for them as well.

Finding myself in a bar with a group of Americans, I had half a pint of beer talking and generally having a laugh with them, when suddenly my beer disappeared.

"Where's my bloody beer gone?" I said to the group, all of them looking around and pretending not to know what I was talking about. So, we carried on chatting, and I reluctantly ordered another half pint. Having taken a few slurps, the next thing I knew was that that one had gone missing too. There was a bit of sniggering from the men around me and I began to realise that they were having a bit of a laugh with me. One of the guys who was laughing the most, I found out later, was the person who was hiding it from me or pouring it into his drink.

"Don't you come that with me!" I said, "How dare you take my beer! In England, that is a real insult." He just laughed even more; I was beginning to feel angry, so I shoved him. Unbeknown to me at that time, this man was some kind of American boxing champion, so he shoved me back and the next thing was that I had hit him, and he hit me back, but I was by then on the floor. Being young, green behind the ears and certainly not to be outdone by anyone, I do no more that get back up on my feet and hit him again, he returns the favour and I'm back on the floor again. I didn't know who he was but by this time I was realising that his boxing skills were probably a bit better than mine! Three times he knocked me down, then in the end, he helped me up amicably and said, "Look, we were having a bit of fun, don't take it to heart, we haven't come across anyone like you before. Calm down!" With great apologising and hand shaking and a promise to buy me a beer, I calmed down and we were friends again. When I learned about his boxing career he had left behind in America, I felt a bit of a fool as I would have had little chance against him, despite my experience in the boxing ring.

Young blood, eh!

One day I was summoned to the Base gate to find, to my surprise, Florence and my sister Phil had arrived to see me. They had cycled all the way from South London and had no idea that I couldn't just walk out of the base to be with them; this was an operational Base. However, the American Major, to whom I was subject, arranged a private boarding house accommodation for them for the night (as there was no way that they could cycle all the way home again) and gave me leave to spend a few hours with them. I was also able to see them off home on their return journey. It caused me a lot of trouble, but it was great to see them.

I had a particular pal called Ned, who I had made friends with. He came from New York, and he was an air gunner on the Flying Fortress bombers. At that time, they were carrying out raids over France against factories making war products and they were very dangerous missions, but the losses in terms of aircrew and planes at that time were relatively light. I desperately wanted to fly on a Flying Fortress, so he and I schemed with the rest of his crew to get me on a trip with them to France.

I had to ask permission and have a chit signed by Major Wallace, who was a force to be reckoned with. I had quite a good rapport with the Major, so I worked hard to cajole him into allowing the trip. I explained that I had done a gunnery course and would be a useful asset on the trip. I wasn't even part of their unit, so how I got to go on it, I don't know. Reluctantly, Major Wallace signed what was known as a blood chit for me, which allowed me to join them on one of their sorties, at my own risk. He said that nothing usually happens on the sorties as they fly in such tight formation; they look a formidable force to the enemy. So, I was kitted up in flying gear, which comprised thick and luxurious leather trousers and jacket, sheepskin lined, so thick that it was difficult to walk to the aircraft. I accompanied them on an operation flying near to Paris, bombing what I believe was the Renault factory, which at that time had been requisitioned for making parts for German tanks. It was incredibly exciting for me, but as the side gun ports were opened, the cold air entered and I was extremely cold, it was paralysing, realising then why they wore such thick clothing. Other than that, everything went very well. We met no resistance when we were over the target except for some flack, but we were attacked by two Messerschmitt on the way back. I think that the forty machine guns of heavy calibre from our ten Fortresses soon saw them off. At least I had a chance to have a 'squirt' with my gun. But it all happened too fast for me to hit anything of consequence. How anyone could hit another plane in the air with the speed at which they travel is beyond me!

I was not supposed to be on the flight, really. I had cajoled the officer in charge into letting me accompany them on a fairly straightforward mission. On our return flight, one of the planes was hit, but he managed to struggle on home. We eventually got back to the safety of the aerodrome. We had stayed in tight formation throughout and, on our return home, were able to deliver fire upon some German planes with heavy calibre machine guns, so they eventually gave up and turned back. It was ever so exciting – the speed with which it all happened – one moment all was fine, then instantly you see the enemy plane and it's gone – that's how quick it was. For the unpractised eye, not enough time to gather thoughts, aim and fire with any hope of hitting your target. When we got back, we had to report what we had seen and done during the flight and the attack. Of course, I was not meant to be on the flight, so I did not dare to mention my part in it. We were young then, so we seemed to have no fear of anything – we just did it; it was part of our job, our role in protecting our country. The following week twenty planes went off from Bovingdon and only sixteen came back! There were ten guys on each plane. So, forty blokes got killed in one raid and four aeroplanes lost. A bitter blow to the squadron and a terrible loss of life. Not to mention that each of those planes cost a lot of money, tens of thousands of pounds worth each.

Unfortunately, after about six weeks, I learned that my little friend Ned had gone missing somewhere over France and I never saw him again.

Whilst at this base, I met some very interesting people. One day I was in the gunnery practice dome on my own and just using the system for pleasure as much as anything else, when someone came in and sat down next to me and asked me if I had achieved a good gunnery score. We had a chat about it for a short while, and then I realised that I was talking to Major Clark Gable, the film star that I had recently seen in the film 'Gone with the Wind.' I asked him if he was who I thought he was, which he confirmed, and he said that he was now in the US Army Airforce serving his country. He was a big, broad man and very personable, asking me what I was doing at the base and so on before he wished me luck and left.

Later in my time there, I also met Bob Hope when he came to entertain the base personnel.

I was at Bovingdon for quite a while before I was posted to a Servicing Commando who were sent to various aerodromes where there was a push to get planes serviced quickly enough.

On one base in 1942, I can't remember which one now; I was with 135 Squadron who were equipped with the American Bomber called 'B-24 Liberator'. Early RAF Liberators were the first aircraft to cross the Atlantic Ocean as a matter of routine. In comparison with its contemporaries, the B-24 was relatively difficult to fly and had poor low-speed performance. As one of the electrical tradesmen, I had just finished servicing one of them and was tasked to carry out the synchronisation of the generators during the test flight following its major service. This entailed getting into the nose wheel compartment, during the flight, via an access floor panel between the two pilots' seats. The four generator regulators were fitted on the bulkhead under there.

Having got airborne, and after other tests had taken place, I was given permission from the pilot to lift the floor panel, situated between the pilot seats, and get into the compartment below. It was extremely cramped for a person to be in there as it also housed the nose wheel that was operated by hand to be open or closed and covered by a leather cover, held by means of a zip fastener. I was quite slight in stature then, so I could just about fit. Just as I braced myself, so that I could connect my electrical voltmeter across the four regulators, the aircraft banked slightly, causing me to shift my stance. Unbeknown to me, the leather cover over the nose wheel had come undone; this should have been detected during its service and remedied. My foot slipped and was quickly followed by my leg falling into the air below in a 190 mph. airstream. My whole life passed before me as I was being sucked out of the aircraft, and it was only by luck, that I had immediately dropped my meter and grabbed some metal stays, using all my strength to hold myself in place and preventing myself from dropping to the earth, some 3,000 feet below.

I was a bit shaken when I eventually emerged from the cramped compartment; I told the pilot what had happened, but they had been oblivious to my struggles! As ordered, I did file a report in the pertaining paperwork for health and safety reasons.

Just another day at the office, they say! But no joke.

8. Exploding Plane – a lucky escape!

RAF Warboys –

The construction of Warboys Airfield began in 1940. The airfield was built to relieve the congestion at RAF Upwood. The airfield was ready to use at the end of July 1941, and the first squadron to arrive was a detachment of Short Stirlings from 15 Squadron, arriving from RAF Wyton. The first fully operational squadron to arrive at Warboys was 156 Squadron on 5 August 1942. The squadron came from RAF Alconbury with Vickers Wellingtons; in the new year, it re-equipped with Avro Lancasters.

On this one very memorable day, I was sent to Warboys Aerodrome (Cambridgeshire). It happened that there was going to be a bombing raid that night somewhere in Germany. It was about 4 pm by this time. There was one Lancaster aircraft right across on the other side of the aerodrome, probably about a mile away from where I was, which had some kind of engine problem, so some repairs were being undertaken. An Officer came over to me and said that no one had been out to the plane and signed the '700', which is the official document to be signed to say it was safe to fly after its repairs. No one was there to check out the bomb release system on the plane and the Officer asked me to go over and check that it was being or had been done. I told him that if it wasn't being done, I could do the checks myself and I set off to walk straight across the aerodrome, not around the perimeter, because that would have been a very long walk indeed. There was no flying going on, so it was safe to walk across. The aeroplane, a Lancaster, was on a dispersal point, which was a piece of hardstanding or tarmac. There were about six guys working on the engines, fitting it all back together, a couple of other aircraft fitters putting the covers back on the fuselage of the plane and some armourers who were loading the plane up with bombs and target indicator flares (these are one million candle power, about 5-6ft long). When the flares were released, there was a chute at the back of the aircraft along which they travelled, before being dropped, and falling to the ground slowly due to a parachute that enabled the target for the bombing to be lit up and bombed more accurately. This plane was going to drop the target indicators. There were four target indicator flares in the chute, one in each compartment. One of the flares fell out of its compartment and hit the ground; fortunately, it didn't ignite – that would have caused a catastrophe! There was a strong smell of high-octane petrol all around and the plane was full of fuel in readiness for its next mission. Two of the fellas came out and picked up the flare, throwing it back into the plane. I was really feeling nervous then as there were 12,000lb worth of bombs on this plane and a light like that would send us all to our maker if it went off!

"Is that safe?" I shouted.

"Oh yes," came the reply, "We can move them about anywhere, until the fuse gear is set." I wasn't so sure of that!

I then moved to the nose of the plane, where there was a box with lots of connections going into it with an arm. When the arm is set back and a button is pressed, it enables the plane to drop the bombs, so I needed to check that it was working, using a special meter, and then sign off the work with the senior NCO, indicating that I had done that part of the check, that the bomb gear was working and that the bomb release mechanism was working correctly.

As I emerged from the aircraft, I noticed that a girl (a WAAF) had arrived and was parked by the side of the plane, having come to greet us in her truck– she had come to take us all back to the mess or elsewhere on the aerodrome, wherever we wanted to go. The WAAF girl asked me if I was going back to the base, to which I answered that I was hungry, so yes. The girl indicated that the other fellas wouldn't be too long and then she would run us all back to the mess as it was quite a long walk. I looked around at the men and it seemed that they would be quite a while, and, as I had finished my tasks, I decided to walk across the aerodrome – I needed the exercise anyway and an opportunity to stretch my legs. The other men, who had finished their tasks, decided to wait for a lift from the WAAF, so I set off across the airfield. I hadn't gone very far when there was a most almighty explosion, throwing me to the ground on my face along with all sorts of materials falling on top of me. I couldn't hear a thing – I was stone deaf and lay there covered in earth, rocks, bits of plane, etc. When I came to my senses, after a few seconds, I jumped up and ran back to offer some help. Too late - the cluster of bombs had blown up with all the men, the plane, the van, and the girl. The blast had broken every bone in the poor girl's body and stripped her of most of her clothes; the others were all dead too. Possibly about 30 people all told. I was the only one left alive – how lucky can you get! But those poor people.....

There was a court of enquiry over the incident, which I had to attend, of course, being the sole survivor. The court was finding it hard to understand how such an accident could have occurred, leaving only me alive. I told them about the flare incident, but they didn't seem to think that it would have caused the explosion. I told them that I felt that it had to have been the flare that had fallen out and then been thrown back in amongst the bombs. After intensive questioning, it was eventually realised that I had nothing to do with the blast and the enquiry was closed.

This partly affected my hearing for the rest of my life.

9. Weekend Leave After Training

Following our initial RAF training, and after many weeks of hard slog, we were given our first leave - seven whole days and a rail warrant to go wherever we needed to go! Mostly the recruits went home to see their families, but I decided that I would go and visit my girlfriend, Florence.

By then, Florence had returned home to Ashington, Northumberland, to look after her two brothers as there was a bit of a crisis, being that her mother had left home. Her father, who was a coal miner, was finding it problematic with having to work AND look after the two young boys, stopping them from getting into trouble. Mining was essential work during the war. In fact, when men were commissioned to 'join up' in the army, they were often given the choice of army or mines. Lads who went down into the mines were often called Bevan Boys. A lot of ships were driven by coal in those days, so it was necessary to have a large work force mining the coal. So, her father had to call upon the services of his eldest daughter to come and babysit the boys: it was an offence in those days to leave your employment when you were engaged in essential war work, so poor Florence, who worked on ammunitions, had to send in a message to say she was ill as an excuse for being away from her job.

I sent her a telegram to say that I was coming to Ashington to be with her for the week, so could she meet me at Newcastle Station on the train from Manchester that would be arriving at

7 pm on that particular day. We hadn't seen each other in five months. On arrival, I spent over three-quarters of an hour looking for her in the crowds. Hanging around the station and looking about me in every direction gave the Military Police cause to deliver strange looks in my direction, so I decided to get onto the local train towards Ashington. The train was a corridor train, so after searching a few carriages, I soon found a seat. After a short while, I saw this very attractive young lady with two boys in tow coming down the aisle towards me. As she passed me, I thought that she looked familiar, and after what seemed like a few minutes, I realised that she looked rather like Florence; I jumped up and ran after her. She had really grown up in the months that I had been away, and I think I had also grown by a foot in height. It was such a great moment for us, one that was never forgotten as we both realised and were drawn into each other's arms. We then continued on to her father's house, with lots of news to catch up on and two mischievous boys in tow.

Her Dad was waiting for us at their home and, after introducing us for the first time over a cup of tea, he told me that Florence would see to the boys as he had to go to work in the Mine at 10.30 pm and I was to go with him to the working men's club for a pint so that he could get to know me. It was then that I started to feel nervous! I was about to be interrogated by the father of my intended bride-to-be.

We were sat with our pints and chatted away, breaking the ice; I don't think I had ever had a whole pint before. His face then became serious. He told me that he had to work and as I would be alone at night with his daughter while he was working, he hoped I was to be trusted to look after her, “No ‘hanky-panky’ or else you will answer to me and it will be severe!” he said, leaving no doubt in my mind as to what he was saying. I told him that she was the one that I would marry and that I would most certainly look after her with absolute due respect.

We had a great week together on that leave; it was so hard to say goodbye and return to the serious matters of war, knowing that there was a chance that we might not get through it and see each other again.

10. Finally Pilot Training is Agreed - 1941

RAF Waddington

From Bovingdon, I was posted to Waddington and then on to a succession of different Airfields servicing the electrical systems on various Aircraft that had battle damage or required major servicing following far too numerous flying hours, thus wearing out parts. I quite enjoyed these times; it was interesting as one didn't know which aircraft would be on the list to work on next.

After some months of working on aeroplane electrical systems, I felt I had waited long enough to be able to re-take the vision test that I had failed some months before due to a heavy cold. So, I asked to see the Wing Group Captain via the usual method of first requesting in writing. I deliberately gave the reason as 'private' in order to gain his interest and an audience with him. About ten days later, I was granted the appointment, where I was given the chance to explain my former ambition to join the Service as a pilot, my membership of the Air Cadets, a forerunner to the Air Training Corps, my designing and making of flying model aircraft, that the Germans had killed all of my friends and workmates in their raid on Croydon Airport (and many of my neighbours), and that I had joined up to try to prevent this from happening again through my work as a pilot. I explained further that as soon as my age allowed, I had volunteered for the RAF Volunteer Reserve as Aircrew and knew that my eyesight was twenty-twenty. I needed to get back on course for my ultimate aim. He was an amazing listener and had given me his undivided attention without interruption. He then said that because I was a top-class tradesman, and that I was doing a really good job in the field, I was fulfilling everything that the service required of me and that it was difficult for him to have me re-mustered back to finish the Aircrew training. My heart sank at that moment as I had really set my heart on flying. But then he continued, that after listening to me, he fully understood my reasoning and, with some reservations, he would put my application forward. No promises were given but there was a slim chance that I would be able to fly.

RAF Kidlington

It was some months later that, with great excitement and trepidation, I was finally posted off to re-do my vision test, passing with flying colours (forgive the pun!), then a further wait to get posted onto Cottesmore for completing my Aircrew training. I was then posted to Kidlington for flying training on Tiger Moth Aircraft. I had already covered parts of the course earlier on in my preliminary training during the induction into the RAF, so it was easy for me to continue a rather shortened course as a consequence. The courses comprised a series of lectures about the aircraft and its flight, and then we were taken on trips up in it to familiarise us with the aircraft. Before this, in 1941-42, training pilots were sent to Canada for their training and then would return to Britain to participate in the war, but so many new trainees were being lost on the ships on their return to Britain that it was decided to train them here in England. At Kidlington, we learnt to fly a Tiger moth and then our trainers would decide on whether we would continue to fly single-engine or twin-engine planes. I was chosen to fly the latter, so the next thing was that I was flying Air-Speed Oxfords and Avro-Ansons as a co-pilot once my course was finished.

Here we go again!

George, second from right

It is important to note here that previously, whilst a teenager and working at the Acme factory, I realised that to become a pilot, I would require to build my skills in mathematics and navigation. I had received a very elementary education, which had been curtailed due to the onset of war, with nowhere near the mathematical skills I needed for flying. So, whilst training as an air cadet, I got myself on a course at

Croydon Polytechnic to learn these mathematical skills, which I felt would put me in good stead for the future. Little did I know how useful this would prove during the war. Fortunately for me, my pilot training required a good understanding of trigonometry, this meant I was able to pass the course with 'flying' colours!

Moving on again!

RAF Northolt

The practical business of flying was fine for me, as I seemed to take quite naturally to all the control functions. Once the course was finished, I found myself suddenly posted to Northolt to fly Avro Ansons with ADLS squadron (Air Delivery Letter Services), flying up and down the country delivering official war letters, war documents, letters of importance and aircraft parts – for a few months, first flying as a second jockey (co-pilot) and then as pilot. It was a comparatively enjoyable time as the ADLS deliveries took place from Monday to Friday most weeks, which then gave me my weekends free to visit home in Croydon to see my family and my fiancée, Florence. I would just jump on a bus to Ealing and then on a tube and a bus to get me to Thornton Heath, Croydon.

Whilst at Northolt, I did get to visit many of the hundreds of aerodromes across the country, which was a good experience and became of great help later on when navigating in inclement weather, being able to spot landmarks from the sky, a skill that would serve me well on future flight missions. It was enjoyable visiting many of the war time aerodromes across the country. Sometimes these days I look at a map and try to remember all the ones I visited at that time. Impossible after so many years have passed!

Though I was reluctant to leave Northolt, I would, however, have really preferred some 'action', but I did my job well and it kept me safe.

RAF Manston 1942/3

My memory does not always serve me well as far as dates and names of places, but I think it was in late 1942 or early 1943 that I had cause to land at Manston airport, on the Kent coast. We were flying in an Avro Anson aircraft, as part of ADLS Squadron, delivering post and parts etc. We had travelled quite a way that day and landed at Manson, deposited our delivery, and felt it was a bit late in the day to head back, so we decided that we had better stay overnight. Even in those days, we couldn't just run back to our plane, start it up and take off, it all had to be organised, refuelled, and then scheduled into the flight plan. Having spent a pleasant overnight stay there, we arrived back onto the apron of the airfield at about 8 am in readiness to prepare the plane for take-off and return to our base. There was a bit of sea mist coming across the airfield and there were many people about, doing all the things they do on busy airfields. At Manson, we were only eight minutes away across the sea from the enemy territory in France, with the Focke-Wulf able to fly at 300 mph. Suddenly, a pair of German Focke-Wulf fighter pilots came from out of the sea mist at only about 100ft above us, shooting at anyone and everything with cannon fire, scooted down to the end of the airfield, did a tight turnaround and came back over us shooting again before they returned to France. We were all standing there, taken aback by the speed of things as there was no warning of their attack. There was an old BSA machine gun post nearby, which had a motorcycle saddle and two BSA machine guns on a rig that had to be cranked before using. I managed to run to it and jump on the saddle, firing a couple of shots into the sky just as the two enemy planes left back through the mist. Missed! I did look this incident up recently on the internet, but all they have on the records is one incident when they were severely bombed in 1940, but no entry for this incident. I just wanted to verify the dates, but I believe not every encounter was logged or reported for posterity. Fortunately, no one was hurt, and no planes were destroyed. Following that incident, we took off and flew to Hawkinge and Lympne, then back to Northolt, where I was stationed at the time.

I really liked the Anson. One amusing fact about the Anson was that whilst flying it, the undercarriage was manually operated with a hand wheel, with which you had to manually operate the undercarriage to lower the undercarriage and retract the wheels. It makes me laugh, looking back!

RAF Upper Heyford

Following the few months at Northolt, I was suddenly posted to Upper Heyford, an operational training unit, to take a course of training on flying Wellington bombers for conversions as a co-pilot, doing 'circuits and bumps' or Fighter Affiliation, learning greater proficiency of flying this aircraft around the aerodrome and handling the plane in the air. The main purpose of this training was to acquaint new pilots as to the manoeuvrability of fighter planes and how to avoid enemy fighter aircraft whilst in the air. If the bomber crew were to stand a chance against the fighters, then they, too, needed to learn how they could toss and turn a big bomber aircraft around in the sky.

As part of the training, the Wellington bombers would take off with all the crew and special camera guns on board. The bombers would be flying along on the level, and we, in our Miles Martinets (pretending to be German planes), would be flying around them, above and below, just as if we were having a battle in the air, and they would be firing at us with the camera guns then analyse the results to see how many 'hits' they got. That was lots of fun, ducking and diving and spinning around in cloud, dangerous, but fun training. It was fabulous – I couldn't get enough of it. One of the crew said as I went to take the plane out yet again that day, "Not you again! Haven't you had enough of this yet? Don't you get airsick?" To which I replied that I could do it all day and not get bored!

Whilst on the airfield at Heyford, we had other duties. The RAF were paranoid (rightly so) that we would be invaded from the air by planes full of German paratroopers landing all over the countryside, so all the airbases were ensuring that personnel were patrolling the airfield all night long – we all had to take our turn with loaded rifles and a Very pistol with which to warn everyone if there was such an invasion. I'm not sure we would survive if we were spotted as they would pick us off very easily – they were expert paratroopers, so we had heard. There was very little cover on an airfield, so there was nowhere to hide. We had to patrol with our eyes wide open and listen for aircraft overhead. But, of course, the aircraft would release the paratroopers a few miles or so away and they would drift and steer their way down to their destination, so the aircraft might not necessarily be heard directly overhead. Nothing came of it, though – we didn't see any paratroopers. We were bombed, though. The bomb fell just outside one of the barrack blocks, killing one man and injuring another couple. We were fortunate that they did not persist, as there were many planes there, and many men.

Once the 'conversion' training was completed, we had to do 'operations'; this was to ascertain our 'readiness' to fly safely. We were to fly initially as co-pilots in these aircraft to carry out a few 'nickel raids', dropping slivers of aluminium and nickel over France to confuse the enemy radar, and as a means to practicing the new skills for flying Wellington bombers. Sometimes we would drop flares. Generally, it seemed, pilots didn't like doing these types of runs, so it was often left to the newer trainee pilots as part of operations. They would then get us to land at different aerodromes to gain experience of landing on unfamiliar runways and changing plans at the last minute, seeing how we could cope under pressure. One poor chap came back with a 4000lb bomb on board. His plane had been shot, so the bomb release gear had seized and not offloaded the bomb. He got to the end of the runway and crashed, causing a huge explosion and loss of life for the crew and himself. We would then move on to being the main pilot for a further few hours of training, before becoming an accomplished Wellington pilot. These planes were very vulnerable to getting shot down as they were relatively slow and under-armed; fortunately, I was not shot down.

During this busy time in the midst of training, I somehow managed to make it home to see Florence. She was having a hard time with working on night shifts every night through the German bombing campaign. Although she was very afraid, she still worked relentlessly at her ammunition-making machine through it all; that was real courage, something she never lacked.

RAF Turweston

From Upper Heyford, I was posted to Turweston Aerodrome, near Silverstone, Northamptonshire, which was also an Operational training unit for Wellington Bombers. It was whilst there that my good friend, Bernard, who had been with me in Blackpool and had been a wireless Operator/Air gunner, was killed during action. He was an air gunner in the rear turret of the Wellington Bomber. Unfortunately, the centre spindle of the rear turret, which was supposed to have a glued-on safety cushion, was missing. For some inexplicable reason, when the aircraft landed, he stayed in the turret (one was supposed to exit the turret before landing), probably to make a quick exit on landing. The aircraft made a bumpy landing, and the spike of the spindle pierced his skull and killed him. The commanding officer of the Squadron gave me my late friend's effects and asked if I would take them to his family in Romford. Florence and I did this one Saturday and met with his mother and father. They were a Jewish family and Saturday, being their holy day, was perhaps not the best day to call, but between many tears and hugs, they made us most welcome as his good friend. It was a tough trip for us with the many changes of buses from Croydon to Romford but worth it in memory of my late friend, Bernard Weiz.

I thought I would soon get transferred to flying the Mitchell Marauder and The Boston Aircraft, but instead, I was transferred to Wyton on the Mosquitos, tasked with photographic reconnaissance with the PRU.

I had every kind of experience that you could think of; in fact, I think the Air Ministry liked posting me on 'crazy' missions so that my RAF record was all over the place.

Here we go again!

11. Mosquitos at RAF Wyton 1943/44

RAF Wyton & RAF Melksham

WW2 Mosquito with George on the tarmac at The Lincolnshire Heritage Museum 2022

After arriving at Wyton airfield, Cambridgeshire, and having an interview with the Wing Commander, I was sent on yet another course for the new navigational aids: the OBOE (British Aerial Blind Bombing System, based on radio transponder technology); the GEE (a radio navigation system to measure the time delay between two radio signals to produce a fix with accuracy) and a few other courses on the navigational instruments. These courses were in Compton Basset and Melksham in Wiltshire, then I spent five weeks in Dyce, Scotland, completing a conversion course for Mosquitos before returning to Wyton. So, clued up on the latest navigational aids, I was given the new assignment of Photo Reconnaissance in a Mosquito on PRU1 Flight, flying a number of ops mostly to

Cherbourg or St. Nazaire in the Bay of Biscay, France. I loved flying the Mosquito; it was the fastest plane we had during the war. I was looking forward to this leg of my flying journey!

Here is a little more in-depth information about the PRU. In September 1939, the RAF formally took over a civilian photo reconnaissance unit (PRU) based at Heston Aerodrome. The unit had previously been contracted by MI6 to perform clandestine photographic reconnaissance over Europe. In November 1940, it was redesignated No. 1 Photographic Reconnaissance Unit (1PRU) and that is when I was training with them. The unit was equipped with a variety of aircraft modified with cameras for the photographic reconnaissance role, including Spitfires, Blenheims, Lockheed Hudsons and de Havilland Mosquitos. Then, later in the war, 1 PRU was disbanded and the individual Flights of the Unit were redesignated as five separate squadrons, Nos. 540, 541, 542, 543 and 544 Squadrons.

The sole purpose of Photographic Reconnaissance was to provide the most up-to-date critical intelligence to the Admiralty, who used this information to strategically plan the Allied actions in the war. Alongside the information gathered by the Special Operations Executive on the ground, and the Bletchley Park Codebreakers through the airwaves, the Photo Reconnaissance Unit physically captured 20 million images of enemy operations and installations during six years of war. Without this vital information, the success of operations and, ultimately, the outcome of the Second World War could have been very different.

Every aircraft we flew was very different from another, so we all had an Aircraft Flight Manual that would give instructions particular to the type of plane we were flying. Flight manuals contained vital procedural and performance-related information for a particular aircraft or aircraft type. Manuals had to be kept up to date as inaccurate information could compromise the safety of the aircraft. I did keep mine, and my flight log, for many years before they were lost in a fire, along with nearly all of our personal possessions, including the few photos I had taken during the war.

We would get into a plane, and the navigator would read off a long list of instructions for me, the pilot, to check before we would be ready for take-off, even though I knew the procedure by heart. It was quite often dark on take-off, and there were some very dim 'glim' lights to help, but they were difficult to see. We'd get to the end of the runway, clear the trees, and we were off. Some mornings we would take off in 10/10ths cloud cover, flying on instruments only. We would need to get above cloud cover for fear of being shot at by our own as well as enemy planes, and then there would be sunshine above the clouds, flying at about 21,000 feet. The Navy would fire at us with anti-aircraft guns if they did not know what the aircraft was, as did the coastal sites. The only problem was that if we ascended too quickly to reach above cloud level, we would use up too much fuel too quickly. It was also always good to be able to dive into the cloud if we saw the enemy coming, especially as we were unarmed. It was always best to do the ascent more slowly in order to conserve fuel, especially for longer journeys. So at about 6 or 7 miles away from the target we would start our decent to about 3,000 feet, where we were relatively safe from any enemy small-bore guns. In order to take the photographs, we had to fly at a fixed speed, something like 300mph very steadily and at a precise moment, the navigator would say, "Now", and I would count off the seconds that the cameras would be working, approximately 15-second bursts. Then I had to do a barrel roll, another 15 seconds of camera burst and so on so that the other cameras could run and be synchronised with each other and I would get a continuous film of the target. On our return over the sea in the Bay of Biscay and the Channel, we would keep an eye open for any U-boat activity and report back on that too during the de-brief.

I had learnt the German "Focke-Wulf" plane could turn faster, it could turn inside your turn in the Mosquito, get behind and on your tail and could shoot you down. Essentially, if you're in a Mosquito and you're fighting a Focke-Wulf, it could out-turn you. What I found out from those who were at the forefront as fighter pilots was that if a Focke-Wulf got on their tail, they would immediately bang the throttle full on and climb vertically until they got almost to stalling position. He would be coming up fast behind, but he can't climb vertically, so he passes on by. They would then tip the Mosquito over, roll it over before it gets into a flat spin, then they'd find that they would have their

Mosquito on his tail and could then shoot him down. This didn't happen to me, but this is just one of the many tips I picked up from the pilots fighting on the front. You never knew when a piece of information such as this would prove useful.

A friend of mine flew an old walrus; it was an amphibious aircraft, so it could be landed on either water or land; it was often used for air-sea rescue. This Walrus came into an airfield I was visiting, and I was with a group of guys, one of whom was a Sergeant Engine Fitter. They serviced the Walrus and filled it with fuel but as they looked up at the engine, they noticed a fuel leak, which needed seeing to. The Sergeant fellow got a step ladder and as he was adjusting the valve to stop the leak, the petrol was trickling down his arm and the sleeve of his uniform. It evaporated fairly quickly, so normally it wouldn't be a problem, but for whatever reason, there must have been a tiny spark from a tool or something when suddenly "Boom," and his uniform and arm were covered in flames, burning all his arm and shoulder. We managed to get him down and put out the flames. He was taken immediately to the sick bay, but sadly, upon arrival, he died from the shock of it, poor fella. That surprised us as we thought he would survive. He was married with children – very sad.

We were a small group flying Mosquito planes, the latest version. These photo reconnaissance aircraft were completely unarmed as, in place of guns they had cameras. They couldn't have both; otherwise, they would be too heavy and would not be able to reach the maximum speed required to fulfil their task and get away quickly from enemy aircraft. They were the latest Mk 12 version and had a pressurised cabin with 'blisters' on the side so that the pilot could look back, and they had paddle-bladed propellors and Griffin engines (the latest Rolls-Royce engine) instead of the Merlin engines that the previous models had. This plane could really move. The paddle blades meant that you could fly more comfortably at high altitudes – to 25,000 feet and more. There were some fuel-saving controls, such as changing the pitch on the propellers to give maximum speed without too much effort on the engine and they had very accurate navigation aids. It was a plane that you 'flew'; there was no relaxing back and letting the plane fly itself. It was a plane that was potentially dangerous to the inexperienced pilot; you had to get to know the plane in order to handle it effectively. Many of my mates were sadly killed flying Mosquitos in the Photo Reconnaissance Unit. Some didn't get home due to running out of fuel over enemy territory, others were shot down. Later in the war, I did get to fly some planes that were armed, the same plane but they had four cannons (40mm), four machine guns and six rockets; just a bit different to having cameras!

We were carrying out photo reconnaissance of submarine bases along the French coast for the Royal Navy. The plane was kitted out with three cameras built-in to the fuselage, so to record photographs, we would have to roll the plane at an angle overhead of the target. The cameras were synchronised and would take a film of the area. We had to fly over enemy-held territory at a very high altitude and then drop down and take the photographs. We would fly up the English Channel past Cherbourg and Brest to St. Nazaire in the Bay of Biscay. The task was to record the movements of submarines coming in and going out of the submarine pens, and any changes in their movements or routines. The flight would have to take off very early in the morning, at about 3.30/4 am, to catch the submarines in their pens as they emerged for the day. Getting up early to put on our 'silks' and flying gear, we would then have a cup of tea and head off to flying control for a briefing and weather update. The range of the Mosquito was 1,500 miles.

The weather was quite often very cold, with thick cloud and drizzly at that time in the morning (it must have been winter). We would get in the aircraft, taxi out along the runway following the glim lights (small, dim, blue lights only switched on for take-off and landing in the dark or bad weather), and take off into the low cloud base. We'd check the compass and set the navigation equipment and be on our way. We would soon climb above the cloud to the clearer skies and visibility.

Our Mosquitos would arrive over the target just before dawn and photograph 'wolf packs' of submarines going off in different directions. We would fly very high, then dive down over the site and roll the aircraft in order to take the photos, then climb back up to a high altitude again for the journey home. Once landed, the cameras would be taken off, and the film would be removed and processed, and sent off to RAF Medmenham in Buckinghamshire to the Central Interpretation Unit (CIU). The

CIU was involved in the planning stages of practically every operation of the war, and in every aspect of intelligence. Towards the end of the war, the daily intake of material averaged 25,000 negatives and 60,000 prints. When the war ended, the print library, which documented and stored worldwide cover, held 5,000,000 prints from which 40,000 reports had been produced.

Following close examination of our surveillance photographs, other aircraft were then assigned to drop bombs into the pens to stop the submarines, and any of our ships could be alerted as to their probable arrival in their vicinity. It was a dangerous business as we would be unarmed and try our utmost to avoid any enemy planes sighting us, often diving into cloud cover if any enemy aircraft were spotted.

It was about a 1200-mile round trip, so we had to always be aware of the amount of fuel we had left in our tanks, assuming, of course, that the tanks were completely full to start with! Once we had completed our mission, we were to return home via the safest route. This would, of course, be over the sea, back the way we came. Some crews, particularly if they were running short of fuel or sometimes even just to save time, would decide to fly back over land, straight across France. This was a shorter distance but definitely more dangerous. I found that if you kept the plane at a steady speed and climbed slowly, often staying within the cloud, then you didn't use the fuel so much. Some of the guys liked to be above the cloud for greater visibility, but that would then use more fuel, up to three times as much. Of course, flying in cloud had its dangers, too, as you never knew what aircraft were flying around in those days.

It was advantageous to be familiar with all the airfields in operation during wartime. I'm so glad that I had the opportunity to familiarise myself with so many airfields during my flying with ADLS. On occasion, we had to land in Perranporth or another airfield on the South Coast, or Benson closer to home, as we were running so low on fuel. We would refuel and continue onward to our home airfield, Wyton.

Accurate navigation was key to keeping safe. Of course, we did not have the use of satellite navigation in those days, so recognising landmarks, use of a compass and a stopwatch, the sun, stars, or a sextant were some of the ways in which we would find our way around. We needed a good knowledge of trigonometry for navigation. Thank goodness I had taken myself off to college when I left school to study higher maths; it was absolutely necessary for the tasks I needed to do whilst serving in the RAF.

Sometimes we were tasked to drop a series of flares to light up an area over enemy territory in order that the Lancaster bombers, whose navigation aids were not so precise, could see the target and drop their bombs more accurately.

We were constantly open to attack by their Focke-Wulf FW190s and anti-aircraft fire, which was pretty accurate. Visibility could also be non-existent at times. Some mornings we would wake up, and it would be freezing cold, with 10/10 cloud cover, rain, and snow. Not pleasant, and we definitely needed to use our navigational skills to the utmost as we would be flying on instruments only. We would aim to get above the cloud, but then the plane would start to freeze up. The runway only had little glim lamps that lit with a blue light as you were taking off or coming in to land; they were hardly recognisable when the weather was throwing all it could, at you. If the engine cut out, that would be it!

When I think about it now, it was suicidal!

There was an enemy jet fighter called the Me-262, which was brought in later in the war, in 1944, which was very fast indeed. The Me-262 was faster and more heavily armed than any Allied fighter. Its flight endurance, however, was short, only about 20 minutes in all, as it burned up fuel very fast. If one of them had spotted you, then they could easily catch up with you and shoot you down, there was very little chance of accelerating away from it. However, the Me-262 was not very manoeuvrable, so it was possible to escape by using the many tricks we Mosquitos employed at the last second to avoid being shot down. Me-262 pilots claimed a total of 542 Allied aircraft which were shot down. The Allies also countered its effectiveness in the air by attacking the aircraft on the ground and during take-off and landing.

According to intelligence gathered via photo reconnaissance, it was found that there was some unusual large disturbances of groundworks and manufacturing going on in German-held territory. It transpired that the Germans were building a 'super-gun'. The V-3 (Vengeance Weapon 3) was a large-calibre gun working on a multi-charge principle whereby additional propellant charges are added to the bomb as it is fired and moves along the barrel of the gun to add greater speed and range to it. The Germans had planned to use the weapon to bombard London from two large bunkers in northern France. It was designed to fire every five minutes, day and night, and was aimed at London. Following surveillance of the area by the PRU, a number of Lancaster bombers were tasked with their destruction using another 'superbomb' designed by Barnes-Wallace (the inventor of the 'bouncing bomb'), and they were rendered unusable before they were completed by Allied bombing raids.

It was on one of these reconnaissance operations that we had a large part of the canopy of the Mosquito blown off by anti-aircraft fire. This was a desperate thing to happen as the cockpit was pressurised, so suddenly, at 27,000 feet, we found ourselves without oxygen. My oxygen mask, which had been dangling around my neck, was blown off in the blast. It only took us a couple of minutes to drop down to 7,000 feet in order to get breathable air, but that frightening feeling of gasping for air seemed to last for ages before I could take a full breath. As frightening as it was, we soon got over it at the time, but this was to deeply affect me in later life, giving me nightmares and panic attacks for many years.

On an air base, you'd meet a new crew or crew member one day and get to know them over a drink or whilst awaiting orders, then the next day or a week or so later, they'd go on an operation and not return. It may be that they had crashed, were shot down, or were hit by anti-aircraft fire. Memos would go around that this person or that crew had 'bought it'. That was the attitude, and it became a very sad part of our daily life in the Forces.

At the Crack of Dawn – by George Pritchard

A knock on the door with a nice cup of tea,

My pre-arranged morning call for half past three.

Get up, get dressed - flying kit and scarf of blue,

Feeling overloaded in sheepskin and uniform too.

Off to Control - more briefing and weather report,

Ceiling very low, rain, sleet and ice of some sort.

Visibility nought. Take off time four thirty am, plane de-iced,

Control locks removed, check the fuel load, twice!

Climbing aboard then pre-flight checks, start up the engines, boys,

Exhaust flames lighting each rain droplet - one hell of a noise.

Set up the prop pitch and get this sweet 'Mossie' in trim,

Brakes released, off we go, instrument lighting down to dim.

Head along the runway, glim lamps alight and so hard to see,

Flying control tower flashes the Aldis over to me.

We race like a tormented bee up the shortening runway,

Up into complete blackness t'ward the first light of day.

Set the compass, head fast to south-west,

Altitude reached - 21k will be best.

Goodbye to Cambridge. Target - Cherbourg, arrive at dawn,

We hope the flak gunners are all having a yawn.

We dive to our target into the barrage at mile five,

Hoping the Almighty will keep us alive.

Over the Penns, cameras on, U-boat sightings the main prize,

The fuselage rattling from close shell hits, not that that is a surprise!

Didn't know I was screaming, flying circles then back into the Bay,

And quickly gain altitude through the cloud of the day.

Assessment carried out for damage and fuel check,

We have enough to get to Wyton and see us onto the deck.

Landed at last, reported sightings and detailed de-brief,

Off to the Mess for breakfast and tea, then bed for an hour of relief.

Then back to Operations and find out what's next to do.

It was a strange life in those days, in 1942!

12. The Avro York at RAF Lyneham

I clearly remember this one adventure, which came sometime in 1943. We were flying Dakotas and were about to do an air test following a major overhaul on one of the aircraft. Flight Lieutenant Thomas was the pilot on this occasion, and we headed off across the aerodrome to where the aircraft was waiting after all the work that had been done on it. The maintenance crew was busy finishing off and clearing away, and we were ready to sign the 'Form 700', which showed what had been done to the aircraft and any special repairs. That signed, we set about doing a quick visual check before take-off.

George with 437 Squadron and a Dakota, circa 1943. George back row far right

We had just got airborne at about 800ft on the plane when the whole nose rose up from its hinges in front of the windscreen, obliterating our field of vision. These planes had a split nose (like a beak), the bottom part housing the radar apparatus, and someone had not replaced all the fastenings following its service. We could only see sideways, to the left and right, but not ahead. We radioed the base, telling them of our dilemma and told them of our plan to try to circle the airfield to gain altitude, put it in a stall, and then try to shake the nose down. We had to gain altitude in order to do this, so that we had time to come out of any spin that might have ensued. That didn't work. We set about working on plan two. The pilot suggested that I lean out of the astrodome and try to push it down! I was not too happy with that as it would be difficult for him to hold my legs, and if I was to slip, I would be straight into the propeller blades; no, thank you! We then tried some more stall stunts, dipping suddenly to try to get the nose down.

We finally decided that the only thing we could do would be to try to land with a limited view of the landing strip through the side windows. The airfield was informed of our decision and the fire crew and ambulances were positioned in readiness for a landing problem. It was a harrowing experience, flying and landing virtually blind, but we made it safely and saved the aircraft too. We were lucky to survive that! We then trekked across the airfield to see the maintenance people and see if we could ascertain who had not replaced the fastenings.

There was a court enquiry about it, and the radar mechanic was found to be guilty of not replacing the fixings after he had been working on it. Apparently, he did the service on the radar on the aircraft, and then it was lunch time, and he disappeared off. He thought he would have time to go and get lunch and come back and replace the fixings, but, in his time away, an air test was planned, taking off without the nose being bolted back in place correctly. He was trying to blame the flight sergeant, who was in charge of maintenance, for not checking that everything had been done properly. He got 90 days in the cooler for that.

RAF Lyneham

At this time, there was a surplus of pilots, so I found myself on 'loan' from my squadron to Lyneham from RAF Wyton. My role in this instance was in supporting and training Canadian pilots in navigation over Britain, pointing out landmarks as we travelled. I had received much experience in the use of my geographical knowledge to help with navigation across Britain due to my time spent in ADLS, delivering materials, letters, etc., to the various airfields across the length of the country.

I soon found myself in yet another 'situation'. The things we were doing were generally quite routine, but one day in January, we were flying in a Dakota Aircraft on a very cold and dismal day, where the sky was tinged with an eerie yellowish glow. The two Canadian pilots and I were chatting about how they were going to a Village dance that evening and did I want to go with them. Those village dances were great fun and afforded some great light relief to our flying antics during the war. There would always be a number of locals, including a lot of young ladies, at the dance with live music where everyone would dance a lot of country dances, which we would enjoy learning with a willing partner.

The Canadian pilot and co-pilot were strapped into their seats flying the plane, and I was standing between them, describing how they could get to the Village dance hall.

It began to snow heavily, and it wasn't long before the ground was a complete white-out, and we were lost, due to not paying attention and navigating properly. We circled the sky a few times to try and locate our whereabouts by observation of landmarks. Fortunately, I knew the area well, so I pointed to Swindon Town, which was just visible through the snow clouds due to the smoke from hundreds of chimneys, as was the way in those days with coal fires. Once there, from 800 ft up in the air, I was able to point out the railway line that we followed and which led us out to the Village, called Dauntsey, which was near the Airfield base. A soot marker had been run along the length of the runway in the snow, so we did a circuit and prepared to land. As we were approaching the ground, the Canadians were still chatting away, not looking, and so dropped below the minimum landing speed (about 70mph) as they put the flaps down for landing. They were coming in far too slow, causing us to drop rapidly and fall, fortunately in a slightly upright position, just making it to the start of the runway and hitting the ground with a mighty 'crunch' and breaking off part of the undercarriage. That sent the plane spinning up the runway at speed, with parts breaking off right, left, and centre. Fortunately for us, there was lots of snow and ice, which enabled the plane to slide rather than create much friction, whereby we would have burnt to a cinder. The two Canadians were strapped in, but as I was standing un-belted, I was sent careering up the inside of the Plane hitting everything in my path. When we finally came to a stop at the end of the runway, the rescue services came and jacked open the door and took one look at me and said, "This one's dead", as I had been almost knocked out and was covered in blood and minor cuts. I soon proved them wrong as I stood and, feeling somewhat shaken and grazed, climbed off the plane. Thanks to the ice on the runway, we all survived but had a lot of explaining to do at the ensuing enquiry!

The plane, unfortunately, was a right-off.

We certainly had some adventures in those planes!

On another particular day, December in 1944, I had dressed warmly, as flying in military aircraft in those days was a very cold affair in aircraft which were unheated. Under my uniform jacket, I wore a heavy turtle-neck sweater, and lamb's wool lined flying boots that were very well worn; these I had repaired at the cobblers in the village of Dauntsey nearby.

We were going to carry out a fuel consumption test and many other tests, on a seven-hour flight down to Cornwall; then up the Irish sea to Inverness; across to the east coast; then back down the centre of Britain back to Lyneham.

The aircraft was an Avro York, a converted Lancaster Bomber design. This aircraft was going to be used in February to fly some special VIPs (Churchill & Anthony Eden) to Yalta in the Soviet Union for a conference with other world leaders, taking a route to avoid enemy air fire, and we needed to do an air test on it to be sure it would go the whole distance and be exceedingly reliable.

Arriving at the crew hut for briefing, I conversed with the test pilot, Flight Lieutenant Ian Frazer and explained the tests he needed to do. I knew the pilot very well, having flown with him on occasion beforehand, but I didn't know the rest of the crew, the co-pilot, the Fight Engineer, and a radio operator. Also with us was another guy who was an instruments engineer; he was to carry out adjustments and checks on the aircraft's many instruments during the flight.

Take-off was scheduled for 8-45am. I went over to the aircraft, which was standing about a hundred yards away, and there I met the Flight Sergeant in charge of the major service to be carried out on this aircraft. He inspected the form 700, all duly signed, and I read any notes on them. The pilot came over and did the same, and the aircraft was officially signed for by him.

We then all boarded the aircraft, the crew having checked the outside of the aircraft to ensure that there were no tail or other locks left in place and the tyres were in good working condition. The wings were then coated with de-icer fluid, and the wheel chocks were pulled clear. With all four Rolls Royce Merlin engines started, to get them warmed up before take-off, the pilot, referred to as 'Skipper', asked me to go up to the cockpit for a word.

On arriving at the cockpit, and standing between the pilot and co-pilot's seats, he told me that there had been a last-minute change of plan, in that we were going to go to Knott's Corner RAF base in Northern Ireland. He asked that whilst the crew were getting themselves fed in the officers' mess there, would I go to a farm and try to get a dozen chickens and some eggs for their officer's mess back in Lyneham, as Christmas was in about a week's time? If I wanted some, that was fine, and he would pay for mine too. I realised that it might be difficult to get off the base to do this and shared this doubt with him. His reply was, "You are a resourceful fellow, do your best." He went on to say that he would do it himself, but he had checks to do on the plane, plus it would be bad form at his rank to do so.

We taxied out for take-off, and I returned to my seat in the main cabin. There were only two other seats, everything else had been stripped down to bare metal in the cabin so as to be able to carry freight. Following take-off, there were some words of disagreement between the Skipper and Flight Engineer. I hadn't followed their conversation, but I had noticed that there was a charged atmosphere between them. I recalled that this officer, the Flight Engineer, was a little overbearing and not a man to cross, according to some. He had caused some considerable trouble one night when acting as Orderly Officer. (Some months later, he was to disappear over the Bay of Biscay in another aircraft that was never found).

We had a steady flight down to Cornwall; visibility was excellent, and it was a really pleasant flight observing the countryside of England below so neatly formed like a patchwork blanket. At one stage, we were 'buzzed' by a Spitfire Mk.1X. around Plymouth. It was great to get such a view of this fabulous aircraft in flight AND a grin from the pilot as he came very close, almost under our wings. It was one of the very latest Spitfires, so it must have been from one of the other test establishments. It had a contra-rotating 6-bladed prop, a beautiful machine; the pilot waved to us as he passed us by.

A lot of turbulence was apparent just off the north coast of Wales and we experienced severe buffeting. It was very cold, and I remember wishing that we could get landed soon, so that we could get warmed up with a cup of tea and some food. We had been airborne by this time for some hours.

Ireland, the 'Emerald Isle', was every bit as green as its name suggests as we made our approach and landed at Knott's Corner air base. On instructions, we taxied to a point near to the control tower and shut off the engines. Opening the main door of the aircraft, we lowered the aluminium ladder, and we all climbed out, to be met by the usual soft top 15cwt van driven by a rather 'butch' looking WAAF girl. The skipper gave me two white Fivers for the chickens, and we arranged to meet back at the aircraft in two hours' time. All of us climbed into the vehicle, to be taken to our respective messes.

Once the flight crew had left us, and the WAAF had started to head with me to my designated mess for lunch, I explained to her the task given to me and the lack of tasty and substantial food back on the mainland in those days. Food seemed much more plentiful in Ireland. I asked her if she knew of a way that I could get off the Airfield, go to a farm and get back within the hour and a half available to me. To my surprise, she said that she would take me through the gates and on to a farm that she often went to for chickens and eggs, for the various messes at this base. With luck, I might get back for a little food before we took off back to Lyneham again.

Getting out of the guarded gatehouse was not easy, and if I had been on my own, I would not have made it. Our WAAF driver was well known to the S.P's in the gatehouse and she persuaded them to give me an hour, telling them what it was I was up to. Time wasn't on our side, so she drove very fast down these narrow country roads around the Airfield for about ten miles before arriving at a small farm, a really ramshackle place, in a sea of black mud, about four inches deep. We found this out to our cost, as we almost fell into it numerous times. My poor boots! Arriving at the main door of this tumbledown farm, we knocked for some minutes before the door was eventually opened by the farmer's daughter, a pretty fourteen-year-old, dressed in an oversized man's striped shirt, mud-stained, woollen skirt and wearing a scarf and mittens. We explained why we were there and asked for the Farmer.

She recognized our WAAF driver, whom she called Barney; for some reason. I never found out why, as our driver's name was Barbara.

'Daughter', as that's what the Farmer called her, screamed out "DAAAAAAAAD, there's people here for eggs!" a couple of times at the top of her voice in a very high pitch, wrecking our eardrums. A few minutes later, a man appeared, the Farmer. He was short and broad, wearing very dirty clothes, and with an Ulster accent that I really could not understand, so we just stood and looked stupid. However, he understood us and took us down a very muddy, slippery path to the other side of a broken-down barn, where we suddenly found ourselves surrounded by at least five hundred chickens all looking for grain. I gathered from our WAAF that he wanted me to strangle my own, but I declined, being a bit squeamish about killing animals. He then moved through the chickens, snapping the necks of ten or more of them, which he shoved to me still kicking, before I put them into an old tea chest, for us to take away. He then set about finding a lid and then some string to tie up the tea chest. By this time, I was getting extremely anxious as the time was going on, and I didn't want to miss the flight back.

Job done, I gave him the Fiver, which he looked at quite suspiciously, then his daughter came with four-dozen eggs in a box lined with newspaper. We must have overpaid him because he smiled a toothy grin and invited us in for tea with his family, which we declined, accepting our plea that we were flying back to England within the hour.

'Barney' drove us back very fast, but it was too late for us to get any lunch, I was terribly hungry by now as we went straight to the Aircraft where the crew was waiting for me. They gave me their sincere thanks, especially at the cheap price we got them for, and I passed over the change. Once boarded with the treasured chickens and eggs, I asked if anyone had got us a sandwich or anything from the mess. Unfortunately, they hadn't, but one of the crew gave me a bar of dark chocolate from the skipper to tide me over a little, decent of him, as chocolate was as rare as square wheels in those days.

We received instructions to taxi out, and, after a five-minute run-up on the engines, we did the pre-take-off checks before heading out to the runway. The weather had begun to deteriorate, as it so suddenly can in those northern latitudes. The wind was gusting at more than forty knots by this time and rising. With nose pointed into the wind, we took off into a leaden sky, heading to Scotland, and continued our basic task of testing the Aircraft. There must have been ten thousand feet of cloud above us, so we flew just under cloud base, lower than three thousand feet I would have estimated.

After about twenty minutes flying, as part of the continuing tests, the port outer engine was shut down, and the propeller feathered, then shortly restarted again successfully. The starboard engine was then dealt with in the same manner. The port inner engine was then shut down and became difficult to restart, coughing and stuttering; it was raining really hard by this time, and at that point, the starboard engine stopped unexpectedly, probably due to a build-up of fuel. We were over the Irish sea at that point and flying on only two engines.

This caused a lot of panic on board, as the aircraft flew badly on just two engines and would not gain height but was gradually losing height. On the pilot's instructions, the Flight Engineer came into the main body of the aircraft to operate the Ki-gas pumps, to inject petrol into the failed engine. All eyes were on him at this crucial time. He was much too fast with the pumping, and his actions proved unsuccessful; the pilot was giving instructions and getting 'commence start' signals back from the Engineer. By this time, things were getting serious, as the waves were almost lapping the undercarriage from the tremendously rough sea in force-9 gale conditions. There was much cursing and many insults being bandied between the crew due to their fear of impending disaster.

I must say I wasn't very happy myself at the thought of a watery grave, as we would have no chance at all coming down in that sea with forty-foot waves and bubbling foam on top due to the wind. Our trip to Ireland was an unscheduled detour - we weren't supposed to fly over the sea, so consequently, there was no safety gear on board, and no one from the base even knew we were there. There was driving rain, and a gale and the plane was consequently rocking all over the place.

There were four controllers which accessed the priming pumps to provide extra fuel for the engines on starting. I could see that the engineer on the pumps was panicking and pumping far too fast, probably flooding the engines. In my frustration at his unsuccessful attempts, I jumped up and pushed the engineer aside, saying, "Just let me do this as I think you're doing it wrong!" I had watched it done many times by other people, and the key was to do this slowly in order to get the desired outcome – the re-ignition of the engines. The process of 'self-preservation' had kicked in! Controlling my fear, adrenalin forcing itself around my body, I pumped slowly. I think the Engineer was shocked at our situation, angry with me, and a bit confused at what just happened, but it did not deter me. The starboard outer engine was again started, and we then concentrated on the port inner, and despite it being slow to respond, we managed to get all engines running, albeit the latter not running too well. At this point, we were only about 50ft above sea level! We were then finally able to gain some altitude. I could feel everyone breathe a sigh of relief as I returned to my seat.

The atmosphere between the crew was now tense, pilot and co-pilot remonstrating with the Flight Engineer for his failure to start the engines at such a crucial moment. The radio operator was also complaining that he should have been allowed to send a 'mayday' signal in any event, despite it being an unscheduled detour that had brought us over the Irish Sea. The skipper thanked me for not panicking and doing a great job, saving their lives, while the Flight Engineer shouted at me, saying that I was ignorant of the seriousness of my actions and that he had more experience than me and I should have left it to him. Just as well, he didn't know that it was my first effort! He was hopeless.

We continued our flight up towards Scotland, and then had to gain altitude to fly over the mountainous terrain. Travelling back down the centre of England, we eventually arrived safely back to base, having completed our tests, and after a very bad flight and dangerous landing in such awful conditions. In all, we were flying for about eight hours. There was a quick de-brief, and we made our report in the form 700. The plane passed the tests and was ready to carry its VIPs on their long trip.

Being by then, after 6.00 pm, we were too late for our well-earned meal, but the cook had saved us some cold corned beef and potatoes, thank goodness! On our return to base, we unloaded the chickens and eggs onto a waiting truck, ready to take them to the mess. "Hang on a minute!" I said, "I would like one, as agreed, as I was the one who had acquired them." They kindly obliged, and I was handed a chicken to do with what I wanted. I should have sold mine to a friendly local, but I decided to send it home to my mother as a treat for the family. I had to work out how best to get it back to my mother. I returned to my quarters, wrapped it in brown paper, and tied it up with string, then, the next day, popped it down to the post office to send it to her. Of course, I didn't even think about the fact that firstly I should have gutted it, and secondly, it would go off during its erratic, war-time postal journey!! Poor mum! She received this parcel, opened it, and couldn't get rid of the smell of rotting chicken for days. She found my note saying, 'Happy Christmas, enjoy the chicken'.

They had a good laugh on me but unfortunately no chicken for Christmas!

Later that evening, I met with my pals in the mess for a laugh and a drink. On the morrow, I would be on an air test with a Canadian crew on a Dakota, another laugh-a-minute!

13. The D-Day Normandy Landings

In 1944 I had returned to Wyton and was then involved in what became known as D-Day. The Normandy landings were the landing operations and associated airborne operations, which took place on Tuesday, 6 June 1944. It was known as the Allied invasion of Normandy in 'Operation Overlord', often referred to as 'D-Day'. It was apparently the largest seaborne invasion in history. The operation began the liberation of German-occupied France and laid the foundations of the Allied victory on the Western Front.

2TAF, the 2nd Tactical Airforce, was formed in June 1943 in connection with preparations to train groups to invade Europe a year later. It took units from both Fighter Command and Bomber Command in order to form a force capable of supporting the Army in the field. No.140 Squadron, of which I was now a member, was to provide strategic photo reconnaissance.

At that time, I had been moved on to Benson Aerodrome. I flew over Normandy on D-Day 6 (12 June 1944, the sixth day into D-Day) in the evening with another pilot. Where we were flying above the clouds, it was bright sunshine, but down below, it was dark due to the angle of the sun as it was setting. As we looked down, we could see fire and gun flashes on the ground below from all the fighting that was going on down there. We were flying in a circle, about 20 or 30 miles into France near Caen, doing our photo reconnaissance, observing any reinforcements that were heading towards the coast. We all felt for those trapped between the Germans and the sea and did all we could to alleviate the situation until they could be further re-enforced.

Some weeks later, I happened to be standing near to the plane we had tested when an entourage of people were being escorted onto the plane. It was none other than Winston Churchill and Anthony Eden. They passed right by me – I felt really honoured to have seen such a great man. They were going off to attend the Yalta Conference with The Soviet Union. For information, the Yalta Conference was held on February 4th – 11th, 1945, and was the World War II meeting of the heads of government of the United States, the United Kingdom, and the Soviet Union to discuss the post-war reorganisation of Germany and Europe. The three states were represented by President Franklin D. Roosevelt, Prime Minister Winston Churchill, and Premier Joseph Stalin, respectively. The conference was held near Yalta in Crimea, Soviet Union. The aim of the conference was to shape a post-war peace that represented not just a collective security order but a plan to give self-determination to the liberated peoples of post-Nazi Europe. The meeting was intended mainly to discuss the re-establishment of the nations of war-torn Europe.

14. The Ghost of Blakehill Farm

On this one night, I was returning from leave in London. I managed to get on a steam train, and it was very late at night when I arrived at Didcot, near Swindon, then, I would have a very long walk to the base. I needed to get back to RAF Blakehill Farm; I had to be back by 6 am, and by this time, it was 2 am. I was looking around in the hope of grabbing a lift off someone. I saw a van with an ATS girl who was delivering mail to the train and picking up the next lot for delivery to the Army camps.

"Are you going anywhere near Blakehill Farm Aerodrome?" I asked, hopefully.

"OOOh! no," she said, "I can't give you a lift; it's not allowed. This is Government mail, and we are not allowed to give anyone a lift. Sorry."

"Oh well!" I said, "I've got a 15-mile walk then." After a few minutes of thinking time, the girl returned and said, "Look, you can jump in the back as long as nobody sees you, and I will take you as far as I can, then you'll have to walk the rest of the way."

She took me about five miles up the road, and then I had to get out as she was going in another direction. At least I only had about ten miles left to walk now. I felt sure I could do it in three hours to get there by 6 am. It was a cold, clear, frosty night, so I set off along the road at a fast pace to keep warm. I headed off down the quiet country lanes; it was a lovely, frosty, moonlit night, so I could see pretty well, and there was no one on the roads, of course, at that hour. I was striding it out along the lane, knowing that I had to get there in time. As I was walking along, I could hear footsteps behind me! I thought, "Who would that be, out here at this time of night?" I looked around but couldn't see anyone. Every time I stopped, the footsteps stopped, and I couldn't hear anything. Thinking it was just a figment of my over-active imagination, I continued to walk on, but the footsteps started up again. After a few minutes of this, I was starting to get a bit worried, as I was miles from anywhere, and every time I looked around, there was nothing to be seen. It couldn't have been my footsteps echoing, could it? I stamped my foot just to convince myself that the steps I heard were not me. Suddenly I jumped sideways with fear as there, in a break in the hedge and in the moonlight, was a great white horse that had been following me on the other side of the hedge. It looked like a great, white ghost and made me nearly jump out of my skin. I went over to it and stroked its soft muzzle, talking to it softly. It was obviously lonely and looking for a treat of some kind which it found in my hand, the remains of a biscuit from earlier in the day.

He made my day!

15. RAF Blakehill Farm and on to Arnhem 1944

At RAF Blakehill Farm, Swindon, I was attached to the 2nd Parachute Regiment, Airbourne Division. They had a job for me that they thought would suit me down to the ground. I was seconded to the Second Airborne Division, where I was to be handling a squadron of men as a sort of platoon commander to travel to Arnhem, Holland, and prepare special runways for our planes, as the ground in Arnhem was really boggy and made the landing of planes rather treacherous.

The Battle of Arnhem was a major battle of the Second World War, often referred to as 'Operation Market Garden'. It was fought in and around the Dutch towns of Arnhem, Oosterbeek, Wolfheze, Driel, and the surrounding countryside from 17th –26th September 1944. The prime aim of Operation Market Garden was to establish the northern end of a 'pincer' ready to project deeper into Germany. It was planned that allied forces would project north from Belgium, 60 miles (97 km) through the Netherlands, across the Rhine, and consolidate north of Arnhem on the Dutch/German border, ready to close the pincer.

Our role, had that operation been successful, was for our unit to service the planes that were to fly to Arnhem. But first, we had to travel to Arnhem by special gliders and put down a kind of mesh and steel plate on the ground to make temporary runways so that our fighter planes could land safely on the soft, soggy ground in Holland. The fighter planes we had then, the

Typhoons and the Tempest were quite heavy; they were bigger than Spitfires or Hurricanes. These were the only planes that could knock out German tanks as they had 4-inch rockets on them – these needed to land at Arnhem, where the earth was too muddy and soft without the runways we were to lay.

We were duly kitted out with special Army uniforms, machine pistols, and hand grenades and told that we were to travel in Gliders, towed by Aircraft, to Arnhem to carry out our tasks. I had been issued a special 'Sten' gun, of which I was very proud. The Sten gun is a family of British submachine guns which were used extensively by British and Commonwealth forces throughout World War II. They had a simple design and very low production cost, making them effective insurgency weapons for resistance groups, and they continue to see usage to this day by irregular military forces.

Later in my life, in 2005, I was privileged to have been invited to join a reunion of Arnhem War Veterans when a special commemorative stone to honour those lost from the Canadian Royal Air Force was being set in the ground at Blakehill Farm, near Cricklade. During the ceremony, I scanned all the veteran faces, hoping to spot someone I knew from wartime. It was so difficult as many decades had passed since the war. I took the opportunity to talk to the mayor of Cricklade, who was honouring the event. I explained that I could see no one that I knew in the war at all, and he offered to ask the audience during his speech. As promised, at the end of his speech, he asked if anyone there knew George Pritchard. There was silence. However, after the speech, whilst we were all mingling and eating from the buffet, I came across a one-armed veteran who, it transpired, I did know. He had flown in Dakotas, dropping supplies to troops on the ground. His plane was shot down by the Germans, taking its wing off as the plane hurtled to the ground. As it crash- landed, he was thrown out, ripping part of his arm. The Germans found him bleeding profusely and quickly applied a tourniquet, saving his life. He was well looked after in the German hospital and returned to tell the tale. It was great to finally find someone who I had served with.

Arnhem Veterans Reunion, George centre

Just before going on the operation to Arnhem, I received a 48-hour pass for leave to see Florence, who was still in Ashington, Northumberland. I set off, travelling by train from London. Trains in those times were absolutely packed, people everywhere, even sleeping in the luggage racks if they could get up there. All along the corridor were people sitting or standing, so it was impossible to try to get through everyone if you wanted to go along and find a space in a compartment or use the toilet. Everyone seemed to smoke on the train, so the air was thick with smoke and filled mainly with troops. There I was with all my latest kit, Sten-gun, grenades, rounds of bullets, kit bags, travelling on this train. It wouldn't be allowed nowadays, but it was a commonplace sight in those days. Life was entirely different. Everyone always got on; it's like we were all mates, even though we were, in reality, strangers. We all had this bond, a camaraderie about us. There was always someone to chat to on the train and to share a laugh and an anecdote about life in the forces.

It was a steam train, and the journey was a very long one, as the train would shunt into a station and fill up with water or coal for the next leg of the journey, then move out, sometimes swap carriages or have to stop in mid-countryside, or worse still, under the cover of a railway platform roof whilst a bombing raid was taking place overhead. You would never know if the train would get shot up by a German warplane on its route, particularly if you were travelling in the South or East of Britain and closer to the coast near France. Steam trains released steam from the heated water. They had a fire (obviously) which would glow at night, plus a stream of smoke from the fire, a dead giveaway that it was a train heading across the dark countryside to some marauding German planes at night. On arrival, Florence was very pleased to see me, and her brothers were excited to be so close to guns and grenades. "Hands off!" was my warning to them as they scampered away. The 48-hour break was much needed and enjoyed; one never knew when or whether there would be another break in the coming months.

To harden us up at Blakehill Farm Aerodrome, in readiness for this task in Arnhem, we had to dig ditches and live in tents in nightmarish weather. It was freezing as it was winter. We were given a tent that was not more than about ten feet square for six men. We had to dig a trench all the way round to hold the groundwater and prevent it from getting into the tent. For sleeping, we had to lay on a ground sheet with a couple of blankets and our overcoat over us at night. The living conditions through that winter in the tents were so hard, and day-to-day life became a nightmare. Many soldiers went down with pneumonia and other such infections due to the severe cold. We were given a daily Rum ration, but that didn't help the cold, damp and icy conditions.

There were military police all around us day and night because of the secrecy of these missions. We had to wait until the area we were to land in, near Arnhem, had been cleared of enemy by our troops before we could go in. When the message came, they loaded us up onto gliders to head for Arnhem. On this one day, we were all sitting ready and waiting on the glider to be called for take-off. It was 6 am and we sat there until about 10 am at which time we were called down as it wasn't going to happen that day and we'd try again the next day. We then were able to go to the tea wagon, which had arrived on the airfield, and try to relax and just wait. The next day we were called at 3 am to get ready for a 4 am take-off – all our kit on with stem guns, ammunition, and everything ready to go. Then came the message that it was a washout, they'd not managed to complete their task in Arnhem, and we had to stand down again. They needed us to leave at 3 or 4 am as then it would still be quite dark when we arrived, and that would give us better cover. By this time, we were getting really keyed up. Eventually, for the third time, it was all 'on' again and they got the glider hooked up to the plane. The plane engines were running, then suddenly it all stopped, and we were called down again. The mission had been finally abandoned. There had been failures to get the forces and services in place in Arnhem, and the fighting had moved on further through the country, so the planned operation had to be stopped; the areas designated for landing were no longer on boggy ground, so no longer required our runway-laying services.

Yet again, I had a lucky escape because if I had landed there, I would have most certainly been captured and possibly killed.

We were then called to get on the wagons heading down to Tilbury Docks with all our kit. We were off to Germany!

Here we go again!

It took a day to get from Swindon to Tilbury docks in convoy, arriving by late in the afternoon, whereupon we drove all the vehicles onto the ship. The men, about 110 in our squadron, all stood on the decks, along with many other military personnel, all kitted up with guns and backpacks, waiting for the ship to finish being loaded before setting sail at 9 pm, when the tide was right. It was a flat-bottomed vessel whose purpose was normally that of a tank landing ship, so that it could get close into the shore.

As we went down the River towards the North Sea, the Captain, standing on the ship's bridge, called everyone to attention using a large megaphone. He stood waving a large, 45 calibre, Naval revolver, telling us the sad tale of the last lot of troops that sailed on his ship the previous week. They had been nervous and spooked by the German E-boats that had been spotted off the starboard bows. One soldier had been nervous and had called out to everyone to abandon the ship. Like lemmings, many jumped overboard. The German E-boats didn't attack in the end, but the ship was unable to pick up the men overboard, so they probably lost their lives by not following official orders. The captain then raised his gun and proclaimed that he would personally shoot anyone who shouted out "Jump off the ship" if we were attacked by German E-boats. That was us warned!

It was quite a distance across to Oostende, and the boat was moving at some speed when, about two-thirds of the way across, in the distance, we could hear some other sea vessels. The E-boats were a very fast-moving torpedo boats, so you could hear their engines screaming from quite a way away. We were all feeling nervous as we realised that if the torpedo boat was aware of our position, then it would be the end for us, either by the direct hit and explosion of the torpedo or by the ship sinking and leaving us to swim to who knows where? There were some life rafts on the ship, but they were possibly not adequate in these war-torn waters. Our ship just carried on regardless, though very quietly. We weren't allowed to smoke or talk in case of being seen or heard, and there were no lights to be used on the ship, so it was pitch dark. The only small light was a feint blue light on the instrument panel on the bridge. Luckily for us, the E-boats didn't come near us or detect our presence, so we managed to get to our destination.

16. Holland

On arrival at the harbour wall, some 'runners' were put out to provide a narrow pathway to allow the vehicles to disembark. These vehicles were Canadian Chevrolet lorries, with windscreens that sloped inwards from the top. The vehicles were driven off the ship by a couple of men via the 'runners', and all personnel were advised to disembark on foot, for safety reasons, otherwise, the lorries would be too heavy for the runners if fully loaded with men. That was a fortunate rule for us on this occasion.

It was the middle of the night in Oostende. It was very dark with only a couple of very dim lights with which to see. The first lorry to negotiate the runners was going well when suddenly it missed the planks and fell overboard into the water of the harbour. The poor guys never got out as it was punishingly cold, and two men drowned. Everyone was shouting and screaming at the next lorry to make sure it didn't go the same way. As we watched the lorries being off-loaded, our hearts were in our mouths. No need to have worried – our drivers were not going to make that mistake again! They were safely on land, we were loaded onto the lorries and then driven a few miles up the road to Blankenburg, where we got out of the lorry and into a hotel, well, what remained of a hotel after the Germans had given it a bit of a beating, but the ground and first floors were alright and prepared for us. It afforded us at least some protection from the weather. At least there was a clean and warm floor that we all fell headlong onto, leaving our guns all stacked around. Four hours later, it was 6 am the next morning when we were awakened and put into the wagons heading towards Arnhem. We found out afterwards that the upstairs of the hotel we had stayed in was a brothel.

"You might have told us!" some of the fellas complained. The hotel had provided a 'red-light' district for the German army.

It was hard going as there were many obstructions and mines planted on the roads, which were already potholed and almost impassable. At that time, the Germans were still occupying Arnhem, so we got as far as Nijmegen and Enscharde, until our troops had freed Arnhem and we could move on. In Enschede, they had found us some huts to stay in, that had been erected by the Germans, so we had a roof over our heads at least. We had some time to kill whilst there, so I had a wander around the town. Amazingly there was a shop open selling lovely goods, and the handbags caught my eye, so I decided to get one for Florence. The shopkeeper didn't want money; he was more than happy with a tin of coffee, a pack of cigarettes, and a bar of soap! All the ladies and children around the place wanted to offer us all sorts of goods, towels, jewellery etc., in return for soap, coffee and such like. A tin of coffee, if they sold it (one lady told me), would keep them going for about four weeks in food and everything. I gave her and her friends three bars of soap, though food was what they really wanted.

We set up camp and a cook house for the duration of our stay, and, of course, the soldiers would leave some remains of their meals, slices of bread, and such like, which would all go into the bins. When we came out of the mess, we'd see lots of children all diving down into the bins to see what food they could find and then eating it hungrily. They were skinny and starving! Then the men began buttering a piece of bread and handing it out to the children. We didn't want to see them delving into bins. It was so hard for them.

All too soon, we were sent on to the Rhine to offer our support for our troops who were gradually advancing into Germany, pushing the German army back.

Enschede

We were following a convoy of lorries from Ostend. The British army, meanwhile, had managed to fight its way onwards to Enschede and free it from German occupation. The terrain then changed to a more chalk-based substrate, and now it was very clear why we were no longer required to lay the track as the ground was much firmer, and our planes could land easily.

We eventually arrived in a small Dutch town called Enschede. The people there were glad to see us but were in a terribly bad state, suffering from hunger and lack of many basic requisites. Seeing the state they were in, we gave them all we could in the way of food, coffee, and soap. They had not seen anything like it for years and were most thankful. Whilst there, I traded a tin of coffee for a delightful hand-made dress for Florence (my daughter still has it!).

Germany – and across the Rhine

From there, we followed up the Infantry and got across the Rhine. Every place was devastated. Land mines were everywhere, and there were many dead bodies in various stages of decomposition and from both sides lining the road; used ammunition was all over the place. An extremely dangerous place altogether, I did not want this role that had now become largely unnecessary. I wanted to get back to my Squadron now that there was no need for us, being here.

Having crossed the Rhine behind the Infantry, there were lots of intense fights going on in pockets of the area. The infantry was the 51st Highland Division and 1st Guards Brigade that we were following up. They were pinned down by Tiger Tanks dug into some small gulches in the valleys of the undulating countryside. Our Infantry were under cover of a dense forest, but there was only 200 yards of grass, then a road, then another 70 yards of grass between them and the Germans. This was the scene when I arrived through the forest to meet the Army Major who had called up for air support. I had been sent to assist with the spotting and directing of troops by radio using our Mosquito Aircraft.

Accompanied by an Army Signaller and a heavy radio transmitter, we were told to creep up a small, fern-covered hill adjacent to and overlooking the battle area. I could clearly see the tanks that were dug in and covered in brush and also the German troops behind them. The going was a bit hairy as we were under sniper fire the whole time that we were crawling up the hill. We were an easy target as we were displacing the fern fronds as we moved. Bullets were snapping past our ears from time to time, so our noses were in the dirt, and we were progressing very slowly. We hadn't quite made the top of the hill when we heard our own aircraft overhead. The Flight Squadron Leader contacted me through the radio (the signaller having passed me the phone from his radio) and asked for details of what we could see. He wanted blue, and red smoke grenades fired to where the tanks were situated. I passed the relevant information on to him. He then told me that I was to report on their accuracy after the first aircraft attacked. I acknowledged, and the first plane came screaming down to where the blue and red smoke grenades were and skip dropped 250 lb bombs onto the tank emplacements, blowing earth and the tank tracks into the air. The Flight Squadron Leader was duly informed as to his timely elimination of the tanks. This was then followed by the rest of the Mosquitos bombing the other tanks. They then flew around and again attacked with rockets and cannon fire. The noise of this operation was deafening; bullets and 40mm cannon shells were flying everywhere. Sniper bullets were cracking past me and my companion while we lay there and continued as we eventually slithered back down the hill. With the tanks knocked out, our troops charged forward and established themselves, advancing onwards. We stayed with them for several hours, waiting for a Jeep to take us back to our airfield.

Handorf

Eventually, we arrived north of Munster, a town flattened by intense bombing and artillery fire, finishing up in a small village called Handorf, which was adjacent to a large airfield with a good, concrete runway. Most of the main buildings on the site had been shelled and bombed, so we had to pitch tents. I was fed-up with billeting in tents, so, after a brief recce, I soon found myself a room in an old Stately home on the edge of the town that had been abandoned. I billeted myself in the old building. The building had been hit with artillery fire, and some of it was in very poor condition, but there were some decent rooms that were certainly preferable to a standard issue bivouac tent! I found a decent room on one of the upper floors and fixed up the room with lighting, a bed, and a cupboard to make it more homely. I was very happy there except for the sound of a piano that began playing for an hour or so, starting at midnight, every night. It was very well played fine classical music, obviously being played by a talented musician. I did struggle to work out from where this music was coming. There were no buildings nearby, and the music certainly sounded as if it was within the building I was occupying. Feeling a little unnerved by the experience, I decided to investigate the pianist, who was waking me up every night, and find out where in the building it was coming from. I pushed my way into a large ballroom that had a very damaged and dusty grand piano at its centre. There was no way that it could have played a tune due to its state, and the strings within it were completely broken. I moved some bits of debris around and found some old sheet music lying underneath that I took away with me. This place was miles from any other habitation, so it was a mystery as to where the sound came from. After taking in the state of the piano and removing the sheet music, I never heard that beautiful sound again. Spooky!

Going back one night at about 11.30 pm, after some night flying, I was walking along the corridor to my room in pitch black darkness, when I heard a slight shuffle and sensed that someone else was there. I carefully crept along with my back to the wall to get to my room, where I had a torch and a loaded pistol. As I dived into the room and got my gun from under the pillow, I heard a rush of steps along the corridor, which then stopped. Now, armed with a torch and pistol, I searched each room in turn, eventually ending up down the stairs in the courtyard, but found no one. I searched all around without success and then retired to bed, feeling rather unnerved. In the morning I realised that the man must have escaped by hanging from the banister stays until I had given up my search. I must have passed him several times. Fortunately for me he gave up too! I did find, however, that my watch and many other personal things that I had bought in Brussels for Florence, my wife, had been stolen.

Remarkably, many years later, I met a young German girl who was living with my daughter in London and working as an Au Pair. Whilst chatting to her about her home in Germany, we soon discovered that she had actually gone to school in that very same building that I had been billeted in. After the war, this building subsequently became a school and college. How coincidental!

17. The End of the War is Announced

I was at Handorf, in Germany, just north of Munster.

On Tuesday, 8th May 1945, the message came through that the war in Europe was over and had all been signed off. We were happy for our friends and family in Britain, but as far as we were concerned, we had to keep going until we were stood down. It was later that evening, at about 11 pm, that we were officially stood down from the war. We had a squadron meeting later that day, which discussed with us the official end of the war in Europe but to prepare to be sent out to join our allies in the war with Japan. We didn't celebrate. We were so run down, with boils and feeling so tired and weary of war; we hadn't even had a proper meal for many months, other than corned beef with everything, so we were not really in any mood to celebrate, and in any case, we knew that the war was still going on in Burma for some.

Whilst in Handorf, that had been recently captured by our allies, I was on patrol on the airfield and came across an aircraft hangar. The German army had been through there fairly recently as it was all in a bit of a state, having been bombed and shot up by the allied forces. As I walked into the hangar, I noticed that there was an office at the side and decided to investigate. I entered the office and saw that there was a dead German at the desk because the roof of the hangar had fallen on top of him, killing him outright. On his desk was a dagger and a silver letter opener, which I rather fancied and kept as a souvenir. I touched nothing personal, of course, in fact, I felt rather sorry for the officer, wondering about his life and family, and being killed so close to the end of the war. I then reported that he was there to those in authority so that he could be taken and buried before the flies got to him.

Our Squadron leaders told us that we were to get ready for a long voyage on a ship out to Burma, or some such place, but not to worry about u-boats until we meet the Indian Ocean, where the Japanese u-boats would still be in action. Before that came to fruition, the Americans had their nuclear bomb in their armament ready. They then threatened the Japanese government, saying if they didn't surrender, then there would be a bombing campaign like no other, as a means to an end of the war. That didn't work; the Japanese would have fought to the death anyway.

At this time, by chance, I met a lovely, pretty, Dutch girl who was about 20 years old and was what they called a 'displaced person'. She had been taken for slave labour in southern Germany and had been very badly treated. The Americans had freed people in the south and in parts of Italy. She had gathered a few things and had walked all the way from there, in the south, back to Holland. She was only 30 miles from Holland when we met up with her. I was sat by the side of the road on a motorbike and could see someone walking towards me. She looked a bit wary at first, and I asked if she was alright. She could speak good English, so we got chatting and then she told me her story. She then asked if I knew of any barns or safe places where she might stay for the night, and I informed her of one that was nearby. She was also looking for some food, so I offered to go and find her some food and bring it to the barn on my motorbike. The chunky sandwiches I had made for her disappeared really quickly; I don't think she had eaten for a week! I hoped she would be OK, but she told me that she could handle herself – she'd got that far. I told her where we were living, above the butcher's shop, and offered to help if she needed any. She didn't require any help, and I didn't see her again. Hopefully, she arrived at her destination safely.

On August 6 and 9, 1945, the United States dropped atomic bombs on Hiroshima and Nagasaki, respectively. On August 9, the Soviet Union declared war on Japan. The Japanese government, on August 10, communicated its intention to surrender under the terms of the Potsdam Declaration.

The Japanese surrendered on August 15th, 1945.

As soon as the war ended, all of the countries in Europe started to pick themselves up quite quickly and began to do well. But in Britain, Churchill was out of Office, and Atlee was in. He promised that they would really look after everyone in the services, take care of the working man, and life was going to be wonderful for everyone. Of course, when we got back, for the next eight years after the war, there was rationing and clothing coupons, you couldn't get anything, and life was really miserable. Once labour was out of Office, then, things started to pick up. It was such a stark contrast between Britain and Europe when I was on leave. There was all the rationing in

Britain, and then I returned to Belgium, where they had plenty of everything you needed. That was the one thing I was not looking forward to once I was demobbed. It was really disheartening.

18. A Victory Wedding – 21st May 1945

It was now May 1945, and the war was finally over for Europe, but not quite for the rest of the world.

We had decided to get married at the end of the war. I had been given a travel warrant for a few days to return home, and so the plan was for a Victory Wedding, on May 21st, 1945. We had both been putting money and other things away in readiness for our future life together, and Florence had found a room for us with the mother of my sister's boyfriend. It was very small, being the second bedroom in a small, terraced house, but it would be the start of our new life together.

Our wedding was held in Ashington, Northumberland, Florence's hometown. It was such a fabulous wedding, with more than sixty guests; many friends, relatives, and neighbours had contributed their rations of food together in order to have plenty of food for the reception, including a wedding cake made by one of the neighbours. We were married in an old, quaint church and had the reception in the town's recreation hall. The people of Ashington were very friendly indeed and had created a grand affair.

My mother, sister, and father came up in his car, which we used as the wedding car. There were some drunken gate crashers that my father and I threw out of the place, but other than that, it was a fabulous celebration for all concerned.

We stayed the night in Florence's next-door neighbours, which was an empty house, too drunk to care but sleep it off. The next morning, after breakfast with Florence's mother and father, I received a telegram to return to Belgium immediately via an aircraft that evening from RAF Blackbush, near west London. Our honeymoon was non-existent, and we would have to wait.

My parents had returned earlier that day, so I couldn't get a lift from them. I had to just grab my kit and leave to get the first train from Newcastle to London, a quick hug and I was off; we didn't meet up again for eleven months. Eventually, the war ended but it was another two years before I was finally Demobbed and could pick up my life where I had left off.

19. Gütersloh, 1945-1947

After the war had ended, I continued serving in the forces in Germany for a further two years. It was there that I learnt to speak German quite fluently.

German plane junkyard

During my time back in Handorf, I had to shoot at some so-called 'Werewolves', a group of German resistors, who were trying to sabotage the main power supply transformer for the Airfield. From the blood seen on the ground around the transformer, someone was hit and wounded but had been quickly dragged away by his companions. I didn't chase them far, that would have been foolhardy and dangerous.

I was in Detmold and given a team of German ex-servicemen (as I could speak German) to oversee doing a few tasks. One such task was to repair a huge petrol tank which was buried underground and had stopped working. There was a huge screw cap that needed to be taken off. We used crowbars and eventually got it off and unscrewed it. There was a little ladder going down inside, and I asked for a volunteer to go inside and check out the motor. They all refused, and no amount of cajoling would entice them down. They said it was too risky with too many petrol fumes around and the motor being tested with the meter, too dangerous, so they refused. The motor was normally submerged in the petrol, and due to lack of oxygen, it would be safe from igniting. In the end, I went down into the tank. The fumes were overpowering, to say the least, but I managed to repair the motor as there was a loose wire which I tightened up, checked the motor, and all was good. I began to feel a bit light-headed from the fumes, so, happy that all was good, I went to exit, but the men had closed the cap and shut me in the tank. I was yelling and banging for some minutes inside the tank, all the time feeling my consciousness slipping away when they decided to open it to let me out; they'd had their fun. As I climbed out, they were all laughing as they thought it was a good joke. The guy that had allowed it to happen was a sergeant major. I was taking deep breaths to clear my head, then walked straight up to him and thumped him one. He apologised, saying it was only a joke, whereupon I pointed out that I didn't find it funny. They didn't do anything like it again!

Belsen

We were part of the air support for the 51st Highland Division and the 1st Guards Brigade. On this one particular day a few of us decided to go to the concentration camp in Belsen that we had heard about. We borrowed a jeep and set off. As we drew near to Belsen, we noticed that there were no birds singing, no animals, and a strange smell in the air, which became stronger as we came nearer. As we neared the gates of the camp, I do not exaggerate when I say there were at least a thousand dead bodies lying on the roadside, ditches, and the land around us. All emaciated and skeletal; some recently dead and some dead for some time. It was shocking, abhorrent, and repugnant all in one. There were as many 'inmates' still alive, just, and in a terrible state. The smell that permeated everywhere was something that would stay with me for a long time.

The army medical officer told us that they were doing all they could to help, but they couldn't give them good food yet. All they could give them for the moment was weak soup; it was all that their bodies could take until they could slowly build up their ability to take in good, rich nutritious food. They hadn't had solid food for so long. Many of them had typhus or some other disease and fleas, lice, and a multitude of other afflictions to add to their complications. They couldn't walk free, yet, as they wouldn't survive travelling any distance, plus the fact that they would be passing on dangerous illnesses to the people they meet on their journey. This they all understood and took in their stride. How could a fellow human treat another human in such a way? It doesn't bear thinking about.

We ended up staying there the night with the army personnel, sleeping in chairs, after having had a few drinks with the lads. The following morning, we had to go back, so we got in the jeep and headed back to base. Just after setting off, we saw a man lying in the road, so we pulled over to check it out. He was a very big, burly German who was definitely dead. It wasn't a very pleasant sight at all. We decided to call the German police, who arrived soon enough, asking us to wait around whilst they checked out the body, and then an ambulance (of sorts) came and took the body away. When we enquired as to what had happened to the man, the policeman said that he had been beaten to death and that they knew who the perpetrators were; it was a couple of guys in the concentration camp.

Apparently, what had happened was when the war was still going on, the camp commandant would send groups of prisoners out to local farms to work on the land or with the animals. This one group had gone to a pig farm to work for the now-dead farmer, and he had unmercifully beaten them all day whilst they were trying to carry out their tasks of shovelling the pig muck around, and other such unsavoury jobs on the farm. He had kept them working non-stop for over twelve hours with no food or drink allowed to pass their lips. A couple of the prisoners died from his maltreatment. In return, they'd made a resolution to get their own back if they ever got the chance. Three of them did get that chance, and took it wholeheartedly, to beat the life out of him. It must have taken a lot out of those prisoners, as thin as they were, to beat up and kill such a brute of a man. Seems like he got his just desserts!

It took about five months to get the prisoners into a condition where they were able to leave the camp. They were fed to build their strength, de-loused, given vaccines and medication to relieve them of their ailments and conditions, and finally given clothes, soap, and a bit of money to help them to find loved ones and possibly their home. Many of those poor people lost everything. There were some organisations in Palestine, run by Jews, who organised for people to collect prisoners from the camps and surrounding districts to help them return to Israel on ships, to start a new life.

So sad!

Once a person had been to see Belsen, in those times just after the war had ended, they would never forget it, and it left a lasting impression of 'man's inhumanity to man' on one's brain.

Berlin Air Lift

The airlift of food and supplies to Berlin had been going on since the end of the war in May 1945. The allied forces had been delivering food and emergency supplies to Berlin via planes for many months (long before the official Berlin air lift), but gradually it was getting harder and harder to carry out the task safely whilst the Russians were making it increasingly more difficult for us. Our role in this was to fly goods from Blackbush airfield north of Heathrow. The plane would get loaded up with food and supplies and fly over to Handorf, in Germany, stopping off there to refuel before flying into RAF Gatow in Berlin via the 'safe corridor'.

That operation led to me receiving the Berlin airlift medal.

1945 Bomber Command Berlin Air-Lift medal

Later, just after my time in the RAF, the Russians created a full Blockade on Berlin (26th June 1948 – 12th May 1949), which was one of the first major international crises post World War II. During the multinational occupation of Germany at that time, the Soviet Union had blocked the Western Allies' railway, road and canal access to the areas of Berlin which were under Western control. Following diplomatic discussions, the Soviets then offered to create an air corridor to enable planes to fly over Eastern Germany to gain access to West Berlin, so bringing essential supplies to the people living there.

The Allied Forces then began a joint operation in support of the entire city. Aircrews from many international air forces joined them and in total flew over 200,000 sorties in one year, providing urgently required necessities, such as fuel and food, to the West Berliners. The Soviets did not disrupt the airlift for fear that this might lead to open conflict, even though they far outnumbered the allies in Germany and especially Berlin. At the height of the Airlift, one plane reached West Berlin every thirty seconds.

On 12 May 1949, the USSR finally lifted the blockade of West Berlin.

....

I was with my Mosquito Squadron, based at Detmold in Germany. Whilst returning to my lodgings one night, I was crossing some scrub in a large field when out of nowhere appeared three scruffy Yugoslavs who menacingly asked me for a light for their cigarettes. Had I gone near them to oblige, they would have surely stabbed me for very little reason other than to take what they could. But I was too wise for that and, instead of reaching for matches, I pulled my gun out quickly and said, "Want a light from this!" and fired a shot over their heads from my Luger pistol. They broke the Olympic track record in running away, but in continuing my journey, I took great care to check that they had not followed me.

Gütersloh

I was later moved over to 21 squadron in Gütersloh. During this time, I did many reconnaissance flights over Minden on the east side of Germany and the surrounding countries. On one occasion, I looked down from the aircraft and saw row after row after row of T34 tanks on the Russian borders, thousands of them, all lined up and ready to come and have a go at us and

Germany, it seemed. It all looked very dodgy to me and didn't bode well for the future of the area!

It was a few weeks later, and I was coming towards the end of my time in the RAF and about to be de-mobbed, that my commanding officer, who was Group Captain of 140 wing, called me into his office and said, "I hear you are being de-mobbed then? Well, I think you should stay with us for a further five years. We need men like you and your specific skills are sorely needed out here. I can give you a promotion, a house, you can bring your wife over, you'll be fine here." I replied that I did not want to be there, with a wife and family, with all those Russian tanks amassing, all lined up not far away, as much as I loved my life in the Service and my duty to my country. I explained we'd had enough with the war and living in London throughout it, and I wouldn't bring her into it as it seems that any minute now, these Russians are going to 'try it on'. He didn't really believe my suspicions and tossed my doubts aside, but he accepted that no amount of persuading would entice me to stay.

So, the day came when I finally received my papers to say that I was to report to Padgate for demobbing. Whilst I was keen to get back to England and my Florence, I had many regrets in leaving all my many comrades, especially Ginger Meats, with whom I had had many good times and adventures. We had become very good friends and did a lot of things together out and about in our 'down' time. He was flying in similar aircraft to me, tasked with the same jobs, and he was a motorbike enthusiast; I have a number of photos taken of us on the bikes. On our movements around the area, we often travelled on a main road called the 240 Up. Along this road in the ditches were many broken, and shot-up machines where we would find parts for creating our own motorbikes. We would gather up the parts (army side-valve engine Nortons) and put them together to make one that would get us around to explore our surroundings. It had a 500cc engine and could do about 50-60mph.

One day, we were driving along the road on the motorbike (no helmets) when we hit something, and we both came off the bike. Miraculously, apart from a few small cuts and grazes, we were both fine. Someone had strung a length of barbed wire across the road – we could have been seriously injured if not killed! We picked up the bike, which was also not seriously damaged and headed off on our journey, making sure that the barbed wire was taken off the road to make it safe for others.

In one other incident, I was driving the bike and on the back was a Russian girl who was an interpreter for the Commanding Officer, she spoke many languages. It was October time, and at night when we were hurtling along a towpath beside the river Weser passing through mud and up and down small 'hillocks' like on a switchback. It was great fun. We were just talking about getting back to the mess for our meal when suddenly we hit some mud or a stone or something. Suddenly the front wheel went, and both of us and the bike were thrown into the air and landed straight in the fast-flowing and freezing river. We managed to swim to the bank; fortunately, we were good swimmers. We marked the place where the bike was and walked about 4 miles back to the camp, whereupon we got changed and went to the mess. Ginger wasn't happy at all. The next day we went to the river armed with rope, stripped off down to underwear, and set about trying to find the bike in the river. Using the rope, we somehow managed to pull the bike out. We were freezing cold and keen to get dressed, sharing a towel to dry off as best we could. The bike was amazingly undamaged. We then had to push the bike back and allow it to dry off. Fortunately, we were soon able to use the bike again.

We also began to re-build one from German parts from BMW, but we never got that one off the ground as we couldn't find all the parts required. We also built a motor boat. Ginger and I had found a serviceable boat that we fitted with a mower engine and propeller. We drove it up the river Weser to a Gastoff (Guesthouse), situated on its own island in the middle of the river. This place was full of disarmed German soldiers drinking weak beer. We soon made good friends with them and went there often, taking British and Belgian beer with us, which was most definitely preferred to the weak, watered-down beer they were used to, so that made us very popular amongst the beer-drinking fraternity. Unfortunately, my pal, Ginger, when a little drunk, would start a fight with them, and we had to make a rapid exit. But we always went back again, apologised for our behaviour whilst brandishing some whisky, which we shared with them, and therefore continued our friendship. Ginger and I had so many adventures together.

I would have actually liked to have stayed in the RAF because I enjoyed it after the war had ended, as there were many jobs to do, dropping off people, picking up cargo, backwards and forwards to Berlin etc. It was an enjoyable life when there wasn't a war on. I loved the freedom of flying – it really got to you and was hard to give up when I came to be de-mobbed. I had grown-up whilst I was in the RAF; I was only 17½ when I started and 24 when I came out, with a lot of flying experience and many other useful proficiencies under my belt.

A million men and women supported Bomber Command on the ground throughout World War Two. Their tasks included engineering, scientific developments, the loading of bombs, air traffic control, plotting, map creation and a myriad of other essential roles. 70,000 men and women were killed. Gone. And many more than that were injured. Of the 125,000 Aircrew who served, 72% were killed, seriously injured or taken Prisoner of War. Of Bomber Command, more than 44% were killed whilst serving, giving the highest rate of destruction of any Allied unit. The PRU, a highly effective unit, suffered horrendous losses too, indeed, records now show that the survival rate was proportionally the second highest of any Allied aerial unit during the entire war. Yet these crews have never been officially recognised, their sacrifices largely unknown. Of the 1,287 men who flew in the PRU, 378 were killed. Many were shot down over France, with 145 of those who died being buried in unmarked graves.

Each man was a volunteer, and their average age of death was only 23. The continual efforts of the RAF Bomber Command are said to have significantly changed the outcome of WWII. Their bombing forays did great damage to German industry. So concerned were the Germans about Bomber Command's capabilities that they permanently stationed more than 1,000 Luftwaffe aircraft for the purpose of fighting the bombers as well as more than 30,000 artillery sections.

A sobering thought!

Part 3 – Life

Moving on-

The highs, the lows, the good times

and the even better times

20. Demobbing and Back to Life, Back to Reality, 1947

The shades of winter and colder days,

the darker nights

We suffer ills that winter brings,

like flu and coughs and other things.

We adapt to suit the icy snow

and find we can't get up and go.

But Christmas day will soon be here

with treats for those we love and know

Travelling by train and then ship, I left Germany with all my kit and headed for Padgate in Lancashire, sending the news by telegram to Florence of my impending return home.

15.4.47 - TELEGRAM – PRITCHARD – 2 SUTHERLAND ROAD WEST CROYDON – ARRIVED HULL HOME BEFORE THURSDAY LOVE GEORGE

Unbeknown to me, she had kept this telegram tucked away in her purse for the rest of her life, from 1947 to 2013, when she died.

It provided very fond memories when I found it whilst going through her belongings some years after she passed away. Many other fond memories returned in that instant. It was quite a poignant moment. Life isn't easy.

It took two days of travelling to get to Padgate; the RAF demob base, where the next day, I was given a brown suit, having handed in my service uniforms and kit. We were also given a railway warrant, and I got £400 demob money to keep Florence and me afloat until I could find a job. That was not an easy task, with three million others demobbed and also seeking work. It was now 1947, with no flying jobs available and not much other work either.

I was amazed to find that, unlike in Belgium, Holland and France, rationing was still in force in England for literally everything, including clothes. Even fruit and vegetables were in short supply, whereas elsewhere in the world, everything could be obtained fairly easily. This was all down to a strong left-wing labour Government and went on for eight more miserable years before they were thrown out and rationing came to an end. That was worth celebrating!

Home

When I was on leave, the Christmas before being demobbed, I had brought a bottle of schnapps back from Germany. We thought we'd save it for a rainy day. One evening the following Christmas, we had decided that it was a 'rainy day' and to break into this bottle at home, when all of a sudden we heard this

"Bang, Bang, Bang," on the door and it was Florence's friends from work.

"Come on Florence, come and have a drink with us as it's nearly Christmas!"

We staggered out, and there were all these girls and lads from work, our eyes were hanging out – I remember it very well. We drank the whole bottle of schnapps between us. Good times!

I had to start again, from scratch; find a day job with regular hours; work inside instead of in the big outdoors; work in a quieter atmosphere, most probably. It was a very different life to the life I had been leading and somewhat difficult to adjust to at first. Life was tough for many years, bringing up a family.

When I came out of the RAF, there was virtually no work, well, only jobs that no one wanted. I hunted high and low, but my resilience paid out, and I eventually found a job. This first job I found was with the 'Melody Maker' pop magazine as a reporter. The first interview I did was of the 'Blue Stone Band' in a venue in Streatham where they were performing. I showed them my card, and then they were interested in being interviewed, telling of the type of music they played, where they were performing, what next, and so on. The report would then be sent in to the editors, and I would be sent to the next venue to do an interview and so on. This entailed much night work with very poor pay, despite going and pleading to the director to up the pay and the roll-out of jobs. I gave it up after a month of reporting on the latest Bands and pop stars. The boss expected me to work very long hours for very little or no pay, and the work was not regular enough. We couldn't live on the money coming in.

One day my good friend Ginger turned up having written me a letter a week beforehand saying he had some leave coming and could he come and visit as he was driving the motorbike home from Germany. I hadn't seen him since we were demobbed, so we had a lot to catch up on. He had arrived with terrible asthma, and he could hardly breathe. He was in a terrible state, probably due to the cold weather on the bike. We couldn't let him drive home on his motorbike all the way back to Swanage in the state he was in, so, although it was a bit awkward, we let him sleep on the couch, and we slept in the bed. It was a bit difficult as we only had the one room, but we managed. We had to both go to work the next day, so we left everything for him and told him to rest and we'd see him later after work. On return from work, he seemed a bit better and we were able to have a bit of a laugh and catch up on old times over a drink. The following day, still feeling under the weather, he was able to set off for home, wishing us well and that we'd catch up again soon. We never saw or heard from him again. We did try to write to him and track him down.

I always wondered what had happened to him.

Iron Foundry Work

The only trade I had was in the electrical field, through my pre-war experience and my training in the RAF, so naturally, I jumped at the first job I was offered in this field, which was as the maintenance electrician in an Iron Foundry. This was a really tough job. I had to get there at 7 am when all the furnaces were running, and the iron was ready to be poured. All the blokes would be on the floor on their hands and knees, working the sand into the moulds. You had to be ever so careful, as they were all like little sandcastles, then the molten iron was poured into the moulds. You could easily put your foot in the molten iron as it is poured, and it could burn your foot off. Very dangerous!

I was wiring up places with annealing ovens where the temperature in the rooms reached about 60 °C or higher. My task was to change the junction box or wire up a switch. The smell of the coke fumes was overpowering, and the heat was killing; you'd come out absolutely drenched. There were no baths or showers, so every night, I would wipe the blackened sweat from my face before getting on my bike to ride a few miles home.

At the time, we had our little one-roomed flat in Sutherland Road, Croydon, about 9ftx10ft, where we had to eat, sleep, cook and wash. It had a paraffin stove to cook on, which used to create an unpleasant (and probably unhealthy) smell in the room. Eventually, we bought a little Belling electric cooker which made meal preparation far easier and with no smell or health issues. I would arrive home late at night, and I'd be black from head to toe. Florence would have a piece of newspaper ready at the door for me to take my dirty outer clothes off before

I entered the flat. Then I would strip off the rest of my clothes over more newspaper, and she would have a bowl of warm, soapy water ready for me to have a strip wash in. Then she would get another bowl to wash again in as it would take two or three washes to get most of the black iron dust off my body and out of my hair. All told, it took about three-quarters of an hour to get cleaned up before I could step into the flat and have my supper.

Florence was wonderful in doing everything needed to prepare our meals and do most of the household chores. We had to take our washing to my mother's and clean up in a proper bath.

A.E. Deans X-Ray Equipment

After a couple of months, I managed to get a better job making x-ray equipment and soon got promoted to the more technical side of the business. I worked there for about five years. Most of the staff had been at this firm throughout the war, and there was much resentment about us 'veterans', and me in particular, being promoted to a better role in the company, but I had to put up with their grief as Florence, and I needed the money to save for a house of our own, and I needed a more interesting job.

During this time, my father had many businesses with good flats over them, which he rented out to others, but, as usual, and for some reason only known to him, he had no time for me and would not let us live in any of these premises. I tried very hard to find us a better living space, spending every minute of my spare time going around trying but without any luck. This became desperate when Florence found that she was expecting our first child. I badgered the Croydon council every day until, eventually I was given the tenancy of a flat in Raymead Ave, Thornton Heath, which was really the top half of a Tudor-style house. We then had three rooms and a kitchen to furnish, which we did with bits and pieces from parents, friends, and junk shops.

Soon enough, in 1948, our son, George, was born. Florence had a terrible time giving birth with many complications and nearly died. Worst still was the epidemic of a serious form of gastroenteritis, which had taken root in the hospital, and baby George came home with it being very, very ill indeed. Florence's mother came down from Ashington to help us with the new baby, and they took turns feeding him glucose and water, nursing him night and day, thus saving his little life. This resulted in a lot of stress and heartache for us and caused Florence to have severe post-natal depression and a virtual breakdown. Poor Florence didn't know what was happening to her.

I came home every lunchtime from work (that was five miles away) on my bike to check on her. On one occasion, I found her running down the road pushing the pram with George in it. I caught up with her just in time to stop her from running into the main road traffic in a frenzy. She never knew!

Eventually, baby George got better from this gastroenteritis bug, and we had no further concerns with his eating or health. Of course, that greatly helped Florence to get her health back on track. Fortunately, she recovered well and was soon back to her old self with a growing lad to run around after.

I realised that this job was going nowhere, I had got to the top, and there was no way that I would be able to improve my wages unless I did something about it. I was married with a small child, and we were struggling with the wages I earned. I needed some more training to better myself in my career, so it was then that I decided to get myself on a college course. I knew I had to really knuckle down and start from scratch, education-wise, as my schooling had been cut rather short due to the onset of war, and in any case, it did not have the depth and breadth that modern day school courses have.

I was to embark upon an electronics HND, which was to eventually take 12 years through night school. It was very hard work at that time with a job, a family, childcare to organise and a college course, along with all the travelling and homework that entailed. I was exhausted!

Once I had started the course, in 1948/49, I found a job as an AID Inspector for the Government (Aeronautical Inspection Directorate) and I went to work for a firm in Mitcham, who were making parts for aeroplanes.

With my new job as an AID inspector, I was now responsible to the Air Ministry and not the Company that employed me so my judgement on the quality of parts made for the air ministry was independent. I was very strict and passed only the perfect parts that were produced. I would not pass them if they were even very slightly out of specification, unlike some of the other inspectors, as these parts were for Aircraft Engines, so safety must be paramount. I was a tyrant! Having flown in a whole range of aircraft during the war, I knew that I would not want to be flying in any plane which had parts that were sub-standard. This did not go down very well with the management of the company, as these 'sub-specification' parts had to be scrapped and therefore caused a financial loss. Consequently, I found that the attitude towards me, from both the workers and the management, was constantly hostile, so I decided to look for alternative employment.

The man from the Air Ministry was ex-RAF, and we always got on very well when he visited me at my workplace. I told him of my situation and that I'd had enough of the management at this company and was looking to leave. He mentioned that he knew of a vacancy for a very good job going at Rotax, part of Lucas Aerospace in Acton, that was right up my street, and that he would recommend me to the company. He was well thought of there and told me that I needed to write a letter to them. True to his word, he did recommend me, and I duly received a letter to go to Acton in north-west London for an interview.

The interview was technically tough, but I was able to give the correct answers due to the knowledge gained on the courses in electrical engineering I was attending at the polytechnic in order to acquire qualifications. The wage offered was very good, and it was a great career chance for me to accept the job, but it did mean a lot of travelling each day by train, tube, and bus from Croydon to Acton.

Getting up at 6 am, Florence would get George ready then we'd put him on a bike seat I had made. I'd leave very early, whereupon I would cycle him to a creche. I would then have a four-mile cycle to Croydon station, tie up the bike and get on a train to Victoria, then Acton, and start work at 9 am. Working there till 6 pm, I would then head towards home, going on to night school most nights before finally arriving home at about 9.45, whereupon Florence would have a bowl of soup waiting for me. Florence was working too, at Phillips-Mullard in their transport office, so she would pick up George when her shift ended. At weekends I had to spend much of my time studying. Somehow, we managed, but it was stressful and exhausting for us both, particularly with a young child.

At one point, Florence had a job working on the 'tote' at various racecourses. These races usually took place on Saturdays and Wednesdays. She would have to leave very early in the morning, whereupon she was picked up by coach or given a train ticket to a racecourse, such as Doncaster, Oxford, Towcester. At the racecourse, she would be in a small cubicle or booth where people could buy a tote ticket. She had to be very good and very quick at mental maths to do that job as there were many different types of bets. She would never bet herself, but the company paid good money for the job.

Whilst living in Raymead Avenue, the people in the flat below us started to cause us some irritating troubles. We tolerated it for a while, but in spite of Florence's protests, it got worse; they continued to harass us. I was forced to go downstairs and give the man a big piece of my mind, and a bit more! After that they were very quiet and, not long afterwards, they left the place believing me to be dangerous! We then tried to buy the whole house from the Council, but one of the Councillors saw the opportunity and bought it himself, moving us into a new 'Prefab' in Addington, Surrey. This gave us a nice new place with a large garden in which young George could play, and we would grow many of our own vegetables.

We lived there for about seven or eight years until I had nearly finished my night-school HND course.

We decided to put an advert in the paper looking for anyone who also had a council property and who lived near Acton (where I was working) who would like to swap with us. We received a reply to our advert very quickly, the swap was approved by the council, and the move was on. And so, in 1955, we moved to a prefab at 67, Rectory Park Avenue, in Northolt, much closer to Acton. Prefabs (prefabricated houses) were bungalow style, flat-pack, quick-build properties that were erected post-war to rehouse those who had lost their homes during the Blitz or servicemen coming back from the war and their young families. They had all the modern conveniences of their time. This made a big difference to us and gave us far more quality time together as a family. I also managed to change to study my course at a Polytechnic nearer to where I was to be living. I had already done the HNC to an Ordinary level, achieving distinctions and merits on my passes, and now I had booked on to complete the HND course.

We then bought a Car to get me to work, only a distance of five miles away. The car was an old Austin 10, but it was a good car and, due to not being used much during the war, had not done many miles and was in good condition. It afforded us more freedom, and we were able to go away to Ashington in it to visit Florence's parents and to other places, and even on holiday!

In 1956, not long after arriving and settling into the new home, Florence found that our dreams had been realised, and she was expecting child number two. With much joy, we had our wish, and, after an easy birth, we had a daughter, Penelope Amanda (Penny), who became the light of our lives.

Florence was an excellent seamstress and was always busy making dresses, shorts, and dungarees for our daughter. We had a good-sized garden and grew lots of vegetables and flowers; Florence loved nothing better than to busy herself with the children in the garden; she was very green-fingered.

Both of us worked hard and saved hard towards buying our own home as soon as we were able. Florence, meanwhile, had organised a group of women to make dresses and other clothes part-time for a London company in Oxford Street, Richard Shops. She worked hard, spending long hours at the sewing machine, consequently making very good money towards our savings, all to enable us to get our own house.

In 1961, five years after Penny, we had some more great news – the birth of another son, John. With our joint incomes and savings, we soon had enough saved for a deposit on a house with some left over for us all to go on a good holiday. There was a nice estate of houses being built nearby; we had set our hearts on buying one of these houses as we excitedly perused the building plans. The decision was made, and I went to see the builder to try to buy one but was told that they were all sold. It was such a blow to us as we had set our hearts on one of these lovely semi-detached houses.

At the time, I was teaching mathematics to our doctor's son, who was struggling for a university placement. I happened to mention the business of the house to the doctor in the course of our conversation. To my surprise, he said that the builder was a personal friend of his and he would have a word with him on my behalf. Within a few days, this builder phoned me with a completely different attitude offering me any choice of the few houses they had left. We couldn't believe our luck, and within six weeks, we moved into our very own house, our first home of our own. It was now 1963. The house was in Northolt, in a road called Lilliput Avenue. We were all very happy there, and it made for a far better quality of life, bedrooms for all of us and a brand-new property that was like gold dust in those days. I was also able to buy Florence her first car and give her driving lessons.

We had super neighbours, except for one immediate neighbour who repeatedly tried to bully us by doing the strangest of things, such as shunting his car up and down the short, shared driveway all hours of the night, playing his piano and running his model railway in his loft for hours after midnight and just creating a nuisance of himself. I soon helped him to correct his ways!

The neighbours, Ruby and Stan, who adjoined him on his other side, were also at their wits end with all the noise and disturbances, and his wife was suffering with her nerves as a consequence. They decided to move away from this antisocial neighbour. They had found two new houses in Hayes that had been built by the same builder on opposite sides of the road and they were both detached and stood on a reasonably sized plot of land. They were very keen for us to move to the other one, which is what we did. We were neighbours again! It was a lovely house with no attached, noisy neighbours, and we lived opposite our best friends. We were very happy there and Florence continued to work from home as a seamstress for a little while longer.

By this time, I was earning lots of money for us, so Florence was able to eventually give up her sewing business and spend her time with the children and in the garden. In 1966 we had the lovely gift of another baby daughter, Vicki. Our first-born, George, was now 18 years of age and was delighted to be able to take Vicki out in the pram and show her off to the girls, pretending that she was his!

Life was good. Moving on up!

21. Post – War Holidays

We had very little money when the factory holidays came but, for our very first holiday in about 1950, we managed to find a very cheap, small caravan for rent on Haling Island. Taking the train, we were amazed to find that the holiday home was nicely decorated but very, very small. However, we had a great week there except that poor little George burned his hand on the little gas cooker that was on the floor of the caravan to save space.

Some years later, some lovely times were spent on our holidays in Cornwall and camping with close friends of ours, Rosemary, Jimmy and family, running about on the beach, walking and playing games together. We met Rosemary and Jimmy in hospital in 1956 when both families were having a baby; we had Penny and they had David. We remained life-long friends and our children spent much of their early childhood together and are still in touch.

On these annual holidays we often stopped overnight at various places en-route to Cornwall as it was such a long way to go with little children. We had a fortnight and two days' holiday to spend each summer. Ford Poplar cars were our mode of transport, and these only reached 45 mph top speed. In those days there were no motorways or dual carriageways, so the journey to Cornwall was in excess of 13 hours if you travelled overnight.

On this one particular occasion, we planned that our first stop would be Cheddar Gorge. There were no motorways, just little winding roads. We found a very large camp site on a farm where there were already quite a lot of people staying in their tents. There were, what seemed like, thousands of chickens on this farm, which was a big egg producer for the area. Finding a good spot to set up camp, we put up the tent and all the cooking equipment. Florence lit the primus stove and we had a great fry-up as it began to get dark. The paraffin lamp was lit and we all got ready to go to bed for the night. We had two children at that time, George, who was about 11, and Penny, who was about 3 years old. Rosemary and Jimmy had four. Following a good night's sleep, we were awakened fairly early in the morning to the sound of lots of chickens, which sounded like they were trying to get into the tent. On opening the flap of the tent and looking out, I was amazed to see a sea of chickens all over the campsite and in everyone's tent. It was about 5 o'clock in the morning! Sleepy people were beginning to look out of their tent flaps with great consternation at the scene before them. And there, in the midst of the mayhem, who do I see in her nightdress? Penny! Unbeknown to us, she had woken up, got out of the tent through the flap, gone over to the chickens and undone all their cages so they all came out. I didn't know what to do – I was planning the best way to get her back to the tent without anyone noticing. "Nooooo! of course it wasn't her," I said as I headed over to Penny to coax her back into the tent. "I don't know what's happened here, mate," would be my reply to the stares and comments from the other somewhat sleepy campers, who were complaining vehemently about the chicken situation. "That bloody farmer wants shooting!" came my retort, "He charges us half a crown to come and camp here and then ..this...!" We hurriedly packed up our things and shot off down to Devon on the next leg of our journey.

There was also the time, some years later, as we were camping with Rosemary and Jimmy when in the night, at about 2am, some teenage boys were putting their hands under the tents to pinch the girls in our friend's tent. They did it to the girls in another tent too and this fella understandably took great exception to it and shouted over to warn us, whereupon we all set out running after these kids, who turned out to be 15 or 16 years of age. We chased them off, couldn't catch up with them of course. Pranksters!

We had lots of laughs on those holidays! Sadly, Jimmy died in the 1980's and Rosemary passed away in May 2020 at the grand old age of 97! Jimmy's wartime exploits were enthralling. He flew in Lancasters, as a wireless operator air gunner during the war and was one of the only people I know to have received a double DFM (Distinguished Flying Medal). He did over 100 operations over Germany in a very famous Lancaster called Johnny Walker. Most people never even managed 10 'ops' before their time was up so it was a remarkable achievement.

Rosemary had a good life and a very interesting one too. During the war she was a radio and radar operator for the WAAF, that's how they met - at radio school. She had started work at Dollis Hill Research Centre, as a Telephone Operator.

(It was there that the world's first electronic computer, used for codebreaking, was created). By 1941 she was working at the Ministry of Aircraft Production, at Millbank taking calls for Lord Beaverbrook and for Winston Churchill. She had the perfect excuse for not going home, as her rotating shifts meant that she sometimes had to sleep in the underground rooms there. It does seem that that Rosemary spent the early War Years carousing in London with her friends and frequenting the famous 'Lyons Corner House' for breakfast.

In 1943 she wrote in her journal, "We were returning from a jaunt in the West End celebrating my friend's departure to join the WAAF, the (Women's Auxiliary Airforce) and we started talking about the exciting adventure she was about to embark upon. After I had retired to bed, I lay thinking about our conversation, and the very next day I sent in my application to join up". She joined the WAAF as a Wireless Operator just two days after her 21st birthday. She then joined the 139 Pathfinder Squadron where she worked on tuning the top-secret 'oboe' radar system, which guided pathfinders to their exact targets.

The chain of attack started with Aerial reconnaissance photographing targets, (that would be me), the Pathfinders using that intelligence to plan and execute raids to mark targets (guided in part by oboe, Rosemary's task), the heavy bombers (Jimmy's task) would then attempt to bomb onto the markers dropped by the Pathfinders, and finally the photo reconnaissance (me again) would return to photograph the effectiveness of the raid. Florence made the ammunition. So when the four of us met up we shared our experiences as unknown collaborators! How amazing is that!

22. About My Father

As a family living in the 1930s, my parents had just started to save to get a bit of money together to move to a decent house, and things had just started to go right for us and then the bloody war came along!

That put paid to any future plans!

When I was young, my father, George Wellesley Pritchard, was a fish porter at Billingsgate Market, carrying baskets of fish on his head. He worked hard there, being available for any work he could find, however hard or menial, earning sometimes only a shilling a day. There were all sorts of crooks around in the Billingsgate market area who were looking to offload their 'stuff'. Dad would sometimes come home with an item, like a ruby ring, which he would give to my mother. But the next week, it would be in the pawn shop in exchange for money so that she could feed us. Dad would go berserk if she couldn't meet the pawn date because she could not pay for it in time. Then there'd be an argument about money and feeding the kids. One thing about my mother was that she would struggle like mad but always manage to feed us, just about. Though we always had a good Sunday dinner as that was the day that our father would be home for dinner.

Eventually, my father was taken on full-time in the market as he was a smart and reliable fellow. He soon found himself being promoted to a salesman, which he was very good at, selling more fish than most of the others, so he soon became sales manager, and then general manager of a fish business in the market.

The gentleman who owned the business, a man called Rook, wanted to retire through ill health, so he sold the business to my father, on terms that he could afford. It was arranged that he pay so much a month over the course of a few years. My father never looked back on this arrangement, and his businesses went from strength to strength. Sadly, Rook died, so my father didn't have to pay him anymore, and he continued to run the business for a few more years.

He then sold the business and bought restaurants, shops and a factory. The factory-made Bailey Bridges for the army, but most of his businesses dealt with the food industry. He was then asked to become the Food Distribution Executive for Oxfordshire, Buckinghamshire and Berkshire. He did very well for himself. During the war, he always seemed to know the right people and would often turn up with a tin of fruit or a bag of raisins or something of similar ilk. We never went completely without as children, though there were very many lean times, when a bread and sugar sandwich was the main meal of the day. What I eat in one day now would have kept me for a week back in those days of the 1930s-1945. There were no fat people around.

My father liked to have a bit of a joke with his customers. One of the favourite fish in those days was Devon Hake. A woman came in and asked for some Hake, and he asked her, "How many f's in Hake?" and she said, "There's no f in hake!!!!"

"That's right!" he agreed. How rude!

He was a bit of a Joker!

I should have paid more attention to what my father did for a living. When I joined up and was sent to Weston Super Mare, we were asked what our fathers did for a living. Well, I just said that he was a fishmonger in my ignorance. If I had told them that he was a successful businessman and a food distribution executive for three counties, maybe I would have started a few rungs up the ladder.

George and sister, Phyllis

By the time I came out of the RAF, he had three fish shops, and my mother was the cashier in one of them, and she did all his accounting. My brother, Charlie, was a partner in one of the fish shops in Coulsdon, and he had two or three restaurants (working peoples cafes), two in and around Coulsdon and one in the Borough Market.

About two years after the war, once I had returned from Germany, my father had purchased an ex-post office Morris Minor van, which he had kitted out to use to transport his fresh fish from Billingsgate to his shops. He would leave between 3 and 4 am to get the fish a few days each week. He was having some problems with the car, as the steering joints were going, so it was proving difficult to steer the car. In those days, there were tram tracks everywhere on the roads, so if you did have steering problems, the tracks could help you steer, but you had to follow the tracks and keep out of the way of trams. He had told me about his car problems, and I said I could do that for him; it was the knuckle joints and bearings that needed changing. He left it in a garage over at one of the shops for me to repair. I was generally working during the day, so I managed to take half a day off to repair it and hopefully finish it in the evening. The day was arranged, and I bought the parts and went over to the garage where it was parked. It was quite a job to take it all apart; take the steering wheel out, the steering box and all the knuckle joints. I was in the middle of all this when my father arrived and started pushing me to get on with it and was anxiously hovering over me, saying I had to 'hurry up' as he had decided to take my mother to the Grand Theatre to see a show. He could see that I was struggling to finish to his agenda. He then gave up and decided to go by bus back home to get his other car, a Jaguar, and head off to the theatre, giving the key to me to lock up the premises. I finally finished at some incredibly late hour, locked up and set off for home. At 6 am the next morning, there was a phone call from him, "What are you bloody doing to me, I can't drive the bloody car…." Shouted my father down the road. He'd got to the garage at 4 am, got in the car and driven off, but the car only steered in one direction! I had put the pin in the rack and pinion with the steering pointing to one side. He'd got as far as the road but couldn't understand what was up with the car; at 4 am in the morning, "What am I going to do to get it back?" It had taken him till 6 am to get hold of someone who worked in the shop to come and help him hold up the front of the car to get it back into the garage. So embarrassing! I had to go over there right away to put it right. It didn't take long – that'll teach him not to pressure me when I'm helping him out. I got home, and Florence and I laughed our socks off at the thought of him going around in circles!

My father was strange sometimes– I believe it was all to do with the fact that he was having an affair at the time. He left my mother when I was about 25, which came as quite a shock! He came to see me and said he had a proposition for me and asked if I had any money put away. I told him we had a bit, which was mostly my £450 demob money that we were saving for a deposit on a house of our own. He asked if he could borrow it with 10% interest, and that he'd return it in a few weeks. I told him I had to discuss it with Florence first, and she agreed as it was my father; he wouldn't cheat on us, would he? So, we drew it out from the bank and gave it to him. Then, a few days later, whilst I was at work (at Deans), one of the guys from the office came to me saying that my mother was outside, wanting to speak to me. I wondered to what I owed the pleasure as my mother never came to see me at work! When I arrived at the reception, she was in a bit of a state and said, "You'd better read this note. Your father has left me; he's taken all the money. I don't know where he's gone. What am I supposed to do?" At the time, she wasn't working, so didn't know how she would pay the rent. I consoled her and told her not to worry as we'd all help her. He had completely disappeared out of the country, we think, and no one knew where he was for a very long time. Needless to say, we were very worried as he had all our savings, and we were not sure if we would ever get them back; we had to struggle on with no financial backup. We were too trusting!

About two years later, I received a telephone call from my Aunt Marjorie, my father's sister, to say that he was seriously ill in hospital in Dublin, with a ruptured duodenal ulcer. That was the first we had heard of his whereabouts. My aunt swore us to secrecy about his whereabouts, but he wanted me to know where he was in case anything happened to him. I didn't like keeping this from my mother but thought I'd better keep the secret.

He recovered, and quite a long time after that, I received another call from Marjorie saying that my father was coming over to England and desperately wanted to meet with me in Blackpool, and would I go? It was a long way to go, but I decided

I better go and at least find out where he was and how he was doing, getting some kind of explanation for his disappearing behaviour and the whereabouts of our money. We met in Wheeler's Bar one Saturday. He ordered me a pint of Guinness and a plate of oysters (not something I really like) and then handed me a large envelope with all my money in it, including the 10% interest.

"Here you are, here's your money," he said, "I'm sorry it took so long and for disappearing like that, but I had to disappear; otherwise, I would have had to pay your mother, and I didn't have any money. Please don't tell her anything as I'm not too well, and I couldn't cope." As it happens, my brother was after him as well because he had run off with money belonging to him too. My brother found out where he was, and he and my mother took him to court for abandonment and owing money. He, of course, dressed the part of the 'old man', took his teeth out and maintained to the court that he had no money. But he had a hotel/pub and a sweet shop in County Wicklow, in Ireland, that he ran with his lady friend, Phyllis, making a load of money. He was a terrible gambler, and despite making lots of money on all the various businesses over the years, he'd lose it just as quickly on the horses and then get into debt so lose his businesses to pay off the debts. Later, for some reason, he sold the hotel and bought a tobacconist and newsagents in Dublin. Again after some years he suddenly sold up in Ireland and returned to England, purchasing a book shop selling rare books, in Hornsey, London. Once the bookshop profits started to decline he sold it. His next enterprise was to buy a fish and chip shop in Norwich, where he was certain that he'd make a fortune. What he didn't realise was that he had a lot of hard work to do in preparation for serving his fish and chips; the potatoes had to be peeled and chopped, and the fish prepared, and the oil that had to be cleaned and replaced. That business finished, and then he bought an eel and pie shop in Limehouse, London. That was a disaster! His next enterprise was getting himself a job as a sales manager for a cooked meats company in Bletchley, to where he moved. He did quite well at this job for quite some time as he was a good salesperson. When he'd had enough of that job (or a dispute with the boss) he set off to Eastbourne and lived there until he died in 1975, living off his pension. It was just before Christmas, in 1975, that my brother, Peter and I, set off for Eastbourne with a turkey for our father for Christmas; we thought we'd surprise him. On arrival at his flat, the door was answered by his lady friend, Phyllis, who informed us that he'd died a few weeks earlier, and was sorry, but he didn't want family at the funeral. We hadn't even been informed of his death, so I could not attend his funeral; I didn't even know where he was buried. He was a very strange person at times! We did, however, maintain a kind of friendship with Phyllis until she died some years later.

My mother outlived him. She found a lovely job working for Paynes Chocolates near to where she lived. She had been a bookkeeper for Lyons Corner House on the Strand in the 1920s when she met my father, and was skilled in business financial matters and accounting, so she became a bookkeeper for Paynes for many years, and they really looked after her well, both whilst she worked there and long after she retired; they always sent around gifts of chocolates for her and cards for her birthday and Christmas. She was lucky enough to find love again in later life and married a lovely man called Fred at 73 years of age. Sadly, she only had a few years with him before he died. Although she did re-marry again at 80, to a chap called Chequers, we were not so keen on him, and many years later, he died, leaving her a widow again. Her health declined when she was in her 80s, so she lived with her daughter, Phyllis, until her death in 1989 at the age of 89.

23. Employment at Rotax – Lucas Aerospace 1950s

The job with Lucas Aerospace, Rotax, was brilliant – it was right up my street, and I was soon to move upwards within the company, taking on more and more responsibility alongside the more interesting tasks. At first, I worked alongside Tony Crombie, and we had a specialist department where we designed and made all the high-altitude switch gear for the 'V' bombers; the 'Valiant', the 'Vulcan' and the 'Victor'. These were all jet-engine bombers designed to deliver nuclear bombs made during the 'Cold War'. (Ironically, my son-in-law's father worked for Handley-Page on the 'Victor'). We were specialists in our field at that time, and along with one man in America and another in Japan, we were reckoned to be the world experts on specialist switches.

Aeroplanes usually worked with a Direct Current (DC) system before the jet-engine age. Switches were normally operated on 110V DC, but at high altitude, the switch did not 'break' the circuit and maintained an 'arc' of electrical power, thus keeping the switch 'on'. This was due to the decrease in air pressure at high altitudes. Obviously, this caused serious problems. Our job was to unravel this phenomenon and come up with a solution to the problem. We solved this problem using the magnetic blowout system and other methods. A new range of switches were designed to operate on alternating current (AC), which would automatically cut off the switch. Jet-engine planes were then designed using AC systems to cope with the switching gear. DC generators would not cope with the high rotational speed produced by jet engines, these were then changed to AC alternators, thus solving the switching problems of sustained arcing. We built a special vacuum chamber in which to test our switches successfully. We went on to make many other specialist switches for various industries.

I ended up working under Dr Clarke, who was the chief scientist for the whole of the Lucas group, which was by now the seventh biggest company in the world. The chairman of the group was Sir Bertram-Waring, who really took to me and gave me some very interesting projects to do. In all, I worked for Lucas-Rotax for about ten years.

The Jet engine Conundrum

One of the 'big projects' we were working on was with jet engines. There is a difference in the speed of rotation of a jet engine compared to a petrol engine. The generator used on a petrol engine aircraft, which produces the electricity for the aircraft, couldn't cope with the speed required for a jet engine. If gears were used to help the generator cope with the difference, then every gear put in would reduce the engine's efficiency, so everything would run at about 30% efficiency, which was no good. So, the idea was for us to devise a system wherein the engine could run at a very high speed and still get the result required with full efficiency. One Austrian chap designed an electric generator and charged Lucas Aerospace a lot of money for it. The model was working very well and looked like it would do the task in hand, so they paid him for it, but when they came to build it to full size, it didn't work. There would be great kudos to anyone who could figure out a way of doing it.

Tony Crombie, my friend and colleague, decided that he had figured it out by using 'epicyclic gearing', so that he could raise the efficiency to around 75% or better (epicyclic gearing is a very complex form of gearing, somewhat like planetary orbits and requires some very advanced maths in order to work it out). I helped Tony work out the maths by helping him check the accuracy of his calculations, but in doing so I realised that his design was not going to work, and I told him so. He was adamant that it would work, and that he was not wrong. Sure enough, his mathematical version gave the impression that he was right, but he wasn't, which I proved with my mathematical model using calculus. I did warn him, but he just wouldn't hear it.

He continued to build his model, but instead of building it at the factory, he built it at home. He was employed as an electrical engineering developer, not as a mechanical engineer. This model was mechanical, so he thought he would benefit greatly by showing his mechanical expertise to add to his portfolio. He approached the top people in the company, telling them that he had devised a system with 75% efficiency, to which they were very excited and agreed to visit his home in order to view it. Tony told them that before they visit, he wanted them to appreciate that this is a mechanical engineering system and that he had put a lot of work into it in his own time at home, not the company's and he wants some recompense for it. He would like a raise in salary, a more senior position in the company and a new car. Their response was that if this design was what he said it was, then the company would have no problem making those changes. They were a bit sceptical as to whether it would work, but Tony was insistent. Tony insisted they attend to his wishes prior to them seeing the model work.

They weren't too happy; however, they did as he asked, and then four of the most senior engineers, and the company director, went over to Tony's home. He started it up and got it running, and they asked him to explain it to them, which he did and to prove it, he showed them the maths. These engineers were top in their trade and, of course, were experts in the field of maths, whereupon they laughed at the fundamental mistakes he had made with his calculations, making him feel very small indeed. His prior demands for bettering his career were dropped, and indeed, he didn't then get the jobs coming up in the future, like making the pacemaker and heart-lung machines. Instead, they gave them to me. This meant that I couldn't work with Tony any longer, and I became senior to him. Tony wasn't happy with me and felt I hadn't supported him in his venture, but I told him that he had refused to listen to me and became all 'bolshy'; I had tried. I felt so sorry for him as he had made himself look like a fool. We had always got along really well, and I was saddened by this incident as it had tainted our close friendship. We worked together for a while afterwards, and there was no animosity between us. He knew that I had tried to put him right.

Pacemaker and Heart-Lung Machines 1959/60

The senior engineer running the Special Projects Group for Lucas-Rotax was asked by the company chairman to find the most likely person to be able to help investigate some problems in the field of cardiac support systems. That turned out to be me.

I was assigned as Development Engineer to work for the Queen Elizabeth Hospital, in Birmingham, on pacemakers and heart-lung machines, among other tasks. Whilst there, I was working with Professor Leon Abrams, who was their top cardiothoracic surgeon, to discuss the possibility of making an electronic means of providing signals to stimulate the body's heartbeats – the pacemaker. Up until now, the design had coils that had been coated in nylon, which was not working as the copper coils were corroding. I discussed with him that the only material I knew of that he could coat them with that would not be rejected by the body was PTFE. He was not sure about this as PTFE had not been tried or tested before inside the human body. I told him that I knew a couple of very good chemists, one of whom was Gerry Pollack, who had agreed to test out my hypothesis if I could get him the raw materials I wanted to use. The project had to be first agreed upon by the chairman of Lucas. During a meeting with the chairman, we discussed the initial costs of manufacturing a prototype for Professor Abrams (up to £5,000 was the agreed sum) and the project was given the go-ahead. I made up the prototype case and the electronics, working out a rough circuit board, and then passed it on to Peter, my draughtsman, who would draw out the finer details and dimensions.

The testing was done, and PTFE was trialled and shown to be non-reactive inside the human body and furthermore prevented the coils from corroding. I believe they may still use PTFE to coat metals placed inside the body.

Following several meetings, during which I was gathering all the medical requirements, data and medical understanding I needed to undertake the task, I began to realise that this was a very difficult task, entailing the use of specialist materials and cutting-edge technology. With the medical team's help, I managed to design and make the pacemaker, producing fine working models, the designs of which went on to save many lives.

Following many discussions with Professor Abrams, who enlightened me as to the types of materials that would be deemed best for being non-corrosive within the human body and be able to sustain the life of the person as they were intended, the unit was given a coating of PTFE and special, pure, stainless-steel, nickel-free braid was used for the suture wires, the likes of which did not exist at that moment in time, so I had to get it made. The wires were very fine (one-fifth of a millimetre in diameter), and initially, I had to find a company that could extrude such fine wire with the purity that was required. I approached British Steel in the hope of getting them to make the quality of steel I required; it took a while to convince them to take on this task as it would be the 'drawing' of the steel to such a fine gauge that would be the most difficult task for them. (The 'drawing' of a metal through a draw plate is where the metal thins as it is extruded or pulled through a hole in a drawplate. Between each extrusion, the metal requires to be annealed, or heated, to soften it as the extrusion process hardens the metal). After some deliberation, they agreed and made me a reel of the special steel. The company I found for braiding the steel wire was Alcock's in Redditch, which was a company that generally made fishing tackle. They made a very fine stainless-steel braided wire for fishing purposes. I knew this as I was into fishing and had regularly bought my fishing tackle from them. They had the technique of braiding a very fine wire which they then welded onto hooks for catching strong fish, like pike. I would require the wire to be welded onto specialist fine needles. Following a lengthy discussion with the managing director, I filled him in on my interesting proposal, and I was invited to visit the factory, whereupon I explained my design idea and asked if their company would be able to attach the steel wire to the needles, but they decided that they would require some assistance with the welding needed for the job. The next company I contacted was the British Welding Institute, where I spoke to the top man there, who suggested what we could use and wanted to try out his technique on a sample of wire and needle. This I duly supplied him with, whereupon he electrically welded it. The work was agreed upon, completed, and stocks delivered.

Returning to meet with Professor Abrams, the next item required for the installation of a pacemaker into a body was something to assist in finding the best position for the placement of the pacemaker. He usually used a pair of probes, but he decided that it would be far quicker and easier to have a specialised glove with two electrodes and a battery system so that he could use it to find the best position for the pacemaker nodes on the heart. Off I go again to design and make the gloves. Much to my amazement, he demonstrated these to me on a live heart during a surgical procedure to install a pacemaker, whereby he tested their usefulness using my oscilloscope to determine the best contact point for the pacemaker nodes to be attached in the heart. I was there to give advice on the accurate reading of the oscilloscope during the procedure. The operation was over four hours long. I did this in further operations on patients.

The idea for the development of the pacemaker was Professor Abrams'. I helped with the design and provided the electronics know-how to make his dream a reality. For this reason, it is his name in the history books regarding the first patient-controlled variable-rate heart pacemaker in 1960, though I believe my name was mentioned in connection with it when Professor Abrams wrote a paper on it for The Lancet medical journal. I have recently found out that there is a plaque on the wall at The Queen Elizabeth Hospital, Birmingham, mentioning Professor Abrams, and George Pritchard (me) with regard to developing the original pacemaker. There is also the prototype preserved in a frame for all to see. Amazing that it is still there!

The pacemaker worked very well; indeed, I was soon to find out, as I was involved directly in the medical surgery where a pacemaker was fitted into a person on two separate occasions. Florence and I were eating our evening meal one evening, when the phone rang. It was the Consultant and senior surgeon at Bethnal Green Hospital. He explained that he had a man in surgery who had come in with no heart rate and was being kept alive on a machine. The surgeon had arranged to have one of the pacemakers couriered to him from Birmingham and was going to fit this pacemaker into the patient. He asked if I could go over to the hospital now and support him with my knowledge of the pacemaker and its fitting into the human body, as I had witnessed this when working with one that was fitted into a patient by Professor Abrams and his team in Birmingham. Professor Abrams had suggested that I attend as I was nearer. Setting off immediately to Bethnal Green Hospital, I was met by the team and prepared for the operation by having a team conference to explain all that I could about the pacemaker. I was then gowned up and allowed to watch the procedure, giving support where my expertise was required in finding the correct place to attach the pacemaker. The operation took many hours to suture the pacemaker in place, put the coil in the intercostal space and, after checking the heart's signal and starting the heart, closing up the patient. The way it worked was by attaching another coil to the outside of the skin exactly over the coil that was inside the body. This made a kind of transformer. This was all connected to a box, which was worn around the waist of the patient. It had an on/off switch and a rate controller in the box, plus all the electronics and a rechargeable battery. As it happened, I have the world patent on that particular type of recharging unit that charges the battery (it allowed the changing of the battery without losing charge for the pacemaker). The operation was over; it was now after 3 am, so the consultant insisted that it was a bit late to be travelling home, so, he found me a bed to sleep in and asked if I would join him for breakfast. In the morning, after a pleasant breakfast spent chatting to the Consultant, we went to pay a visit to the patient, a postman, who, to my amazement, was sitting up in bed and smiling. Before I left to go home, the consultant asked if I could come back in a few weeks to discuss the pacemaker with a few of his staff at the hospital, to which I agreed.

Some weeks later, I received a phone call from the Consultant inviting me to go and give a talk to a few doctors, which I duly did, explaining the developmental process and my work with Professor Abrams. I also got to meet with the patient again, who was still recovering from his major surgery, but who was doing really well and looking forward to returning to work as a postman, and to the golf course in the not-too-distant future. He was joking about the fact that when he plays golf, he can just turn up the speed of the heart when he has to walk up the hill! I then met his wife, who flung her arms around my neck, saying, "Thank you for giving me my husband back." These early pacemaker patients made good recoveries and returned to a high quality of life. By 1966, 56 patients had undergone implantation, with one surviving for over five years.

Off the back of this meeting with the doctors at Bethnal Green, an invitation came through to me to give another lecture at Shotley Bridge Cardiac Centre about the pacemaker. Florence and I decided to make the journey together and combine it with a visit to her hometown in Ashington, Northumberland, which was not too far from Shotley Bridge. The children were deposited with the mother-in-law, and we headed to Shotley bridge for my talk. Unbeknown to me, there were not just a few people around a table, as I had imagined, but a large auditorium full of 300-400 people, experts in their medical fields, to whom I was going to talk as part of a big convention! I felt nervous at first, thinking that my prepared talk would only last about fifteen minutes. But I needn't have worried as in the end, I was talking about the pacemaker and then answering questions for over 90 minutes. I explained that I was not a doctor, I was an engineer, so I was going to discuss this pacemaker in terms of electrics and hydraulics. I went on to explain the development of the product and all those people and companies involved in the procurement of the specialised materials and the whole process of getting this made down to its success in the few patients who had so far had it fitted. I hadn't realised how much a lecture like that could take out of you! I felt exhausted and drained, but also exhilarated in having had the opportunity to help create such an amazing piece of technology that would benefit the human race for many years to come.

It's strange how word does get around; when I came to get a pacemaker fitted into my own body and mentioned 'casually' how I happened to be involved in the original pacemakers, I found that some of the people knew about my involvement of that original pacemaker, as it had been written up in The Lancet at some point and my name was mentioned alongside Professor Abrams at the Queen Elizabeth Hospital in Birmingham.

Following this, I was involved with the development of a few other machines for the NHS, namely a machine to help diagnose and distinguish 'Mitral regurgitation' from 'Mitral stenosis' in patients, a foetal heart detector, radio pills, defibrillators, autoclaving open-heart surgery defibrillators and 'potted' copper coils in PTFE (rather than Perspex). As far as I know, I was the first to find a way to completely encase an object in PTFE, in this case, copper coils.

I was then asked to go to The Central Middlesex Hospital by Sir Bertram-Waring, where my help was needed as they had a problem with their oxygenator machine and wanted me to join the team to design a new one to supersede the current Perspex model they had, which was not working efficiently. They had had a young man on a machine, who was a rather over-large person, and who had died because they thought the nurse may have assembled it incorrectly. I was to work with a fellow called Dr Melrose to develop a new design of a machine that would be more efficient and more straightforward to set up. Melrose was medically trained, so he could provide all the information I would require to create a product that would be up to the mark medically as regards the materials and outcome that would be required. The new machine had roller pumps; everything about it was controllable, and it could determine the rate of flow, levels of oxygen, blood temperature and so on. It was about 3ft high by about 2ft wide and could be wheeled around. It is now the universally used machine called the Melrose Heart-Lung machine, which oxygenates the blood for patients whilst they are having heart surgery. Melrose got the credit; such is life! It is amazing to think of all the lives that have been saved by these machines over the years.

I was not too sure if I was very keen on Sir Bertram-Waring, the chairman, anymore. After I had worked and developed the pacemaker, and it had been publicised and written up in The Lancet, I was put forward for an OBE by Professor Abrams at the QE Hospital in Birmingham, with whom I had been liaising throughout its development. But because the Lucas company and the chairman had put up the money for its development and had employed me to do it, the chairman got the OBE, not me. Much to the annoyance and chagrin of the professor and the medical people I had worked with. I became very well known by anyone in the heart/medical business for my work on the pacemaker and all the other medical electronic gadgets that had been developed to help people survive, what were, major life-threatening ailments of our time.

I now have one installed in my own body! In fact, I am on my second one!

Joining The Freemasons

Whatever I did, I vowed to succeed and get to the top, in everything. In the Freemasons, I got to the top and became a Worshipful Master.

I was working at Lucas-Rotax at this time, in the 1960s, and a lot of the top engineers were all in Freemasonry. I knew one of the guys I worked closely with was involved in it, as he used to often tell me he was leaving work early on that day to go to his lodge meeting. I decided to ask him what it was he had to do to get into it. He asked if I was interested in it and told me that to become a member, I had to ask him to propose me. This he did, and I went to an interview where I was 'grilled' in order that they could check on my character. I was accepted and was in it for 15-20 years. Towards the end of my membership, after I had reached the top as 'Worshipful Master', I ran into a situation whereby we didn't have much money. In the Freemasons, there is a lot of charity work, and I was always having to dip my hand into my pocket and give up one afternoon and evening a week for meetings, so this had begun to become difficult for me to do for a while, as we were going through some lean times.

I had been asked to design and build a fingerprint machine for Scotland Yard. There were quite a few freemasons who were detectives or police inspectors working at Scotland Yard. They knew my field of work and asked if I could do this task of making a machine that could store fingerprint data on a computer for easy access instead of the outdated card system they had at the time.

My colleague, Gordon, and I set to work designing and making a prototype machine for fingerprinting, working out a system whereby the machine would scan and interrogate the fingerprint looking for all the identification points and then come up with a match. We handed in a proposal, which was studied at Scotland Yard, and they showed a keen interest in the design. I spent three months in Scotland Yard designing the fingerprint machine, about six hours a day, which only left me a couple of hours a day left to earn a living (Scotland Yard were not going to pay me until it was completed). My Freemason friends, the detectives, were always trying to get us to go across the road to the pub, joining them for drinks, for which, more often than not, we would have to fork out for the round! The Yard had been informed that it would take four months to make this computer, upload information and have it ready and working, and we provided them with a report on it.

George as Worshipful Master

I was then waiting for feedback on our report so that we could start the job and begin to get some money back from the job. Sometime later, I learned that they had bypassed me and had given all the designs and work I had done to some other company to make the machine. All that hard work for very little return! These guys were supposedly my Freemason friends, and they did this to me. It really put me off going to my lodge, as their behaviour went entirely against the values upheld in Freemasonry, so I gave it all up. I was really incensed by it all and never saw them again.

We did have interesting times at the lodge, and I did make a lot of good friendships, which were to last the rest of my life. Unfortunately, those friends have all gone now, and I am the only one out of us who is left in the land of the living. We did get invitations to visit other Lodges once I had been a Worshipful Master. On one occasion, we visited the Chelsea lodge where Sir. Lawrence Olivier was the Master. Tommy Trinder and Norman Wisdom were all in this lodge, and it was very interesting meeting them. It was wonderful to see a real 'pro', Sir Lawrence Olivier, conduct his members in his lodge, and I will always remember his voice. A true professional. We would get to a meeting by about 3 pm and meet until 5.30 pm, completing all the serious business for that week, and then we would have a banquet with some speeches and lots to drink. Lots of money was coming out of our pockets and businesses in aid of charity.

Donald Campbell 1966

Following our work on the specialist high-altitude switches, a letter was received by the boss of Lucas-Rotax from Donald Campbell, saying that he was having some trouble in his 'Bluebird' boat with the switch gear, which switched on the jet engine for the boat, could he come and pay us a visit to get some alterations done and provide him with a specialised switch. I had been allocated the job with my working partner, Tony Crombie. On this particular day, two men were brought to our part of the factory in Acton, it was Donald Campbell and his mechanic, Yeo. We recognised him straight away, even before he introduced himself. He explained that he was working on doing a new world record in his boat at high speed, but that he was having a problem with the switch from the jet engine on start-up as it kept sticking. The mechanic explained more details about their particular requirements and asked if we could make them a switch. I explained that we only make prototypes here, not the 100% finished product. Nevertheless, he was happy that the prototype would be quite satisfactory, as long as they could bolt it onto the bulkhead and it was fit for purpose. It sounded as though the current was so high that it was causing the contacts to weld on and stick in their switch; it was affected by heat and fused the metal contacts. The only thing was – he needed it within two weeks! It was agreed and, after a general chat about his boat and the speeds he was managing to get up to on Lake Coniston, he bade us farewell and looked forward to having a new switching system soon.

I set to work and began to design and make the switch. The contacts were made out of silver cadmium, made by compression of these metals in tiny, microscopic globules so that if anything melted, they would come apart and not fuse the contacts. The switch was put together according to their design brief and was sent off to them. After installing it and giving the boat several runs at high speed, Donald Campbell got back in touch with us to let us know that it was working beautifully, with no problems at all at any speed, and thanked us very much for all our effort. The next thing we heard was that Donald Campbell had been involved in a tragic accident with his Bluebird boat and had been killed whilst travelling at high speed. They are not entirely sure what had happened to the boat as it travelled at world record speeds on Lake Coniston on that fateful day and had caused the boat to overturn and break up into pieces. The cause of the crash has been variously attributed to several possible causes and remains a bit of a mystery.

It took until 2001 before his body was recovered from the lake. Poor chap.

G & E Bradley's

Whilst working at The Lucas Aerospace company, which at the time employed about 8,000 people, the Chairman (Sir Bertram-Waring) sent me to go and work for a while in G & E Bradley's, in Neasden, which had been taken over by Lucas.

The Chairman, there was a Lord, and there was an MD, who was his son-in-law. There were one or two other members of the family working within the firm in high positions and running the business too. I arrived there from Lucas and was sent by the chairman to make a judgement of the company, G & E Bradley, as to its suitability to make some of the medical electronics, including the pacemaker, that I had been developing for Lucas. I was given a part of the factory to take over, in which I was to start the development of electronic medical devices and eventual production. When I got there, I was to work alongside the chief of development and design engineer, who was an Austrian Doctor, and who really didn't like me at all as he felt I was usurping part of his territory. I was placed on the board of directors there, and my role was to set the company up for them to manufacture the pacemaker and other electronic devices for Lucas. Sir Bertram-Waring asked me for my feedback on how the company was doing and whether they were a sound investment. He wanted a report on the directors and the management there and to know what my views were on Bradleys as a business. When sitting on the board of directors there, I must say that I was not impressed at all. Firstly, there was the Doctor who was always trying to put me down as he believed I was beneath him – but I certainly knew more than him about the electronic devices I was developing. He asked me how I would calculate some of the advanced electronics formulae for the devices. I wrote a report all in very high-flown mathematics called 'Laplace Transform' (converts a function of a real variable (often time) to a function of a complex variable (complex frequency)), which he couldn't understand and was very angry with me. I was getting my own back on 'put downs', it seemed.

Eventually, I wrote my report for Sir Bertram-Waring at Lucas, saying that, in my opinion, the board were all 'useless'. They seemed to know nothing about the company technically, and they didn't seem to have grasped what they were there for. The chairman of Bradleys appeared to be forever going out for meals and drinks; his son, the MD, hardly did anything at all. The sales guy was not up to the mark, the accountant was a waste of space as his bookkeeper knew more about the business than he did. Sir Bertram-Waring called me to his office, and he asked me to sit down and tell him about the company. I went on to regale the typical board meeting where, after a few minutes spent talking of the business in hand (to satisfy Lucas), they then would drink copious cups of coffee and have a laugh wasting a lot of time. I ended by saying that I would not give them house room and that it all needed changing around. Sir Bertram-Waring asked me to return to see him the following week in Birmingham, whereupon he told me to go back to Bradleys and to fire them!

"But, But, But I can't do that!" I exclaimed, "He's Lord H, and the rest of his co-workers are mostly family, I can't do that!"

He came back with, "We own the business, so we can hire and fire whoever we like."

I went along to the board meeting at Bradley's and sat there quietly listening to all the usual waffle, and then they finally addressed me.

"Pritchard, have you anything to say?" asked Lord H.

"Yes, I've a lot to say, actually," I said, "I have been directed by the chairman of the group, Sir Bertram-Waring, to tell you that your employment here, yourself (and a few other members of the board that I pointed out) are all dismissed from the company as from the end of the week. We are forthwith disposing of your services. You will get notices in writing from the chairman of the Lucas company to terminate all your employment. I am here to warn you so that you can prepare yourselves to leave, other people will be taking over from you. Furthermore, we expect this to be handed over in a proper and business-like fashion."

"You can't tell us what to do and fire us," said Lord H, starting to get hot under the collar now.

"There's the telephone," I said, "You can phone Sir Bertram-Waring and ask him to confirm what I have told you."

They were all as white as a sheet as Lord H picked up the phone and dialled Sir Bertram-Waring, who gave him short shrift down the phone and confirmed my message.

The whole family were dismissed. I was then left to pick up the pieces and get the company back up and running more efficiently. There were only five members left on the board then who needed a little 'sorting out'.

Another guy, Gibson, came down to Neasden to take over the company. I spoke to the Doctor, who had always talked down to me, and told him in no uncertain terms that he either works with us or goes. He behaved himself afterwards and started to even call me 'sir'!

It was quite convenient for me to work in Neasden as it was not too far from Hayes, where I lived. They had some very good guys in the workforce at Bradley's. There was a foreman who had been there for quite a long time, so I had a conversation with Sir Bertram-Waring about the possibility of making this foreman the works manager of the place as I felt that he would make a really good job of it. It was agreed, so I called the foreman into the office and asked him to sit down, whereupon I told him that we had got rid of most of the board.

“Thank God for that!” he said, “They drove me crazy; in fact I was thinking of leaving, but I have been here for years, from the start, and didn’t really want to sacrifice my good job for the likes of them.” There and then, I promoted him to works manager. He nearly fell off the chair; he couldn’t believe it when I said, “As from Friday, you are Works Manager of this company, your salary will be adjusted accordingly, and you have an office which will be vacated by Friday and ready for you to move in.”

He couldn’t believe his good luck and fortune!

Off to the USA .... Or not!

I received another call from Sir Bertram-Waring again; he wanted to thank me so much for all my hard work in developing the pacemaker, saying I was his ‘top man’.

“George, I have another job for you, you’re just the man. I want you to go to Lockheeds in Burbank, California, USA”. I asked for some more details about the post and where it would be. I would be working in Lockheeds for Lucas, ensuring that the missiles, rocketry and machinery made would be ‘anglicised’, made appropriate to fit with British aircraft. It would be for at least three years. He told me that he would make all arrangements, all I needed to do was to go and get visas and passports for the family. We discussed it at some length. I was a bit dubious as to my own and Florence’s standing on this, so I agreed to go home and talk it through with Florence first and then, if we were interested and in agreement, to go and get visas and passports set up for the whole family. Following a long discussion with Florence, I then returned to Sir. Bertram-Waring's office to discuss the next stage.

"I have decided that I don't want you to go and work at Lockheed anymore, but instead, I want you to go and work on guided missiles in New York. I'm sure you would be able to cope with that, wouldn't you?" I was quite taken aback – this was not what we had agreed at our last meeting, and there was no way I wanted to uproot my family to go to New York! California, we could have handled but not New York. We really didn't want the upheaval of moving the children from their schools to a completely different country. Despite that – here in Britain, I was busy making medical equipment that saved lives and there I was contemplating a job in another country making equipment that took lives. My mind was made up, we were not going to go.

"I don't want to go there, no, New York is not the place for us. Florence would never agree to that, and I am not at all keen either." I told him.

He started to get agitated and then said, "But you have to! You must go!" he said, "You work for me, so you have to do as I tell you!" He was so used to getting his own way.

To try to diffuse this tricky situation I further discussed with him that there were many people in the business who could do the job as well as me. I told him of our decision and that I would rather stay with working on the medical electronic equipment.

I even offered a few names of people who would probably be interested in going to America.

"No, I want you to go," he said, "You work for this company, so you've got to go if I tell you."

"I don't want to go to America, and I have explained my reasons," I responded.

"In that case," he said, "If you can't do as I ask, then you can't work for this company, you'll have to resign." I think he thought he was calling my bluff, and I would then back down, but I was not going to be bullied into doing something as life-changing as moving to another country. I immediately resigned as I was getting rather annoyed with his attitude by then. I packed up my gear and left, leaving him open-mouthed and very angry. How dare he treat me like that after all the business, fame and fortune I had brought him! And an OBE!

So here we go again! It was now the mid '60's, and I was without a job, again. And not much money. I decided that working in a business owned by a worldwide company might not be the best idea for me. I would try and set up my own business.

24. Gemco – 1960's

I had an acquaintance, an industrial chemist and businessman, called Gerry Pollack, who got in touch with me when he heard that I was starting up a business after leaving Lucas-Rotax. Through him, I was introduced to a man called Sam Cordell. When I enlightened him, Sam showed a great interest in what I was intending to do in this new business venture. He then went on to suggest that we go into business together as he was about to start setting up on his own after working for his brother-in-law. So, a new company was born, Gemco Electronics, based in Old Street, Shoreditch, London. We did very well indeed, gaining a solid client base, making good money, and Sam went on to become a great friend and colleague.

In one year, Gemco earnt £90,000, in the bank, which was a fortune then. That business became very successful and is possibly still going strong.

Air-suspended Conveyor Systems

By chance, I got involved in a contract for air-suspended conveyor systems for a large warehouse distribution company. There was a professor I was introduced to at Imperial College who asked me to help with his idea to use an air system to carry packages along a conveyor. He needed a trial system built and had the money upfront for the development of it. He found that the trouble with his previous designs was that however much air was put into the system, the output would be lost as the package moved further along the system as there would not be enough air further along to move the package, therefore it would slow to a standstill. This is where he needed my input. I came up with an idea for the design of having the air only being able to escape through a small number of holes at any one time and, as the package moved past, the holes behind would be shut off, thus maintaining the air pressure all along using small sensors to signal where the package was to shut and open 'gates' to maintain the pressure. The professor had been at his wits end working on a solution to the problem for nearly a year and was stunned that I could come up with that in a few minutes! I talked him into giving the contract to me and made a very successful system that was used in several distribution warehouses on a large scale.

Ultrasonics

I had read an article in an engineering paper about 'ultrasonics' which had captivated my interest, so I had decided to investigate. Ultrasonics involved making a crystal that would operate at the right frequency which, if you vibrated the crystal at a certain frequency, would develop an envelope of transmission at a specific radio frequency and send it off in a direct line. Then you would pick up the signal bouncing back so that you then knew the measurement of distance. By now I would have made millions if I had patented it then. But I didn't. I made this product and wrote an article on it. The crystals were made on a lathe; it was a crystal called lead zirconate tartenate (LZT). It was a very difficult task as an ultra-sharp tool made from tungsten needed to be used to machine the surface of this crystal and mount it with wires etc. to make the product.

I developed this with the help of my colleague, Sam. There was a building opposite to the factory and we tested it by pointing it at the building and it told us the exact distance to an accuracy of +/- 1mm over 600ft. It was really accurate. I didn't realise at the time, but this would prove to be extremely useful for guns and all sorts of instruments where accurate distance measuring is required. Every estate agent now something similar to measure the room and house dimensions. I had originally designed it, but I never got a penny for all my work on this. This was superseded by laser systems later on.

Note to self – must patent good inventions!

Altimeters for the Ministry of Defence

The Ministry of Defence (MOD) telephoned for me to go and pay them a visit, whereupon they offered me a contract to make ultrasonic altimeters, as they wanted to land troops out of helicopters in jungle areas where it was difficult to judge the distance of drop due to the trees. A normal altimeter would pick up ground level as being the tops of the trees which were invariably 60-100ft above the ground; impossible to drop air crew off from the end of a rope. The ultrasonic altimeter would ignore vegetation and give a true helicopter to ground distance. I visited a fellow called Giles and I was asked to design one to suit their needs, they'd pick up all expenses for the prototype which they would then test before we launch into large-scale production. So, I asked that they give me £9,000 as a start and that should be enough to design and make it the prototype initially. That was a lot of money in those days. He transferred the money and I began to make the specialised altimeter. He informed me that anything that goes onto an aircraft must meet all sorts of stringent tests and regulations, so it would need some thorough testing, especially being electronic and having a voltage on it. It would take the MOD a long time to even get as far as testing it out unless I could think of a way to at least check that it works at speed and would be appropriate for the task. Once made, I put the altimeter on the end of a long pole, we were then given special permission to use Farnborough airfield to test it by leaning precariously out of the car window, whilst travelling at the fastest speed possible, and holding the pole so that the gadget was reading changes in distance from itself to the ground as we sped along the runway. We had a long row of straw bales and other items along the track to test the accuracy of the readings from the gadget. Needless to say, it worked very well and very accurately. We linked it to an oscilloscope with a copier attached so that we could see the response from the altimeter. We brought the test design back to Giles, who was very pleased with the result and wanted me to get the design work together so that they could pay me. We discussed a contract for £91,000! I even got design authority from the MOD, which is like getting hold of gold dust. I was asked to make a few prototypes and they were soon ready for testing on aircraft; the only drawback (a rather major one!) is that I was not a MOD approved company with the relevant certification to meet the demands of building electronic gadgets for aircraft and the MOD. When I delivered the prototypes, the fellow delivered a virtual bombshell – I was to hand over the designs and details for a MOD authorised company to make the altimeter, a company that WAS on the MODs list of approved companies. I was not too happy, but the fellow said that they would pay me for the work I had done. I had acquired money from the bank in advance, so was in debt to the bank at this time. I handed over the designs and I received the written contract. After a few weeks he said that they had put my prototype onto a helicopter and had been flying over the New Forest and that it worked very well. “That’s good news,” I agreed with him. Then he told me that they were going to proceed with the other company making them and that unfortunately I didn’t have the contract to manufacture them. I was devastated! He told me that for my design work on it they would pay me £22,000, not the £91,000 initially agreed. Needless to say, I was not very happy at all. I missed out by not patenting the altimeter and then other people were able to benefit from making and developing it into the future. Note to self AGAIN!

High Temperature Switches

Following this set-back I got into making high temperature switches which I sold to the RAF for jet engine deflection plates using special ceramics, so they could work at very high temperatures and still operate as a switch. I got it Patented this time!

Hovercraft

Using a similar system, we produced ultrasonic transducers giving roll and pitch control to Hovercraft made by the Vickers Company for cross-channel ferries. I did write a paper on it for the exhibition at the Horticultural Halls in London and the editor of the Financial Times had my article on it printed.

The Vickers Aircraft Corporation got to hear about the ultrasonics ideas I had been working on with the helicopters, they had heard about it from this article I had written, so they asked me to design a system to control the huge cross-channel hovercraft. They wanted it to put one at each side and the front of the hovercraft so it controlled roll, pitch and yaw. After developing and testing the prototype we found that it worked very well. I eventually made the parts and they were fitted to the hovercraft, of which there were only five at the time. The engineers came to visit me for information on fitting the parts, but they told me they did not need me to go and oversee their work.

I went on to try to sell the idea to the oil companies (Esso) for measuring the height of the oil inside the tanks, which was a problem for them to measure. The apparatus would be screwed onto the top of each tank and would then measure the distance to the oil surface, so calculating the depth of the oil and its relative volume. But there were too many variables with the size of the tank, the changes in pressure, etc, so that idea didn't come off as we couldn't get the accuracy they needed.

It was quite an adventurous time, one way or another.

Transistor Radios and Portable Colour Televisions

We were getting to the point where we needed some kind of investment to enable us to make more of the products that I had been developing. I had made a very good transistor radio with three wave bands in a very neat case (that another friend had made for me by a vacuum forming process). We also made a small portable Radiogram that could be taken anywhere like picnics and for playing 45rpm records. Advertising in the Financial Times for Investors ensured that we received many replies.

Eventually we sold shares to Sir. Patrick Crofton and his outfit. However, the deal was made on great promises that didn't materialise. We had designed and made one of the first portable solid-state television sets. We had employed a friend of mine, who I worked with at Bradley's, he was a real wiz with the dark arts of transmission. Eventually we designed and made the first all transistor television, along with another guy, who was an electronics and radio engineer from Bradley's. This was the first portable, all transistor television that could be carried anywhere and pick up a signal. It could be used whilst camping or on a boat, anywhere in fact. It worked using batteries or could be plugged into the mains. We sold 25 of them to Blake's Holidays (a boating holiday company) and then I approached Fergusons in the hope of them placing an order. But though they were interested, they didn't buy.

I even sold many of these products to Hong Kong!

That product, plus some of the other gadgets I had designed, got Crofton and his pals to cheat us out of our shares. We learned a very sharp lesson, never to trust the gentry!

Sam knew the Mayor of Paddington, Sir. James Collins, who owned a company called Headquarters and General Supplies. Sir James, or Jimmy, had a penthouse suite on top of Whites Hotel. It was during one meeting in his penthouse that he explained that he wanted some electric fires to be made – a 500W portable fire, boxed and that was strong enough to survive the rigours of the postage system and survive any gruelling journey and harsh use wherever it was used. It couldn't cost more than 10 shillings.

I looked around and found a cheap source of steel to buy, which were offcuts from the making of Vauxhalls cars. When I approached the purchasing manager at Vauxhalls regarding buying the offcuts, he was amazed that I was interested in not 1 or 2 bundles but all 30 tons they had available at the time. I bought 30 tons, and had it shipped down to a place in Romford, getting this guy to weld it all to make the fire housings, then had the electrics made and fitted. They were so resilient. I took the fire up to Jimmy, in a substantial box; I had paid 4 pence for the corrugated cardboard box. It cost me six shillings (which is approximately 30p) to make each fire. I handed it to him, and he had a good look at it, plugged it in and switched it on and was very pleased with it. It was a small square shaped fire and had a nice, dark bronze, hammered paint finish to it. He put it back in the box and sealed it up then to my amazement he lifted it right above his head and dropped it. Then he picked it up and threw it against the wall and then took it out of the box and he said "Right, now we will see if it is any good!" He plugged it in and switched it on – it worked no problem at all. He said, "Well it has worked first time, so I am going to try it again, have you got another one?" To which I answered that I hadn't. He went through this rigmarole a few times, testing it each time then re-sealing the box. It still worked and was unscathed.

"I want to order 10,000," he said. We made 30,000 of them in the end.

Another client, Jack Levane, asked us to make some electric dryers that would dry washing on a wooden clothes horse which it supported, and would also stand on edge acting as an electric fire. After much research I was able to source the wooden collapsible clothes horses from Czechoslovakia, bought for a ridiculous price of something like two shillings each. The heaters could be used for all sorts of purposes such as heating, obviously, and putting under a clothes horse to dry clothes etc. In a year, clear net profit into my bank, I made £80,000, which was a fortune in those days – it would be in the many hundreds of thousands today! I had really fallen on my feet. I was even invited onto the board of the Lloyds and Scottish Group company because I had been contracting the making of all these things to them. We used to have five great big lorries every week taking all this stuff to different places, Debenhams, and other such stores. We were turning these out like madmen and the money was coming in. Sam was running all the sales side of things. Now Levane hated James Collins. Sam really messed up because he told Jack Levane that we were also making for James Collins. This information really upset Levane, so overnight Levane's company stopped receiving them and the lorries were turned back. We had to stop making them. We had 18,000 of them in stock! What were we going to do?

We went from riches to rags virtually overnight!

I tried to sell them to the John Bloom organisations as they were selling thousands of cheap washing machines at the time, but he was involved in other attractions to assist his sales. Eventually I sold them to another washing machine outfit at a slight loss managing to pay off my accumulated heavy debts.

Ah well! You win some – you lose some!

25. Fishing in Sam's Yacht

I mentioned that I loved fishing, and so did many of my pals. With Trevor, another of our friends, Sam and I would get into Sam's car and head off to Brightlingsea for the weekend. He had a yacht moored there and had offered to take us out fishing for the weekend. We arrived in Brightlingsea at about 3pm where the yacht was moored further out in the water of the estuary; to get to the yacht we would row out in a small boat. Once on board we settled down to an evening of beer and chat, ready to set off early the next morning to go fishing.

"How do you feel about rowing the boat?" Sam asked me in the early evening, "I thought we could have fish and chips as there's a lovely fish and chip shop on the harbour front. It won't take long. I will get the rest of the food ready for your return." Trevor was a bit of a 'Wally' and, as I was always the more adventurous one, I was the one to go. I headed out to the shore, tying up the boat and queueing for our supper, salivating at the thought of the supper we were about to eat. Little did I know!

It didn't take me long, I soon purchased the goodies and got back in the rowing boat. The only trouble was that by that time a thick sea mist had come rolling in and I couldn't see his yacht at all, but I did know in which direction it lay, only about 300 yards away, so I felt confident that I'd soon find it. I started to row, but soon found that I could neither see the shore nor the yacht. I wasn't too worried as I felt sure that I was rowing straight and in the right direction, I was confident that I would be there very soon. I hoped! I rowed in circles for probably two hours – all the time the water was coming down the river, so I was probably being carried out away from my target. Eventually the yacht loomed in front of me. I've never felt so relieved; I could have lost my way and finished up in the North Sea! Sam and Trevor were getting very worried but felt helpless as I had their only means to get to the shore, they were happy to welcome me back on board with cold fish and chips. We warmed them up and had a few drinks and a laugh before going to bed.

The following morning was promising a beautiful September day whilst we headed out into the North Sea, all sails open, taking us along at a fast pace towards the Thames estuary, where we turned around some five or six hours later to head back towards Brightlingsea. Quite suddenly the weather started to change and there was quite a swell developing, with high winds and choppy seas. We began to get worried as the boat was rising and falling some twelve feet with every wave. Trevor and I were not experienced at sailing and Sam put on a brave face as he concentrated on keeping the boat steady. We eventually arrived near to Brightlingsea and managed to find the buoys that indicated our passage into the river where we were to travel to our mooring.

Suddenly the boat stopped! We were marooned on a sand bank and the tide was running out of the estuary. Sam was worried now as he realised that the boat would tip over before long as the water level steadily went down. That's when he told us we had to put the sea legs on the boat. These two sea legs are planks of timber, about 12ft long, 1ft wide and 4 inches thick (4mx30cmx10cm), attached to the outside hull of the boat by someone, whilst another person bolts them from the inside. 'Muggins' was duly elected to get into the water (Trevor was adamant that he couldn't swim well enough) to attach the sea legs – a very difficult job! The water was freezing plus the fact that there was the tide carrying water out to sea at a fast pace. I was tied to the boat by a rope then I manoeuvred the first plank with not too much trouble, but the second one proved more difficult, probably since I was, by now, numb with cold and shivering violently. Once out of the water I found it so difficult to warm up, even with hot tea, blankets and a tot of rum. We spent the evening having a good laugh about the day and settled down for the night.

At about 4.30am the tide started to turn – that was my cue AGAIN to get into the water and get the sea legs off. I was really not amused that I had to be the one to go in again, especially as I knew how long it would take to get warm again. Over the side I went, undid the nuts, got the legs off and climbed out of the water again. I was truly frozen by then. It was by now 6.30am and we were off the sand bank and heading upriver to our mooring. Sam had the idea of going to shore and knocking up the fellow in the pub (whom he knew as a friend) for some early breakfast, tea and a bit of warmth. Poor fellow! It was a Sunday morning and I was sure he wouldn't be best pleased. He was a bit disgruntled at first but accommodated us and we were at least able to warm up before being fed an amazing breakfast in the warmth.

"Whatever you do, Sam, never take me yachting again," I uttered, between still-chattering teeth.

I really didn't learn my lesson!

Some years later I purchased a small sailing dingy, second-hand, and we took it on its trailer down to Cornwall one holiday to test it out. I remember we were in a bay near Mevagissy and I had unloaded it from its trailer into the sea, I felt the eyes of everyone on the beach watching, and proudly set out to sea, tacking using the wind's energy. I sailed out some distance but then realised that I was past the lee of the cliffs, the wind and waves were now starting to take control and I wasn't at all sure I knew how to turn the boat and tack back to shore! Eventually I managed to manoeuvre the boat around and head back to shore. I prepared to jump out of the boat with the rope in hand and then haul the boat in. But what I hadn't realised was that in the meantime the tide had come in and it was deeper just that short distance from the shoreline. I jumped into what I thought was 3ft of water, but it was 9ft deep and I came up coughing and spluttering, rope still in hand and everyone watching. Many were laughing; I did feel a fool as I swam and then dragged the boat to shore.

It's good to laugh at those antics now!

I didn't see much of Sam after that business. He suddenly decided to go to Brazil of all places! He had sold the boat and was busy packing up.

"What does your wife Sally think about going to Brazil?" I asked him, amazed at his sudden decision.

"I'm not taking her," came his reply. Apparently he hadn't told her that he was leaving. He professed that he had always wanted to go there – first I had heard!

Then suddenly he was gone. We never heard from him again after that. It was a shame as we got on very well as a foursome, we were good friends and Sally was a lovely lady. We did keep in touch with Sally for a while. She was most bemused and upset by his departure, she couldn't understand him leaving to go to Brazil. They had a lovely house, were comfortably off, we got on well together and were very happy.

Ah well.

26. Gadgets for Cinesound

My great friend, Gerry Pollack, had heard about my situation as regards my business and was in touch with me again, saying that he'd introduce me to his other partners as he had a factory in Kensington making Cinesound equipment, but no one to run it at the moment. The factory was bursting at the seams and in need of more space, so I suggested that he might like to try to lease the recently vacated premises of EMI in Hayes, Middlesex. He subsequently secured one of the vast floors of the building and moved his business and machinery over to Hayes.

Gerry was a brilliant chemist but he required someone with the knowledge of electrical supplies to run this business. I decided to go and at least have a look. I liked what I saw but knew I would have my work cut out in 'taming' the workforce. We discussed a reasonable wage and he agreed that I could do the job and installed me in it to oversee the business and the workforce. It was in one hell of a mess though. There were 42 ladies who worked there and one man, and then I came in to take over. That didn't go down too well with the workers. I told Gerry that it may not work too well at first as I would have to come down really hard on them and I might upset a few people in the process as they were well used to ruling the roost themselves and working on their own terms.

"I know they're not an easy bunch to handle; I can't handle them myself, so just do your best," he said.

"Please understand that it is not going to be easy to begin with, but it will get better in time as I bring them into line," I said. He agreed that I could sort it all out in my own way.

The very next day I invited all the workers to stop work and come and bring a chair to sit on whilst I talked to them about my expectations.

"What I like is a nice, happy working environment. A place of work that you enjoy and look forward to coming to each day. I don't want you to come to work feeling stressed or feel that you're not happy in some way," I said, "But, in order to achieve that there have to be some changes and that is that everybody does what they are told, when they are told. If anyone has a complaint, then they must come to me and I will try my utmost to sort it out. I believe in being fair and giving fair treatment, but I will not tolerate any bad work ethics. What I will do for you is, if you cooperate with me, I would like to start a bonus scheme. If we get the production levels up to a good profit level, then some of that will be shared with you in the form of a bonus."

The ladies looked at me and must have been very satisfied with my proposition as, in a very short time, the profits were up, bonuses being shared, and I had them all eating out of my hand. In the end we were doing very well.

One lunchtime I was sitting in my office and I could hear raucous laughter from the factory floor. This went on, at lunchtime, for a couple of days in a row where they were literally beside themselves with laughter, so I decided to investigate. It was a huge factory, set out in blocks, with many glass windows to the side of each block and a gap in between forming an alleyway. The girls were looking down, out of the windows at the only man who worked in our part of the factory, as he lay with one of the girls on a pile of cardboard having a bit of 'quality' time together. The girl was only sixteen! I couldn't leave it at that.

I called him into my office and said, "You don't know this, but I am going to tell you. Everybody here, every day watches you go down there with your sandwich and that little girl and get 'at it'." Well, his face was a picture. He was totally unaware that he was being watched. It did stop (or he went elsewhere) and all seemed to settle down. Some weeks later there was a knock on my door from one of the ladies saying that there was someone here to see me. A very irate lady came into the office saying that her daughter worked here, she's been led astray and has got herself pregnant by somebody here. She was referring to the sixteen-year-old girl, of course. I told her that as soon as I found out I had it stopped and had reprimanded the man, but I have no jurisdiction over what they do in their own time as they are both over sixteen. The lady was really upset and tearful. I kept the girl on for as long as I could and gave her a bit extra in her wage packet when she left; I did feel so sorry for her.

Soon after that I employed a lady formerly from East Germany, called Gurda. She had been a secret police officer, under the East Germans, and was one tough lady. She was aged about 40 and was married and had three children by an English ex-RAF fellow who had defected to the Russians, but who had now left her. It was a very tough life for her, living in an Eastern bloc country with no support, so she went to the British embassy to get her British passports for her and the children, being married at the time to a British man. Eventually, after much deliberation, they provided them for her, then she had to plan how to get out of the country. On one of her days off from work, she dressed up, with her children and set off for the borders where she managed to talk her way through the barrier as she told them that she was visiting her husband's parents. Once into West Germany, she managed to get over to Britain.

She spoke very good English so I decided to take her on in a supervisory role, hoping that she wouldn't upset the applecart, so to speak. But I needn't have worried, as Gurda was an asset to the company, handled them all very well and was readily accepted by the workforce.

One day, at the end of the working day, Gurda asked to see me and asked to have a private word with me. She came in and sat in a chair and said, "I've got to ask you something, do you think I'm attractive?" I knew she liked me, but I was quite taken aback by her forthright question and had to think carefully how to answer this delicately.

"Of course you are attractive, you're a very nice lady," I answered.

"You really do find me attractive then?" she asked again.

"I'm sure there are many men who would find you attractive and an interesting person to get to know. Is that important to you?" I asked.

"Yes," she said, "I needed to know that you find me attractive."

I explained to her that she needed to remember that I was a married man, but I felt sure that there were many men who would be attracted to her and find her to be a lovely person.

"Oh, no! Sorry,' she said, embarrassedly, "Don't get me wrong, I am thinking of going to a marriage bureau and just wanted your honest opinion to see if English men would find me attractive and if I had any chance of finding a good man at my age." I told her that I felt sure that other men would find her attractive, but to be warned to be very careful, as some of the men she might meet from a marriage bureau may not be very nice at all.

Some weeks passed and I hadn't heard any more from her until one day she came to tell me that she had gone to the bureaux for the first time and had met a man for whom it was his first time trying it too. They had been seeing each other regularly and had really 'clicked', getting along very well with him and the children really liked him; he really loved her three little girls too. I was really pleased for her that it was all working out. A few more weeks went by when she suddenly announced that she was leaving on that coming Friday. I was stunned! I had come to rely upon her as she was a great support in the factory and a good worker. It transpired that she was moving in with the man she had met, who had a lovely big house in Ealing and could give her everything she wanted, including his love and affection for her and the girls, and she didn't need to work. I was very saddened that she was leaving, but happy for her. I told her that if it didn't work out then I would have her back in an instant.

Some months later I happened to be in Ealing Broadway, when I chanced upon Gurda in the street. She was so smartly dressed and looked really well, I almost didn't recognise her, and I asked how things were.

"I don't know what happened," she said, "But God must have been looking down upon me the day I went to that marriage bureaux. The man I am with is a builder whose wife had died a few years ago, so he was on his own. We've got a beautiful house; he loves me and the children (and we love him back!) and he would give me anything I want. We go on lovely holidays and I am having the time of my life with someone who really cares and treats me like a lady; I sometimes have to pinch myself." She gave me a hug and wished me farewell. I was so pleased for her; it was about time she had some good luck in her life.

It had been difficult since Gurda had left, so Gerry Pollack decided that I should seek another employee to help within the business. I had interviewed a young man, aged about 30 who, at his interview with me told me that he had been recently released from prison, and was trying to get himself back into work and reforming himself. He was married with a wife and child and was finding it particularly hard to find a job with his background and no specific skills. He had been in prison for two years for stealing, hated prison and vowed he was not going back there ever again. I liked him for his honesty and decided to give him a chance and took him on for which he was very grateful. He was a good worker and got on well with me and with all the staff.

The week's production was shipped out every Friday in the customer's lorry. Although we counted them on the lorry, less units always arrived despite them being counted on by the driver and my storekeeper and counted off at the other end. The discovery of this led to some problems between me and the boss of our customer. I indicated that it must be either their driver or he was stopping somewhere and having them stolen. For some weeks this went on until one day, due to the shortage of parts in a delivery to us, we were quite short on production. At that point my new employee came to me and said quite openly, "Don't worry, I can make the shortage up as I have lots stored in the back storeroom that I nicked for you from their lorry!" I didn't know whether to laugh or cry. I had to face up to telling the customer the whole story. At first, he was furious but then he saw the funny side of it. I told my young man that I appreciated his loyalty to me but that was distorted honesty and I got a promise from him never to do that sort of thing again.

After getting this factory up and running on a sound footing, we had so much business that I found that I could not cope with both running the place and testing the products. We advertised and I took on a Mr. Gordon Chandler. He was able to do the job alright, but couldn't get to work on time any day, so after a few months I had to sack him. Soon afterwards I finished my job running the factory. The directors wanted me to stay but I had ambitions to start a consultancy business with support from a very pleasant and amenable person I had met, called Al Saxon.

27. Starting my own Business

G.W. Pritchard Engineering Ltd – 1960's

Autoclavable Defibrillators

After working with other people and after much thought I decided to start my own business and to do things for myself. The business was called G. W. Pritchard Engineering Ltd, and I began to become quite successful as a design engineer and consultant working from home. I did do some work for Imperial College and, soon afterwards, there was a big write-up about my work in the Financial Times. It wrote about how I had started up in business and the things I had been designing and making in recent months, what great business prospects I had and noting many of the things I had been involved in in the past.

I contacted Professor Brockwell at Central Middlesex Hospital to discuss some of the new medical machinery I was developing. He was the one I had contacted in the past to make the heart-lung machine. I suggested to him that I was going to make some 'autoclavable defibrillators' (they are used when you have open heart surgery to re-start the heart). The terminals that come into contact with the body (the heart) have to be gold or gold plated. I had previously spoken to my friend, Gerry Pollack, who was a very good industrial chemist, and he had found a way to plate gold onto a type of plastic, a necessary requirement for the heart-lung machine. I worked on the design of these these defibrillating machines (and many others forms of medical machinery) and exhibited them in the Royal Horticultural Halls Exhibition. Through exposure at the exhibition, I started to make this machinery for the NHS through Professor Brockwell. Unfortunately, in those days, the NHS took almost a year to pay for equipment provided. This was no good for a small business like mine so unfortunately, I couldn't keep going with orders from them in the long term. I was sorry to leave this form of design work as I had enjoyed developing cutting-edge life-saving machinery.

28. G.W. Pritchard - Consultant Electrical Engineer

Business was good, so, securing an office in Grafton Street, near Tottenham Court Road, I set up my own business as a Consultant Electrical Engineer and set about finding more clients. Soon I was successfully getting design work from top companies and quickly set to making good progress and with great success. Gordon Chandler telephoned me saying that he was desperate for work and asked if I could help. Knowing him and feeling sorry for his wife and small children I took him on, with his promise to mend his tardy ways, which he did, and we worked well together for some years.

Apart from the work for our customers, we developed some other products of our own. One of these was an electronic calculator using Nixie tubes (or cold cathode display, it is an electronic device used for displaying numerals or other information using glow discharge). This was before the transistor driven/LED types that are available now. We had a large order promise from William Hill, the bookmakers, if this machine proved that it could rapidly calculate all of the betting mathematics. We managed to get this machine to do its calculations in seconds, crops, double bets, Yankee bets and all kinds of strange bets. This would save the Bookmakers thousands of pounds and lots of time. Philips Ltd, in Holland, were pleased to offer to make them for us and I thought I would soon make my first million. But after some more investigation of the maths involved, I found that I could use mathematical formulae to do these calculations almost as quickly using pencil and paper. I had to tell the Customer this fact in fairness to them and gave them the details free. They generously paid me all costs.

Within a couple of months, the current 'mini' calculators came onto the market. So, we were saved in the long run from certain disaster, had we gone ahead with our machine.

29. Brooklands Aviation & Booth Engineering 1967-1972

I forged ahead with my consultancy business and was doing reasonably well in my London West End office making a decent profit. Within a year, my staff and I were very busy and becoming well known in the industry as a 'can do the impossible' outfit. One day, soon after this, a man calling himself Air Commodore Grieve, Chairman of Brooklands Aviation Group, saying that he wanted to meet me and had a proposition to make to me telephoned me at home. We arranged to meet in the evening at my house in Hayes. At the meeting he spoke of his company wanting to get into a different field of business, so he offered to buy my business and asked me to run it, as a subsidiary Company of his main Company, as Managing Director with an appropriate salary and car with expenses. Following some discussion with Florence, I accepted and was given the opportunity of starting a factory either in Surrey or Northamptonshire. We decided on the latter as it would be situated in the centre of the country, useful for distribution, and more beneficial for our children in so many ways. We were given financial help to find a house and premises and to relocate. I was given £10,000 for the business, plus a job, money to get the business up and running, a car and a factory.

So here I go again on a new venture that's full of promise and hard work!

Putting some things in an overnight bag, I set off to Northampton by train. I was met at the Station and taken to

Brooklands office and Boardroom. There, I was quizzed and cross-questioned about everything and asked what my intentions were in improving their business, before being taken to a local Inn to book-in to a room. The following day I was taken and shown an empty factory and told to get going from scratch. I was given a car, a Ford saloon that ran very well. This was the extent of help towards the venture.

After having spent a week there, I went back to our home in Hayes for the weekend and then took my family up to Northampton to size up the factory and look around the area with a view to purchasing a property.

With hard work and dedication, coupled with some pressure from Brooklands Directors, I had things up and running well enough in a short space of time and the business was named Booth Engineering. I spent every weekend at home in Hayes. It wasn't too long before we were doing very well, and the factory was too small for the work I was producing. So, with an increased staff, we had to move into better and much larger premises. By then I had large contracts, with many top Companies, like Rolls Royce. With the aid of my staff, I had designed variable speed electric motor inverters. These were used to produce the machined parts for Concorde, and we spent many weeks at the British Aircraft Factory in Preston on this very interesting task. These inverters were unique at that time as they could produce high frequencies giving very fast electric motor speeds aiding the smooth cutting finish for the metallic parts. We also supplied systems for many of the Water Authorities around Britain.

A year passed and eventually the family moved from London to Tiffield, a lovely village near Northampton, into an old sixteenth century house that had been totally modernised. It was a lovely place and we liked it there so much, but when a new housing estate was built near-by, we decided to move elsewhere.

Brooklands Aviation were a bit 'stuffy'; they had been in the business for many years, but did not really keep up with the times, making it more and more difficult for me to run the business successfully. They didn't really appreciate that to start up a new part to the business and run it in the way that I felt it should be run, doing the things that they wanted, would take time and money. All the profits that my part of the company made, were used to support other branches of the company, instead of being used, in part, for developing my part of the business further. By the end of my time with them, my part of the business was making far more money that the rest of Brooklands Aviation.

After all this effort in developing the company, I was suddenly told by the Directors of the parent company, that I was to run just the technical side and they were installing an Ex-Naval Commander to take over everything else. I was not happy! Within a few days he came and took over my office. He was quite a nice man but was completely out of his depth with our advanced technical business. We found out that he drank large cups of whisky all day long and soon became a joke with the workers. He lasted just one month before he was thrown out and I was reinstated.

30. Dosing pumps for Water Authorities, 1972

By now we were supplying systems to many water authorities around the country for 'dosing pumps' (designed to pump a very precise flow rate of a chemical or substance into either water, steam or a gas flow) that I had designed. These would be responsible for adding precise chemicals to the water at the water treatment plants for many of the water authorities, such as Thames Water and South-West Water Authority. My son, John and I were also involved in making a unit for the pumping station at Hemel Hempstead. This pumping station was situated over an underground river or body of water percolated through the Chiltern Hills over many hundreds of years. When the water board analysed it at that time it was remarkably pure water. Our job was to get the water pumped up through the shafts from deep underground, installing the machinery and controls for this. Each pump was 500 horsepower and worked very effectively. John was the liaison engineer for the manufacturing company and he had involved me in designing and making a system for them to pump water from the underground river into the treatment plant and off to the surrounding homes. We had designed it all, installed it, tested it and were ready to be paid for the work we had done for them. We had been sub-contracted by the main company who had the contract to do the work but they refused to pay us saying that it didn't work as well as they wanted. I asked the chief engineer at the plant what his view was on the apparatus installed by me.

"Great, it works really well and efficiently, why do you ask?" he said. I relayed the issues I was having with the company about them refusing to pay us.

"But that's not true! They can't get away with that!" came his response.

I employed a solicitor and a QC in Northampton and the company had to attend court over the matter. The judge heard both sides as our cases were stated, then he said to them, "You are nothing but a load of crooks and liars, you should be ashamed of yourselves, you should not be in business." He really gave them a dressing down. He continued, "The water company have made a statement to the effect that they are more than happy with the works carried out, so I make the judgement in the favour of Mr. Pritchard." I told my barrister that I was sure they still would not pay me despite the judge's decision unless he got a court judgement. The barrister stood up and told the judge that these people were not to be trusted, so the money had to be paid into the courts who would then pay me – this was a fail-safe way for me to obtain my money owed. If they didn't pay it, they would be in contempt of court and would be arrested. They had to pay all the money within seven days, plus costs. They were not happy that I had won the case.

Water pumping station, Hemel Hempstead

One strange experience that I had was that another company had supplied pumping machinery to a water company in Cambridgeshire, but once they had finished they were afraid to switch it on and were at a bit of a stalemate with the water company so wanted me to go and check it all before they put the machinery into action. They wanted an assessment of the installation from me. I agreed and then double and triple checked everything with meters of various sorts and then told them that we were switching on at 10am. I was happy with the work that had been installed. Everyone was a bit 'twitchy' before the start button was activated. I pressed the button and it started just fine. I couldn't understand how a firm could make something and then be afraid of using the machine or not want to start it up. Maybe they had had a bad experience in the past or something.

My final words to them were, "There you go, make sure you pay my bill."

31. Crystal Growing Machines, 1975

Whilst running the business, Booth Engineering (which was owned by Brooklands Aviation), we were involved in designing machinery with Rolls-Royce, to make turbine blades, using crystal-growing machines, with input from metallurgical specialists. Up until that time, turbine blades were a bit unpredictable and would easily break, causing industry a lot of time and money in replacing them. To make this new form of blade we used a mixture of various metallic crystals (palladium, chromium etc) to 'grow' the blades. The machine that we designed would magnetically influence and control the stress lines in the crystals and would create the turbine blades, which were perfectly formed. It was a £3 million contract from Rolls Royce to build and install these crystal-growing furnace machines, each of which required a controller cabinet and a power supply cabinet. My equipment was used in controlling the growing of crystals and making turbine blades for jet engines in use all over the world. I wonder if they have updated it yet, forty or more years on!

Turbine Blades - single crystal-growing system

I was also involved in a project making parts for Concorde with B.A. (British Aircraft Constructors).

I had always found work and contracts through Rolls Royce for many of the companies I worked for and for my own companies. Fellow businessmen were astonished that a small business like mine would attract contracts from such a large company like Rolls Royce. I think it is all about one's approach to these large companies, or maybe I just have the 'gift of the gab'. I achieved contracts from large companies like GEC, British Gas, UK Water companies, MOD, etc. It wasn't an impossible task; you've just got to aim high.

There were many projects involving Rolls Royce, and much of the control equipment I installed in their premises is still being used today. Initially, in the 1960's, I designed a specialist lighting system, which would switch on individual lights as a person passed along a long corridor, or from room to room, negating the need to keep switching lights on and off. The control system originated from a gold-plated control unit situated in the main foyer at Rolls Royce and was still in use when I last visited there a few years ago.

We also designed and made a very large pumping system for jet aircraft fuel at Heathrow. Locally, I had made a special fuel-pumping aircraft fuelling system used on Boeing and jumbo jets for Timken Bearings in Northampton and which was also used in another of their companies in France.

Business was now going forward nicely, but, as I was sitting in my office one afternoon in the factory in Weedon Road, a man called (who I had never seen before) and walked straight into my office without knocking or being announced. He said to me, "I work for an asset stripping company and I am now in charge of this place of business, we are closing it down as we have taken over Brooklands Aviation and all of its assets of which this business is one."

I immediately stood, exclaiming, "Oh no you are not! I set up this part of the business and I have heavily invested in it." Of course, seeing that I wasn't a push-over, he then began to explain that he was the managing director of the asset stripping Company and they had bought out all the businesses linked to Brooklands Aviation, including Sywell flying club. I then explained that I was a director and shareholder of the Company and had not, up to that moment in time, been informed of this by the other Directors. He then informed me that I would need to take it up with the other directors and furthermore, if I didn't leave then I would be thrown out. To his consternation I then threw him out, I was really mad at the treacherous way I had been treated by the company.

When I went to the main Brooklands office and gave them a real mouthful, their excuse was that they did not have to tell me about their negotiations, that had been going on for months, as I might have upset their upcoming deals and, according to the Stock Exchange rule book, they were legally within their rights. Furthermore, as my part of the business was being closed down, I would get no money out of it, just a little redundancy pay. I informed them that they really did not know who they were toying with and that I was not going to let them get away with daylight robbery. Their reply was, "Take it to court then!"

I knew that I would have no chance against such powerful people in a court of law, never mind the costs in money and time that such a process would consume. So, after a fitful night's sleep, that 'lightbulb' in my head came on and I came up with an answer to my problem that would scuttle them completely.

The following morning, I phoned all the companies that we had supplied expensive equipment to over the past two years and explained my problem. This included phone calls to the Thames, the Devon and the Three Rivers Water Authorities, British Timken, The Ford Motor Company, British Gas and a few others. I explained that if the company was closed down, they would of course, then find that their warranties for the equipment we installed would expire with the business shut down that was planned. But, if they could support me by telephoning the Brooklands Directors, then, if I get to continue the company on my own, I will support their warranties through the business. I asked them all to say that they would sue Brooklands for millions of pounds due to loss of the back-up warranty, as any problems with the dosing pumps would potentially cause losses in water supply around the country at a cost of millions of pounds.

Amazingly every one of the companies carried out this task immediately. Within a couple of hours, I was asked to go to a meeting urgently with the whole group of Brooklands and Asset Stripper Directors. They said that what I had done was contrary to my agreement and documentation as a director of the company, and that I had given away information that I should not rightfully have disclosed...etc, etc. They were obviously becoming very unnerved by all the phone calls they had been having in the past few hours. They continued to believe that they could just shut my part of the business down and throw me out on a limb with nothing.

"If you do that," I said, "You'll find yourself in court for Fraud." Their faces began to change. "You have known about closing the business down for the past six months and at no time have you thought to have this conversation with me. You have allowed me to make legally binding contracts with companies, with an agreement to service, maintain and repair or guarantee any equipment with a warranty for two years; that's fraud. So, either they will all be sending their equipment back to you, plus a writ for all the loss of business, or they will sue you for breach of contract. You are probably looking at a 10

– 15-million-pound suit!" Gradually the penny dropped, and they appeared stunned by the dawning realisation that the only way out of it would be to let me continue with my business. I then laughingly said, "Ok, I am willing to take on the warranties, but to do so I want the whole of my part of my business in my name, plus all of its tools and equipment, in fact all of it plus £35,000 left in my name in the Bank account." You could hear a pin drop! At that point I turned on my heel and left them to think about it.

They tried every stunt possible to defeat me like offering the service contracts to other companies. They did find some companies to do this, but I was already ahead of them, I guessed that they would be trying to find a way out, so I was on the phone again to my customers letting them know what the company was probably planning with regard to passing on the warranties to other companies. I informed them that as these inverters were designed by me and were 'new', no one else would know much about how they work in order to maintain or service them properly. I helped them to understand that they really would only want my company to be carrying out the work. My very loyal customers were well informed when the phone call came from Brookland Aviation and reiterated that they would only accept me doing the warranty work, due to my design and installation experience, and my loyalty towards them. They could put the offer of another contract up their *****. After a week of them trying to find a way out of it, they literally pleaded with me to pay a visit to see the Chairman. I eventually decided to go to London and met up with the Chairman of this group to settle this once and for all. He cheekily offered me a sum of money to pull out, about £20,000, which I duly refused. I reiterated to him that if we were to go along that route, then did he realise that within a few weeks he would have lorry load after lorry load of equipment being returned to him, and companies clamouring at the door for money back and suing for loss of business and services, such as water and gas, to a vast number of dwellings? Not to mention a total financial deficit of well into the millions, well above £20,000. His face went grey. He tried to offer me more. Then I told him what I wanted; the whole of my part of my business in my name, plus all of the goods, tools, equipment, machinery and the books, in fact all of it plus £35,000 left in my name in the Bank account. I also want an undertaking from you that there will be no interference from anyone from your company once this is agreed. Then finally, with a sigh, he agreed totally to my terms and said that I was the only person to have ever defeated him. All of it was signed and documented then and there. The whole business and accounts for Booth Engineering were passed over to me, along with the £35,000, which was what was in the company bank account at that time, a lot of money in those times. The bank was informed of my ownership and keen to support me with any overdraft, if required, and all was now well with the world.

So, I was now in control of everything I needed to get ahead. But the one thing that they thought would catch me out was the fully repairing commitment on the factory lease. I had already foreseen this crafty move and refused to have the lease assigned, especially as there were many problems with subsidence of the building, which had been built on land that had piles of leather clippings from the shoe industry buried in the ground. In view of this I had already started proceedings to move into another factory in Daventry. I was not going to sign the lease – the repairs would have cost me the business. I would leave Brooklands to continue their leasehold – they could foot the bill as I wasn't going to be there. I then moved all staff and machinery into the new factory, much to the annoyance of Brooklands! My new company continued to be called Booth Engineering.

I carried on with the electronic business successfully for some years with many ups and downs, such as the three-day week, brought about by the political troubles of that time. I had taken on a good, young Engineer, Brian Highe, who had a family living in meagre circumstances. I managed to get him a new house from my builder friend, and we continued to work well together to the point where I made him a shareholder in the business. Business was so good that I took on the empty factory next door.

To finance all the material and cost for this new business I went to the Bank for a bigger overdraft jointly with Brian, his security being a lot less than mine. We jointly agreed to the Bank's terms and the bank manager said that he would draw up the paperwork for our signatures. The documents were ready and I went to the Bank and signed. Brian however did not and, out of the blue, told me that he had found another job and was leaving. This went down very badly at the Bank as it left them thinking that one of the Directors did not have confidence in the business. Consequently, I had to take the full financial hit. Worse still was that I was left with massive incomplete contracts with three major customers, Rolls Royce, GEC and Gillette. I had to ask them for an extension of time for completion, Gillette was the only one not to give me more time.

I had to work extremely hard, with long hours, to complete, finish and install all this work. It took me more than a month to complete successfully.

My younger son came to me with the news that he and another lad had been offered retail electrical components shop in Daventry, but they had no money or experience in business or the financial commitment to get it started. It sounded as if it could work out alright, so I bought it from a local businessman who, as it I happened, I knew. It all started off well enough but did not make much money, but I used the losses as a tax loss on my other Company.

My other son then came to me asking if I could employ him too as he had recently lost his business and was in dire need of work to support his family and home. In an attempt to help him as well, and to try to put some effort into building the shop business with his brother I agreed to employ him, to buy him a car and pay him a wage. This had some good results to start with but soon we were to find out that an acquaintance of theirs had been stealing money and goods from the business and the business was often left in the hands of unknown characters while other interests were pursued. It was little wonder that the business was not turning a profit and in fact making a loss. Florence and I were most disappointed with all of this and finally gave up and sold the retail shop and goods for the best price that we could get after advertising it. But we came out of it with a loss of almost seventeen thousand pounds!

A lot of money in those days.

Loughborough College contacted me asking if I could place any for their students doing the BSc course in Engineering. Many of these students were foreign students looking for a placement for work during the holiday period. I agreed to take one or two on. There was an Israeli lad called Jorda, who was a lovely guy, in fact we met up with him and his parents some years later when we visited Israel. Another of the students was Oki, a Nigerian chap, very bright and pleasant, who had done all of his electrical engineering training in Russia. At the time, the Russians had trained a group of students in exchange for a supply of hard wood for making gun stocks. Oki had a BSc in electrical engineering and came to work for me, fitting in well with the guys in the factory and bringing his experience from the Russians to complement the skill set. One day he suddenly announced that he was going back to Nigeria. I was sorry to see him go; I had tried to persuade him to stay. Some months later I received a phone call from the bank manager, sounding quite irate down the phone, "You never told me you were going into liquidation!" he said. I was speechless for a moment. "What are you talking about, I'm not going into liquidation," I queried, feeling quite taken aback.

"Yes, you are," he said, "Your company has been 'gazetted' by the Financial Times, also the Telegraph. I couldn't believe what I was hearing, it was news to me. Bad news! I felt sick with worry.

"In fact," I said, "I was just coming to see you because the business is doing really well and expanding so fast, that I need to talk to you about how we move on from here."

"I'm afraid you've gone bust, to the tune of -£38,000, now those notices have gone into the records you are out of this bank, I have to foreclose on your overdraft right away."

What had happened, I eventually found out, was that the fellow called Oki had returned to Nigeria, printed all my paperwork and leaflets about the business and everything, came back to Britain and pretended he was a company associated to me. He set up a company in Bristol making table lamps, getting all the bases from Stoke on Trent and the tops of the lamps from somewhere else all purchased in my name. The companies looked up my name and because the business was stable and had a good name, they gave him credit. I contacted my accountant; I had no option, there was nothing I could do except to close the business down until I could resolve it.

I went from having a flourishing business to one with a bad name in the space of a few days. Florence and I had to find the sum of £38,000 and pay the bank within a week. It was a nightmare at the time, but we managed. I was able to change the name of my company to Booth Electronics, then it took us two or three years to finally get back on track, losing a few good customers en route, though many did remain loyal once they understood what had happened. I did get on to the Department of Trade and Industry to try to recoup some of the money, but they couldn't do anything as Oki had headed back to Nigeria by then.

Sometimes you do your very best to help someone and then this is the way you are treated in return. Fortunately, the majority of people one meets in one's lifetime are good, honest, law-abiding citizens. The bank and my solicitors vehemently advised me to shut the company down, which I did, but I believe that was probably the wrong advice at the time.

At that point, in 1970, due to deterioration in the area we were living, the building of a modern housing estate behind us in a small village, we decided to sell the house in Tiffield and move into temporary accommodation in Long Buckby whilst I found land to build our own house. I finished up with three plots to choose from in various parts of Northamptonshire and eventually decided on a lovely plot in a small village called Cold Higham, just north of Towcester. Having commissioned some plans to be drawn up, I set about organising the building of a large bungalow there. Trying to do this whilst running the business was quite a challenge, especially as I did lots of the work on the building myself at weekends.

It took nine months to complete before we could all move in and we were all very happy and relieved to at last be settled in that beautiful part of the Northamptonshire countryside.

Peggoty's Restaurant

It was around 1975 and near to where we lived was a lovely old restaurant, called Peggoty's, on the A5 Watling Street, just north of Towcester. It was an old stone building with lots of oak beams and full of character. The restaurant came up for sale and I showed an interest in it as a business venture, it was priced at something like £185,000 for the restaurant, all the furniture and kitchen gear and with a car park, so I was wanting to make an offer. We went to view the property and were shown around by the chef. There was also a residential flat above for the chef or caretaker of the business. I happened to know a very wealthy builder who might be able to look over the property with me and verify that it was a sound property and give me some ideas about what we could do to make it a bit more presentable, as it was looking a bit 'tired'.

The day came when he arrived at the property in his magenta Rolls-Royce! After viewing the property and a lengthy discussion, he offered me a proposition – that he could go halves with me in the business. He would do the building work and add on some rooms in the outbuildings that could be used for bed and breakfast accommodation; Silverstone Racing Circuit was just a few miles away so the accommodation and restaurant would do well. He was going to go away and draw up some plans and I was going to make a start on acquiring the property for us. I organised to borrow the money for the purchase from my bank, who were quite happy to loan me the money, but they would need an assessment of its value and a structural report on the building, to which I agreed.

I went to see a local estate agent, Duncan, who agreed to come and do a report for me. A few weeks went by and then I heard back from Duncan. He had visited the property but had some bad news for me. Apparently, being an old building with possibly very little by way of foundations, the whole building was suffering from subsidence and was moving downhill gradually; sooner or later it was going to start cracking up. I argued that it had been there for hundreds of years and looked fine to me. He countered with the fact that it had been a very dry summer. I rang the bank up and told them of the problems but that I had a builder on board who was able to fix these problems. But the bank refused the loan outright. The deal was off. My builder friend was disappointed but agreed that it would not be a sound investment with such problems.

I then went to meet the chef again and told him of our change of mind in view of the problems with the building and securing a loan. Some weeks later I was to learn that the chef had purchased the property with Duncan and that there was no issue with the building other than the normal issues linked to older properties, certainly not subsidence. Duncan, and his firm of Estate agents, had cheated me out of the deal by giving a negative report on the structure. I don't think that it did them much good though, as the Chef died of a heart attack soon afterwards. It has changed hand several times in the past few years and was never brought up to the standard of the plans I had for it.

Eventually, as the children grew up and left home to start families of their own, Florence and I were left living in Cold Higham on our own. It was a great house for entertaining friends and our growing extended family with all the grandchildren; eventually there were nine of them.

Florence and I made a lot of good friends locally and Florence became a local Councillor, becoming more involved in local church and village activities. We were very happy there, having lived in that small village for nearly thirty years before moving to Duston, on the outskirts of Northampton in 1998.

32. Mr Mamak, the scoundrel!

The business was doing very well, and I had decided to retire. I needed to sell the business and put it up for sale in the Financial Times, where it gained some interest from about eight people. I whittled the list down eventually to one person, a man called Mamak. He was a lecturer at Manchester University in Electrical Engineering and knew a lot about the subject and therefore seemed the best candidate. So, we went ahead, and he began to take over the business with a view to me gradually moving away from it and retiring, with him paying me off a bit at a time. Unbeknown to me, he was a villain as he had bought up about five other companies, all of which he was gradually bleeding dry. He had decided to return to his home in India, taking all the money from the businesses by cashing in on them. He had sold up his lovely house in Chelsea, worth millions, where he lived and had moved into a rented house for the duration. In Sheffield he had acquired a big contract with British Steel whereby he was to do some fitting of a conveyor system whilst the factory was on its annual holiday fortnight, for this is the only time that any maintenance can be carried out in such a factory. He had a team fitting the equipment, but it didn't work, and they were running out of time. He informed me then that he had a factory in Sheffield and explained the problem of the situation regarding the equipment not working for his team and about the time constraints. He asked if I could go and help them out to make it work within the time frame. He explained that the team in Sheffield didn't know how to get the equipment working. Off I go to Sheffield and meet these two men who then filled me in on the fact that Mamak had cut back on their money, they couldn't do the job properly, he was pushing all the time, he seemed only interested in getting his money from British Steel. Having looked at the conveyor system, I told them, "It will never work! The design is all wrong." To which they insisted that it would work and that they knew what they were doing. I told them that if I was going to do it, I would need to do it in my own way, then I could be assured that it would work. So we started from scratch. We went along to the factory that Mamak now owned in Sheffield (it was quite a nice place) and made alterations to the original design so that the system could work. The guys in the factory rushed to make the items required for the job. We gathered tools and the machinery we needed and headed back to the Steelworks, whereupon we endeavoured to re-design and make a working system in the two days we had remaining before the British Steel company returned back to work on the Monday. If we could not get the system fitted by Monday, Mamak would be sued for millions in damages, so we needed to succeed. All this time, I was liaising with Mamak, telling him about the fact that the original design was flawed and that we needed to redesign and make the system. "You will lose Millions if this is not successful, you do realise that don't you? It is insured, I hope?" I asked him.

"Oh dear! Can you sort it?" came the reply from Mamak.

After a very hard two days and very long hours of work, we switched it on and away it went, thank goodness! We then needed to make it compatible with all the other machinery in the factory before we could call it 'Job Done". Needless to say, the system worked and the fellas in Sheffield were most grateful for my help. Finished at last. Mamak was very grateful to me for all the time and effort I had spent on it, "You owe me, mate!" I told him, to which he agreed wholeheartedly.

A week or so went by and he had yet another problem which he shared with me. This time he explained about a job for British Gas, where the costs for the design and make of a new control system were becoming astronomical. On further explanation I agreed that it shouldn't be creating that much in the way of costs, and yet again agreed to intervene on his behalf. This time I was in Herefordshire at a domestic gas pumping station helping to create a control system for 1.5 million houses. With the design and machinery completed, a day was scheduled where I could switch off the old system and switch over to my new system within a few seconds. I had built the new control system and housed it safely within a fibreglass housing, within which was a steel housing to protect it from any vandalism which may occur. No one would ever be able to get in. Come the day, there was a gale blowing and it proved near impossible to have the goods delivered to the site, despite the weight of the gear. Eventually we succeeded between us, not before the poor lorry driver had injured himself on the ankle. The moment for switching it over passed without incident and within seconds the new system was up and working like clockwork. It was such a new and innovative system at that plant, that there were many visitors to view the system from other plants, all wanting the same system installed at their gas control sites. Had Mamak not done his disappearing trick, we would have had big contracts with British Gas installing the new control system for years to come across the whole country.

Soon after that I had reason to visit the directors of the company belonging to Mamak in Sheffield, where I found they were in a right old state, owing to the fact that Mamak was 'unobtainable' and that wages and bills were not being paid to all the companies that had been supplying them over the past few months. It was strange as I had also recently been contacted by a few companies seeking invoices to be settled. Mamak was the one now holding the 'purse-strings'. He had borrowed or hired everything, including the car I had, which had to be returned. I contacted his solicitor who didn't want to know. I'd been 'had' by another 'crook'! Apparently, he had skipped the country and taken all our money with him, leaving the companies he'd acquired stripped of capital and ready to go bust. He owed everyone. And there was no way of finding him.

Fortunately for me, I was not daft, and had taken on another factory building some months before, so that in the event of anything like this going wrong, I could shift all my stuff. I had begun to develop a distrust of him, and suspicions were eventually proven right. The equipment legally belonged to Mamak as I had sold the business to him, but as he had disappeared off without paying me, I could rightfully commandeer equipment that I had not yet been paid for. He should have paid me many, many thousands for the business and I would have retired, but as it was, I had to start all over again, having lost many loyal clients, who had lost faith in the business through his misdealings; it would take many years to rebuild that loyal client base again. I did also contact the department of Trade and Industry and the Inland Revenue to explain what had happened in the hope of some help towards finding Mamak and regaining at least some of my money. But they said that I was wasting my time and throwing my money away if I try to chase him as there was no hope of finding him. He had gone to Hong Kong.

The Threat

Arriving home early one evening and sitting down with my wife and a well-earned cup of tea, I found her looking a little stressed and she proceeded to tell me that she had a strange phone call from a Scottish sounding man who told her to tell me that he was going to kill me unless I paid him £5000.00 that I owed to his friend. But I didn't owe anyone this amount of money. I could see now why she was worried, but I was puzzled and shrugged it off, telling her that it was just someone 'trying it on'. As the week wore on, I subsequently had two more of these calls but knew there was no one that I owed money to. Soon after the last call on the phone from this person threatening me, an auction was held at the factory to sell the remaining assets of Mamaks business that he had taken over from me.

I attended the auction out of interest and, whilst standing there, was approached by a so called 'enforcer', who informed me, in a Scottish accent, that he was there to get either the money or me. I laughed in his face! Was he joking? To say that to ME this fella was asking for a nightmare as I began to feel really incensed, realising that this must be the perpetrator of the threatening phone calls.

"OK, outside you!" I said. He nodded as we both walked toward the exit, but before we got there, he tried to throw a punch at me and missed. Seeing what was enfolding before them, my daughter, Vicki, and my son, George, who had come to the auction with me, appeared at my side. The Enforcer then picked up a steel bar and tried to hit George, breaking George's finger. I then really went berserk and began giving him a good beating (I knew that boxing training in my youth would come in handy one day!) when I was jumped upon by a very large man. So I now found myself dealing with two men, though later I found that he was in fact one of a pair of men trying to break up the fight. Having turned back to sort out this Enforcer, I began to give him a serious thumping.

In the general uproar and confusion, he turned and ran away, jumping into his car. By then I had caught up with him and, as he backed his car away, I threw a large concrete block through his windscreen. The police then made a timely entrance. We knew the Officers and, along with the many onlookers, explained what had happened and how this man had threatened me and my family, injuring my son. The Police knew of this person and went off to arrest him, but as I had seriously made a mess of him and his car, probably breaking his cheekbone and his windscreen, they elected to give him a warning and he was told to leave the area.

I needed to make sure that he wouldn't return bringing more trouble for me or my family. So, I managed to get hold of his address from some acquaintances. At 4 am that morning I went to where he lived, banged on his door and told him to come out as I was about to smash up his car and then I was going to do the same to him. He was afraid to come out and said that he was employed to put frighteners on an old man, never thinking that the old man could look after himself was also a 'madman'. He begged me to leave him alone and that he was going back to Scotland, apologising for any wrongdoing on his part. We never heard from him again. I did, however, find out from him who it was that employed him on a false debt claim. Sorted!

Commodity Selling

After a lot of thought and with a talk to a good friend, he suggested that I tried Commodity selling to help raise some funds. Another person told me that the company Rio-Tinto-Zinc Corp. we're always after metals. Now, here was a small business opportunity! In the past I had bought from the Vauxhall factory in Luton, all of their metal off-cuts from their car production line for a really cheap price and had made electric fires and clothes driers from them in many thousands. With a lot of nerve, I went to the Ellesmere Port factory of RTZ and managed to bull my way into seeing the Buyer. It was like getting an interview with God! I explained that I was looking to help them obtain metals if he would kindly give me his priority list. He laughed and said that they were into hundreds of tons, and was I really serious that I could undertake the sort of deals involved in money and in practice? I said that trying was my forte and asked what his immediate needs were. He then told me that there was a shortage of extrusion grade of aluminium and he would buy any amount I could get. He then said, "Some hope!"

I had hoped that it would be Steel that he wanted not Aluminium. From a contact I had I found out that the Russians might have some. So, I telephoned the Russian Trade Delegation in Highgate, London, and I was invited to go there to meet a representative to discuss it, as it was possible that they had lots of scrap aluminium of the sort that I required, it was from their aircraft industry. RTZ said that they would pay for a shipped sample amount of 1000 tons into Liverpool Docks and they would arrange collection from the Docks. I then got in touch with the Russians and, after much paperwork, finally managed to place the order, having to pay fifty percent of the costs there and then. True to their word it was shipped by them to Liverpool and was collected by RTZ. After a week I was informed that it was of a satisfactory standard and an order was placed for a further lot of 35,000 tons. On the strength of this order I was able to borrow a great deal of money from my Bank. I then had to sweat it out for five weeks until it arrived and was collected by RTZ. RTZ paid me within a further week so that I was able to pay the Bank back and make a decent profit. The following week RTZ ordered two lots of 100,000 tons. This would put me well on track to become a millionaire. I was really pleased with myself for completing such a risky deal and went ahead to order it from the Russians. For such a large order RTZ promised to give me half of the money in advance, that pleased the Bank, and everything was going great. The following week I was contacted by the Russian Trade Delegation who said that the EU had blocked my deal and my annual allowance was limited to just 20,000 tons per annum. RTZ then cancelled the order when told as it was not enough for them.

You can imagine my frustration, no matter how I pleaded the Import/Export Office would not budge. So, again luck deserted me but undaunted I went on with more attempts to procure business opportunities.

After some weeks working on my usual products, I met a Bulgarian man who worked in their Trade Legation. He was trying to sell the Bulgarian version of electric hand drills made under licence from Bosch. They were very cheap, and I would have had no problem in selling them, they looked very good. So, I bought some samples from him to try. They worked very well, for a while. But after twenty minutes of constant use they burned out. Typical Eastern Europeans, they tried to save money by reducing the size of the armature wire and by over stretching its copper wire. I couldn't sell them as they would all be returned within a week and give my company a bad name.

The Bulgarian fellow was undaunted and through him I purchased 100,000 tons of cane sugar from the West Indies. I had found a customer who was interested in buying the product for a wine company in Switzerland, who had vineyards across France. We met in a bar in London to discuss the business venture. There happened to be a group of Swiss men in the bar who must have overheard our conversation and subsequently went ahead and purchased the cane sugar before I got back to my provider.

He next came back to me with the offer of Bulgarian blackcurrant jam. The quality of the jam was well-renowned, and it was offered at a good price to me in either barrels or jars. I took the samples to the Co-op in Manchester having got an interview with their buyer. He put it into their checking Department while I was there and got acceptance from the top if it met with their stringent controls. I had to leave and go back at a later date once they had made their decision on it. After a couple of days, he got back to me saying that they would order 3000 jars once their quality regulations team had visited the factory and approved that it met with European Standards. This would be followed by many further orders. He asked me to arrange the visit with the Bulgarians. When I told my Bulgarian friend, he said that they had no Factory and that the jam was all made by many independent growers and put into jars supplied to them. This was unacceptable to the Co-Op for statutory reasons, so the order was cancelled. I was very disappointed with that news and decided to just concentrate on the business I know completely, Electronics Engineering.

I set up another new business, which was called Booth Static Power. From then on, I progressed rapidly, acquiring more and more business from many top Companies in the Country.

33. Booth Static Power

My new factory was a much smaller place in Daventry, with an office. I changed the company name from Booth Engineering to Booth Static Power. I didn't have enough work to begin with, however I did know one man who worked for the East Midlands Electricity Company who informed me that they were going to replace all their big transformers. These were really large units, as big as a medium sized room, oil filled and carrying a lot of current, found in sub-stations around the area. They had been having problems with many of these transformers, so had decided to replace them as they felt they were wearing out. On reflection, I feel it was probably just down to bad maintenance rather than them wearing out. They had five of these transformers to replace. The guy I knew told me that they were trying to offload them to other companies around the world, as they still had some serviceable life in them, there was a good market for this sort of thing in Africa, South America, India and Eastern-Bloc Countries, and there was an enquiry for one in Mozambique, Africa.

The Admiral and the Submarine

In January 1972, I wrote a paper that was published in the Electrical Times about the advantages of using thyristors to switch machines instead of using open contacts. This is like a big transistor that does heavy switching using these thyristors. I had the opportunity to write the article and have it published which would also give me free advertising of my product. Some months later I received a call asking me to go to the Institute of

Marine Engineers to talk about it to a large group of people. A colleague and I set off to carry out this lecture, equipped with slides, notes and a paper I had produced about the product. We completed the talk and the question time, after which I was approached by a man calling himself, if I remember rightly, Admiral Sinclair, who was very interested in the product, and asked if I could go and meet with him at the Admiralty. To this I agreed, and we arranged that he would telephone me when he could negotiate a suitable time for us both. The following week I received the call from his secretary and a date was arranged for the next week.

The Admiralty is a grand place and I had made sure that I was dressed accordingly. It was very sumptuous and a lovely place to visit. Admiral Sinclair was a top electrical and mechanical engineer for the Navy and had an enormous office within this lovely building. We enjoyed the niceties of tea and biscuits, and a polite chat and then got down to business. He told me that he had read my paper on this specialist switch and asked if there was anything else I could tell him about it; were there any adverse effects? I suggested he come to the factory so that I could show him it actually operating, the biggest one we had could handle 150 to 200 amps, I told him.

"Really! I thought they were only for small items," he exclaimed. "Then I will definitely come and see them. Now, this is a state secret so you will have to sign this paper to say you are aware that these are state secrets, under the official secrets act, that I am about to discuss with you." That done he set about telling me about Britain's submarines that are fighting under water, and also about ships that use depth charges to hit an enemy submarine, if they know that one is nearby. On a submarine, every time a big contactor (switch) is used it makes a loud clunking noise, which can be detected easily and give away the whereabouts of the submarine. These sounds can be detected up to 12 miles away underwater, which makes the submarine vulnerable to attack when on a stealth mission. He realised that my 'switch' did not make a sound, so potentially it could solve this issue if heavy switches on the submarine were replaced with my design of switch. I told him that one other advantage of my switch was that I had eliminated the opportunity for the current change on the switch to be detected electronically. He asked about my company and how many people I employ, and I told him that we were a relatively small company of about 15 people and that we were based in Daventry, Northamptonshire. He wanted to know that we were producing gear that was up to BS standards and then agreed to come and visit us.

We prepared the machine in readiness for his visit and managed to find something big enough on which to demonstrate the switching process using a higher load of about 90 amps. I assured him that this product could go up to 500 amps if need be, but that I didn't have anything on the premises that was anywhere near that strength. I knew it could do that because I had just used one of these thyristors on a job recently completed at London airport for a fuel dispenser used on the

747 aircraft, where it is using an average of 150 amps, peaking up to about 350 amps. The Admiral was duly impressed by this and arranged to meet me back at the Admiralty to discuss what to do next. This time I had a sumptuous meal with him and learned that he wanted to order two of these units from me initially as they needed to be tested inside a submarine before any further units could be ordered. The units had to be able to fit into a sub's hatch, 19x19 inches. They paid for the two prototypes, plus expenses, which came to about at £3,250 in total, and I informed him that they would be a lot cheaper the more that were ordered. They seemed to want them pretty quickly, so, dropping all other jobs I was working on at that moment in time, it took only three or four weeks to complete the prototypes in readiness for testing, with which the Admiral was suitably impressed, as most companies they deal with take months to complete a project. I was asked to crate them and send them to the submarine yard in Glasgow for fitting onto two subs that could then go out to sea and test the results, comparing them with the sounds from the original switches that are normally picked up on the sonar. I passed over all the diagrams, circuit diagrams and instructions on the fitting of these switches so that they could be installed properly.

A month or so passed and I received a phone call from the Admiral who let me know that the units had been fitted and that tests, whilst stationary in the harbour, had been very successful and they were now ready to test them at sea and over greater distances. He asked if I would go out on the submarine to be on call if I was needed for the testing? I agreed that I would, as I wanted to see the submarine and was excited at the prospect of experiencing a ride on one.

In late March, or early April, travelling by train and taxi, I finally found the submarine base and was shown onto the sub and down the hatch. The crew and captain were really busy preparing for the sailing, so after meeting them briefly, I was shown to a cabin and asked to wait until they were ready for me. As exciting as it was, initially, my elation soon dwindled as I waited for two or three hours in this very small cabin, which was all wood veneered and felt like being inside a coffin. It was furnished with only a bunk, a small table and a chair, so I was very bored and restless, eager to see the rest of the sub or at least another person. It was quite claustrophobic, and the air was not at all fresh. Indeed, it was a concoction of diesel oil, sweat and smelly feet - not very pleasant at all! I headed out of the cabin into the gangway and followed the direction of the voices I could hear along the gangway, ending up on the bridge.

"Get off my bloody bridge!" shouted the captain at me, whereupon the Chief Petty Officer very quickly escorted me away to a different room, the Petty Officers Mess. I was really taken aback by the captain shouting and told the Petty Officer of my annoyance, stating that I was not in the Navy and shouldn't be spoken to like that. "It is only on permission of the captain that you can go onto the bridge, it's the rules," he said.

Again, it was a small room but had a couple of tables and chairs, tea and coffee, and a few people walking through. There were a few magazines, but most were not the kind I would read, being 'girly' pin-up magazines. There were a couple of books, which I set about browsing through for another long wait until I was called. We were headed up the deep-water trench between the Scottish mainland and the islands and 90ft under water. It was very smooth going. I was then taken to the Officers Mess for a meal and was joined by the captain, who apologised for shouting, reminding me that no-one goes on the bridge without his knowledge.

"If I had known that then I wouldn't have been there," I said, "But I had been in there for some hours and was wondering what was going on."

"I apologise," he said. "I can tell you that the trials went very, very successfully indeed. The other sub could not pick up when we were switching over on the motor." He explained that we were to go on to Stornaway and would stay there overnight, returning the next day or the day after. I didn't want to stay on the sub any longer than necessary, so asked if I could get off at Stornaway and find a flight back home. This I did and was lucky enough that someone at the base had been informed of my departure and had managed to secure me a flight back to London, for which I was very relieved as I had not expected to be away for more than a day. Finally arriving home in the early hours of the morning after flying to London and then a train to Northampton, I eventually collapsed in bed for a few hours of well-earned sleep.

All had gone well, and I was satisfied that they were very happy with the device, so I rang them the following week to find out what was to happen next. The Admiral congratulated me on the device, that they were very happy with the trials and that they would be going ahead with putting the switches on all their submarines. He assured me that he would get back in touch with me soon.

A number of weeks went by and still no contract. They had paid me the money to cover the making of the prototypes, but I was eager to acquire the contract and fit it into my growing schedule of works. Eventually the call came, "We have come to the conclusion," he said, "that this is a viable and first-class effort. I know we have paid for those two and you have given us the designs. Well, we have everything we need, and I am afraid you haven't got the contract."

I was stunned and really taken aback to hear that my company was not going to get the contract to make the switches, but that it was to be given to another company. The Admiral pointed out that I was not a MOD accredited company, and without that approval I would not be allowed to provide machinery or parts for any of their submarines. I responded that it was my invention, adapted especially for them, they wanted the prototypes quickly, so there was not time to get a patent. In those days you could not claim 'intellectual property', and I didn't have the time to get it patented before they received the prototype. The patent aspect was null and void now because of disclosure to them and the other company. He received a 'lengthy dialogue' from me regarding how unfair this was to a small business like mine and 'how dare they!'

"Oh, don't take it like that, old chap," he said, "You have done your country an admirable service, you should be very pleased with your efforts." With that I hung up. I believe GEC were contracted to make the switches.

I was most aggrieved.

34. Travelling and Working Abroad

Visit to Mozambique

There was an electricity supply company in Mozambique that was showing a lot of interest in getting one of the transformers from the description and they had requested more details on the units. East Midland Electricity was looking for someone to go over there and talk to them about it all. Would I be interested in going out there if I had enough information on the transformers, I was asked? Once I agreed that I could do this, they approved provision of the air tickets, all expenses and a payment for doing this for them. It would take a week or two as there was some travelling to do once there. A meeting in the UK was organised whereby they passed on all the paperwork and reading material to enable me to do this task. I had to fly to Johannesburg and stay in a hotel there and then travel onward by car a distance of about 300 miles. There had been a lot of fighting in Mozambique but that seemed to have settled over recent months, but there were still some very volatile areas and the cities were not very safe; the countryside was even less safe to travel in. There were bandits everywhere, robberies and murders occurring, so one had to be very careful.

Setting off on a 747, I flew out to Johannesburg, the nearest airport to my destination. The African heat and smells really hit me as I alighted the plane. A taxi took me to the hotel, which was really first class – very pleasant. I had some time to spare as it was early evening, so I thought I'd have a stroll around the area. As I reached the door to leave the hotel, I was stopped at the entrance by the commissaire asking where I was going at this time of the evening. I told him my plans for a stroll to which he replied in no uncertain terms that I couldn't go out as the streets were very dangerous after dark and my safety could not be guaranteed. I was told that because I was white and on my own, especially as I was not familiar with the area, I would be a target.

The following day, after an evening spent at the hotel, I was eager to go for a walk and arranged to meet the agent, a Scotsman, at his home nearby. We discussed what I would be doing and arranged to let the customer in Mozambique know when I would be arriving there via Telex, the only way to get in touch with them. The agent discussed my travelling arrangements to my destination. It seems that I had three options; I could travel on three different buses, but that wasn't safe at all; there was not direct rail link but I could get there by a few changes of train, but that may take many days and be equally as dangerous; or I could drive by hiring a car. He very kindly offered to loan me a car, a Jaguar MK10, for a small fee, to which I agreed, as it would definitely be safer to use a well-maintained car rather than a hire car which might let me down. All was agreed and messages sent to the customer of my impending arrival. The journey would take about four hours, so I would need to leave very early in the morning in order to ensure that I would get there in time to discuss the transformer with them. They would need to find me accommodation for the night and then I could return the following day. To my surprise, he then gave me a loaded Makarov pistol, with two spare magazines of ammunition, and a knife for my safety. I sincerely hoped I wouldn't need either of them!

So, fully equipped with driving licence, map, necessary paperwork, safety equipment and plenty of warnings as to what to do and what not to do I was ready for my journey. There was one straight road to my destination, which was the hotel where I would be staying. Once there I could contact the customer regarding my arrival and attend a meeting arranged for 2.30pm with them.

The roads were just dusty, earth roads, so it was impossible to drive at any speed above 40mph, with numerous potholes and such-like. The road travelled mainly through very tall grasses, 8 or 9 feet high, and apparently full of lions, snakes and vigilantes. My Scots agent had forewarned me not to get out of the car for any reason except for an emergency, and certainly not to leave the vicinity of the car. It seemed like I was driving for hours and hours and I started to get anxious about the fuel level in the car, hoping that it would get me to my destination. I finally reached the border, where there were some soldiers who looked over my papers and asked where I was going and what I was doing, using a mixture of Portuguese, French and English. Satisfied with that they let me pass through and it was with a sigh of relief I found the hotel. It was all on a single floor with a thatched roof and a veranda all around it. I was able to meet the customers there, two Portuguese fellas who spoke good English, and discussed their potential purchase, explaining how it worked and its suitability for their purpose, telling them that there was nothing wrong with the units and that they would have many more serviceable years left in them. They were very interested and willing to negotiate a price but needed to get in touch with Eastern Electricity in order to do that as the company had not shared that information with me. What I could tell them was that they would be crated up and shipped over to them in Mozambique. Happy with the information I had provided, they left with a promise to return later and have dinner with me. The hotel was lovely with beautiful scenic views everywhere. We had a great meal and a laugh with far too much to drink. As they left they gave me fair warnings of making sure I travelled safely back to Johannesburg.

Soon after dawn the next day, having had a good breakfast and filled up with petrol, I left the hotel to drive back to Johannesburg. I was doing well and was about half-way, on this rather monotonous journey, as all I could see was tall grass for miles and miles, when suddenly, to my horror, I saw steam rising from the engine. I had to pull over and find out what was wrong. Here I was with a broken-down car, no tools, no garages or anyone to help and in the middle of nowhere. Having checked the car I realised that the thermostat had gone, it had boiled out with this journey. What he hadn't told me was that over such a long distance and in those temperatures, the thermostat and fan just couldn't cope. In the boot I managed to find an old bicycle spanner and a screwdriver with half a handle; with these and my penknife I was just about able to get the thermostat off. This I did and made a new gasket from the back of the map I happened to have and some grease from another part of the engine. Fortunately, there was no leakage from the radiator, but I would need water to top up the system before heading off. I realised that it was dangerous and going against all the safety advice I'd been given, I needed to look for water. I wandered fifty feet either way up the road and happened upon a large, stagnant pond at the side of the road. The water looked vile, but under the green algae was some useable water and, fortunately for me, there happened to be an old tin can beside the pond which I used to transport a few can-fulls of water to my radiator. As I put the bonnet down, I looked in the distance to see five fellas heading towards me down a slope, with AK47 rifles slung on their back, they looked like bandits to me. Crossing my fingers and everything else, I turned the key, praying that it would start – this was my one and only chance. It started! The engine roared and away I drove as fast as I could go, tyres screeching and in a cloud of dust. I managed to get back to Johannesburg without further incident and took the car back to the agent, whereupon I told him my story.

"They'd have killed you for sure, stripped you naked for your clothes and left you to the lions. Furthermore, there could have been anything in that water from hippos to snakes, not to mention that the water was probably poisonous," he said. "You lucky bugger, you got away with it!" I felt more frightened listening to him then than I did at the time.

I was staying at the hotel and I couldn't go home right away because of my air ticket, so I asked the concierge if it was safe to have a walk around the area and see a few sights to while away a few hours. He suggested that he contact a friend of his who could escort me around, he was a taxi driver. He went on to tell me that I would be safe with him as he is a member of the ANC. This chap arrived, we had a chat and then set off. He owned up to me that people in Johannesburg were fond of the English and asked what I would like to do. I admitted that I just wanted to have a look around the area and would leave it up to him. He took me first to a market in Sowetto, where we parked the car and walked to the market. I was the only white man there in sight with everyone staring at me walking alongside my black guide. He was very reassuring and rather proudly kept telling people he knew that I was English, to which everyone acted impressed. I did feel very vulnerable though.

"Do you know what a 'shebeen' is?" To which I answered that I didn't. "We will go and have a drink in a shebeen." It was a very dark place inside, with about five other guys drinking beer. We had a beer and I offered to buy a beer for everyone else in the bar, to which they all perked up and were keen to imbibe, having been introduced to me as 'an English man'. There was a lovely smell of cooking drifting through the room, which I was informed was goat stew on today's menu. The other men looked on eagerly, so I offered to buy them all a meal too. By this time, they wanted me to stay for the night's entertainment and drink with them for longer. I felt it was time to leave and get back to my hotel, particularly once my guide told me of a recent visitor who was held captive in a tyre and set alight! My guide wanted to take me out again and I didn't want to go out, so I invited him to be my guest at the hotel for a meal. He wasn't too keen at first as he said he probably wouldn't be made very welcome, being black, but I insisted and said I would sort out the hotel if there were any problems. We sat in the hotel and had a good chat, talking about our different lives, the police and issues with living in South Africa.

The return flight and arrangements all went smoothly and I was pleased to return to British soil. I always wondered whether the sale went through or not, I did ask but they didn't get back to me. Although they did pay me handsomely for my time and effort, I half wondered if I would have received any commission for it later on!

Visit to Polish-Russian borders – 1976

I was contacted by the Russian embassy in Highgate as they had seen some of the machinery I had been manufacturing recently for other companies and wanted me to pay them a visit to discuss supplying a Russian company with one of these high-speed crankshaft grinding machines. I was asked to explain the workings of my machine so that they could ascertain that it would do exactly what they wanted. Once they had decided that they would have one of these machines, the necessary information was shared with me, a fee was agreed and I was contracted to make the machine and get it shipped out to them.

The machine was made, crated and shipped out with all the information on installation and use of the machine. They duly confirmed that it had arrived and a few weeks later I received payment and thought nothing more of it. After about five weeks I received a telephone call from the embassy saying that it wasn't working and would I go over to the factory on the Polish borders with Russia to sort it out. It was no good speaking to the embassy staff, I really needed to speak to an engineer in order to ask exactly what they had done and to try to rectify the issue over the phone. This was to prove impossible so I was delivered tickets to travel via air to Russia in order to fix the problem.

I was seated on an old converted Aleutian bomber. On landing I was met by three Russian soldiers, with guns, who escorted me to an awaiting vehicle whereupon we set off to our destination. We drove mile after mile through birch tree forests for an hour or so and I was feeling very thirsty. There was a language barrier between the soldiers and I but I thought I had managed to convey the fact that I was thirsty after travelling for so long and could we stop to get a drink of coffee or something? Following some exchange between the soldiers it seemed they understood and they were soon stopping beside a small hill, not a building in sight! Then, suddenly, a door opened in the side of the 'hill' and in we went to find a bar where they were selling brown vodka and strawberry juice on the side. I offered to buy a round (using sign language) which was delivered to us at the bar whereupon the soldiers drank the vodka shot in one go. So

I did the same. I then asked for another round as it seemed to make the soldiers very happy. Three or four shots later we were all feeling a bit 'woozy' and happy. We eventually arrived at the factory where a guy met us at the gates as we piled out of the vehicle, looking a bit unsteady and obviously a bit drunk. These soldiers were severely reprimanded and sent on their way and I was taken into the factory to meet a woman who was to be my interpreter for the duration of my stay. I was taken to an army major who ran the factory who could speak English very well and he explained the problem briefly before sending me on to the hotel as it was starting to get late in the day. I was to book in at the hotel and then take myself to a particular restaurant near to the hotel.

The receptionist wanted to know what money I had and how I was going to pay whilst in Poland. Apparently the meal at the restaurant was paid for in advance by the company, as was the hotel. The room was three floors up in the building – no lift. I was given the best room in the place as it had a carpet on the floor and a separate side room with a toilet and wash basin. But oh, the smell! Despite the temperature outside being about -100C, the smell of the poor plumbing of the toilet made me retch. So much so that I had to use toilet paper and towels to block the smell from seeping under the door at night.

At the restaurant I was shown to a table and I pointed to a dish that looked appetising that someone on a nearby table was eating. It looked like some kind of goulash. It was very nice and the restaurant obviously entertained high-class clientele.

Factories start at 6am so I woke at 5am in order to get ready to go to the factory. There was no breakfast and nowhere to go and find any food. I was picked up and taken the couple of miles to the factory. Inside there were no windows and the floor was just compacted earth. Where machines stood there was a base of concrete for it to stand on. I was introduced properly to Elaina, the interpreter, who showed me to the machine I had provided. I checked it over very carefully and couldn't find anything wrong with it – it had arrived in good order and nothing seemed to be out of place. I switched the power on and it wouldn't work. That's odd, I thought. So I checked it again, this time checking the voltage. There was the problem. This machine had to run on 380 volts but it was only getting about 180 volts through their system. I asked Elaina to locate the electrician in the factory and see if he had a voltmeter. He arrived with one which was from the ark, being about a foot square and very old! I asked him to check and to write down what it recorded, which was 180 volts on each phase. I then asked her to take me to the 'boss' in order for me to explain the problem.

I explained the problem and told him what needed to happen in order to fix it, then asked for my passport back so that I could be on my way home.

"Oh, but it's not started yet," the boss said.

"No, it won't unless you can supply it with 380v. Once that is supplied then it will work, guaranteed."

He would not allow me to leave until he saw it working and that was final. However, he promised me that he would get it done as soon as possible so I was to go back to the machine and wait. And waiting was what I did for the next couple of days. The factory manager came along to talk to me through Elaina. I told him that it was his fault that I was still here and explained that all he needed to do was to get the appropriate supply fitted for the machine to work. Whilst waiting I was able to have a long chat with Elaina and find out a bit more about the factory and living in this area of the world. I found out that her husband was not in favour of the party in government as he used to be a school teacher, he had loved his job, but they made him become a carpenter instead, he had no choice in the matter. There happened to be a young lady working on a machine near to where we were waiting. She was quite slight in stature and was struggling with lifting a certain component. I could see that the fellas working nearby were not going to help her but rather to sit and watch her struggle and laugh at her efforts. So I offered to lift it for her. She was quite taken aback but was grateful for the help. When I queried why no one would offer to help her Elaina explained that as she was getting equal pay then it was deemed that she had to do the same work with no help, despite her struggles. Back in the UK most fellas wouldn't just sit around and watch while someone struggled, they'd help, whoever it was and probably particularly for a woman. It's just the way it was.

I was able to use the works canteen but that wasn't very exciting as the soup was like a bowl of water with a bone floating in it, not very appetising. So after a whole day without food I was looking forward to the restaurant food in the evening. As I was having to stay a few days, Elaina invited me to her flat to have an evening with her and her husband. It was arranged that she would pick me up near to the hotel and get me back in time for the curfew at 10pm. So armed with a bottle of Courvoisier Brandy I got ready to meet Elaina, being reminded at the front desk that I had to be back by 10pm.

The block of flats she lived in looked pretty dismal with concrete patches missing and paper and rags stuffed in the holes to maintain the warmth inside. She had kindly laid out some food and the inevitable bottle of vodka for us all to enjoy and had a few friends and neighbours in to join us. When I brought out my bottle of brandy and poured them all a drink everyone's face lit up, they obviously don't get to drink brandy very often. Everyone was getting very merry, singing songs, joking and laughing that I didn't notice that the time was passed 10pm – curfew time. Elaina couldn't take me back to the hotel as it was curfew for her too. The last thing we needed was the police stopping any of us with the threat of arrest and prison. I managed to safely find my way back to the hotel on foot in the dark streets and was met by a very irate receptionist. I professed my innocence and thankfully got away with it.

Finally, after a couple of days, the cable was fixed and I found myself with quite an audience as I prepared to switch the machine on. Thankfully it started right away whereupon I asked Elaina to let the Major know that all was well and that I would be leaving soon. But yet again my timely exit was prevented as the Major insisted that I stay until the machine had turned out at least two sample crankshafts. I explained that I needed to get back to my wife and family and that I had a business to run. I was not very impressed when he offered to find me a wife in Poland!

This further delay would take another two days; however they were very happy with the two samples produced and thanked me for my patience. I bade farewell to Elaina and told her she was welcome to visit us in England whereupon she told me that she wasn't up to travelling so far but her son, Tony, might like to visit; he was in the Red Army.

On return to England I was contacted by the embassy thanking me for the work I did and saying that they were very pleased with the machine. Tony did come to visit some months later and thoroughly enjoyed his few weeks with us as we showed him a little of our country. The company did order another machine from me a year or so later but fortunately I did not have to go and install it this time.

Visit to Nigeria

We received and enquiry to build a huge, controlled rectifier system for a company in Lagos, Nigeria. Because the company was manufacturing windows for houses in the tropics, and as plastic window frames didn't last, they made aluminium or steel window frames. The manufacturing process involves the metal frames being galvanised by putting them in a huge tank (about 10mx10m) full of sulphuric acid along with zinc plates. A DC electric current would then be passed into the acid which would then galvanise the window frames. I was asked to make and test this equipment and then get it crated and sent out for export to Lagos. Six weeks passed and I received a message to say that it had arrived, but it had unfortunately been dropped at the docks and some damage had been done. They had partially installed it, but it was not switching on due to the damage that had been done. No one else in my company wanted to go to Nigeria, so I was the one elected to go out there and sort out the equipment, much to my annoyance.

Nigeria was not considered a safe place to go at the time and I didn't relish the idea at all. I had to go and get inoculations against all kinds of fevers and diseases. That done I headed to the airport, boarded my plane and set off on my journey.

On arrival at Lagos, at about 9pm, the heat and the smells of Africa hit me as we disembarked the plane and headed into customs and passport control. All travellers from the planes were herded into a very small room, considering the size of the crowd gathering from the planes landing. The heat in the room with all those people was unbearable to someone so unused to the high and humid temperatures. Eventually I got to the immigration desk and there was a Nigerian army officer, a Major, asking for my passport. I duly handed it over and he flicked through all the pages as if looking for something, then said, “Right, go and sit over there,” pointing to a bench at the side. I sat down and waited for ages as more and more plane loads of passengers went straight through passport control. After an hour or two I returned to the desk and asked what was going on and could I be on my way soon?

“Well,” he said, “There wasn’t anything in it, was there?” Then I realised the error of my ways! He returned it to me, and I placed a few notes in between the pages and returned the passport to him. Satisfied, he stamped the book, thanked me and sent me on my way. As I got to the exit there was a soldier with a rifle who barred my way.

“Where are you going?” he asked, the rifle across my path to the exit.

“I am exiting the airport to meet with a business partner who is collecting me in a car,” I answered. He then told me that I couldn’t pass.

“What do you mean I can’t come through, everyone else is walking through the doors to the outside!” I complained, starting to get the hang of this now.

“You can’t come through here, you need a password,” he uttered.

A few more dollars later and I was free of the airport buildings, a bit poorer, but safe in the knowledge that I could go about my business at last.

The factory manager, a very amenable Asian gentleman, met me in his car and proceeded to drive me to the hotel. As we left the airport, I remarked to my colleague about the women who were all waiting in a long line along the street as if to welcome a royal dignitary or something.

"Those are 'ladies of the night'," he explained.

He left me at the hotel and, after checking in, the receptionist gave me a lamp for use in my room. "What do I need this for?" I remarked, "Is there no electricity in the room?"

"Yes," he answered, "There is electricity, but I have put you on the third floor because sometimes robbers enter the room through the window, disconnect the electricity so it goes dark, and then beat the person up and rob them. The lamp helps stop this. There is also an armed guard outside your room on each corridor." With that I took my lamp and headed to my room, not feeling at all safe with the arrangements, though the knowledge of the armed guard outside the room did help a little to allay my fears.

The following morning, after partaking of a very unappetising breakfast, I took a taxi to the factory. The heat inside the factory was incredible, about 110oF (43oC), making us sweat profusely all the time. The machinery was in a bit of a state, the voltmeters were all broken and there were many bits broken off all over the machine. I had only planned to be there for a week, it now looked like it would take much longer! The factory manager gave me four men to help with the machine, so we started writing down all the items we required on a notepad, which then got passed on to the purchasing office for acquisition of the parts. Back at the hotel I was ready for a lovely meal but was disappointed to receive a whole, small, chicken, still in its feathers. It was not to my liking at all, so I asked for a cheese sandwich instead. One stale sandwich later found me sitting in my room. It was 6.30pm and I had nothing to do, no book or game or television.

The following day at the factory was spent discussing how the piece of equipment worked and chatting in general to the four men at my disposal, waiting for the parts to arrive. It was so hot. I had on some overalls and the sweat was dripping down my body and into my shoes causing me to 'squelch' everywhere I walked. Horrible! There was also a very strong smell of sulphuric acid which really made it hard to breathe.

Back at the hotel that night I was not going to order any food, therefore I enquired about places to eat in the vicinity and found that there was a pizza place just a few roads away. Having changed and feeling a bit more comfortable in the evening air, I headed out of the hotel and along the streets to the pizza place, collected my food and headed back to the hotel. The door guard looked at me incredulously and asked why I had been out, going on to tell me how dangerous it was to be out on the street – a white man on his own with no escort! Oh dear, I thought, duly reprimanded, I'd better not go out again then.

Back at the factory I spoke with the manager and stated my concerns about being in the hotel as I was getting rather nervous with all the warnings I had received and the inability to go out anywhere; I didn't feel safe. He then decided to help me find somewhere else that was safer to stay. It was a small apartment in a walled compound which was guarded night and day for everyone's safekeeping, and I had my own houseboy who would cook and clean for me, only a young lad in his early teens. He made a great breakfast and really looked after me. A car was organised to pick me up in the morning and take me back in the evening, so all was well.

One morning I awoke and was having breakfast, chatting to the houseboy, when I could hear loud bangs coming from outside. It was the sound of gunfire from the guards towards some bandits running away, leaving two innocent telecom workers laying shot on the ground, one had been shot dead and one shot in the stomach. As I found out later, the telecom men were there to fit fibre-optics in the area. The one who was shot in the stomach was taken to hospital in Lagos and later repatriated through the British Embassy, to Britain for further treatment. Hopefully he survived.

Again, I discussed what had happened at the compound with the manager and he decided to invite me to stay at his house with his family until we could find a safer place. He also lived in a compound with his family, a wife and a grown-up daughter and son. They did look after me very well, however I had to ask for milder curry.

The parts eventually arrived, and we worked on getting the equipment up and running, checking and testing the working of the machine. The time came to switch it on. I was so worried as I was sweating continually, which does not bode well when working with high voltage electricity! I switched it on and it ran for about ten minutes then stopped. We soon discovered that the circuit breaker, which I had installed in Britain, would stand up to an ambient temperature of up to 38oC, but the temperature in the factory was well in excess of that and therefore it was unable to work. There was no chance of getting an appropriate circuit breaker within a few days. Scratching our heads for ideas we decided to purchase a fan to keep the circuit breaker cool. A great idea as it then continued to work really well.

That evening, the son of the manager decided to invite me out to a really good Indian restaurant in Lagos, the best, he said. He assured me that it would be safe because I was with him, so we set off into Lagos. The buildings that had once been so beautiful were now a shadow of their former selves and really run down. There were many alleyways off the road we were driving along as we came to the restaurant and my fellow passenger told me of incidents when locals would fill a tyre with petrol, set fire to it and roll it on to an oncoming car in order for the car to stop (as it burst into flames from the petrol) and to then rob the burning passengers. It seemed it was a common occurrence; I didn't feel that I fancied witnessing such a horrible scene! He assured me again that he knew how to look after us. There happened to be an armed policeman as we parked the car and he was given some money with a promise of more if he looked after the car for us, to which he agreed.

It was an enormous restaurant with many long tables that everyone sat at. The food was lovely, if a little spicy. After a super meal and a very pleasant evening spent in this man's company, we headed out to the car, paid the police officer who had looked after the car, and set out on our way home. Sure enough the vigilantes were up to their tricks and a fire tyre came rolling out of an alleyway towards us. My friend was a good driver and managed to outmanoeuvre the tyre and we went safely on our way out of Lagos.

Another close shave!

"I don't know how you manage to live here?" I said to the manager later that evening. He then disclosed that he was intending moving back to Mumbai very soon as it was not a safe place and he had to think of his family. He had already been shot by robbers once and ended up in hospital. Not much of a life when you're locked in your own house for fear of being shot.

The job was finished, and I made preparations to leave and go to the airport. The manager said that I needed to go to the airport and tell them that I would be coming the next day, that would ensure my seat was not sold on. We arranged a taxi to take me. The driver set off, but instead of taking me straight to the airport he drove me to a very run-down village and left me in the car for ten to fifteen minutes as he had a quick job to do. I felt really vulnerable sitting there and was very cross with him for this deviation in our journey. In the airport, at the BA desk, I made sure all my papers were in order and left to return to the factory. The following day the manager took me to the airport, I waved goodbye and then had to pay a tip to get into the airport – here we go again. Fortunately, I had made sure that I had plenty of money for all these backhanders in this overly corrupt country. My luggage was checked in – they needed paying, and I arrived at the desk with my ticket when I was told that I was not going to be travelling today. "But my ticket says today!" I questioned.

"No, there are no seats as we have other people going and they are a priority," came the reply.

"What do I do now, then?" I asked, beginning to worry about spending a night in the airport, not a safe place at all! He pointed to the chairs and then continued to his next customer. So they had my bags, my passport and someone had my plane seat. All I could do was to get back to the managers house and then return the following day. I made a quick, sneaky exit, found a taxi and headed back to the compound.

"What are you doing here?" the manager said, amazed to see me and worried that I was now in the country illegally as I had technically left Nigeria once I had left my things at the airport. I told him of my dilemma and he agreed that it was safer, though illegal, to stay with him for the night,

Very early the next morning he came with me to help settle the matter. On arrival at the desk there was no problem at all, and I was handed my passport and ticket and shown the way to the aircraft. I think it is all about 'who you know"! Eventually I was on the plane and sitting next to one of the few British travellers. He was a nervous wreck, telling me that he had only just about managed to 'escape' and that 'they' were after him. Apparently a gang had held him for over a month; they had taken all his money and emptied his bank account before they would let him go. He was in a terrible state.

I was so glad to get home, alive. I vowed that I would not be returning to Africa.

35. Nuclear Power & The Troonvale Company

Back in the 1960's, the Government had set up The Nuclear Power Group which had been going some time before they picked me out to join the group. This group included John Thompson's, a big boiler building company, The General Electric Company (both of those companies were 'giants 'in that time), Smiths Instruments, Honeywell's Instrument Company and my little company. I was one of the originators of nuclear design and had been working with nuclear power companies for many years.

The original nuclear power stations were built soon after the war and used carbon pile reactors, which weren't very efficient at all. The government wanted to build some new nuclear power stations, using the iron bar control system, which is what I created the designs for. This Nuclear Power Group would meet monthly in order to discuss how we were going to build these power stations, where they would be located, what systems were we going to use and other such questions. Before I got involved, they had already had major discussions regarding the type of reactor they required. We designed these power stations and my part in it was to design the instrumentation and the control systems, the most complex and tricky job of the lot, in my opinion. We had another company that we pulled into the group, who would develop the specialist computers, three of them, in order to make sure that if one or two failed there was another one, to cover all events. My involvement in this went on for more than forty years and, of course, still continues.

As well as designing and making the control systems for the reactor, I also designed and made the system to control the cooling of the gases for the reactor and the heavy-water cooling system using cryogenics. This cryogenics machine was one of the most complicated things I had designed and made. It entailed a process of extracting heat from a material and was used in this case to reduce the temperature of heavy water down from 98°C by 16 degrees almost instantly. Perfect for the job. They were sceptical about its success in completing the task in hand. I was given the go-ahead to set up the machine at the Nuclear Power plant and they connected up the water input and output in order to check how well it would work in situ. We switched it on and looked at the temperature gauges which read 98°C on the input side and instantly 16°C lower on the output side. They couldn't believe that this design would work; all their top scientists were stuck on this problem of cooling the heavy water quickly enough to maintain its stability. The fact that I had made it baffled them. Oh, ye of little faith!

I made one for Heysham Power Station, one for Hartlepool Power Station and one for Sizewell B Power Station.

That was probably one of the most complex things I designed and made in my working life.

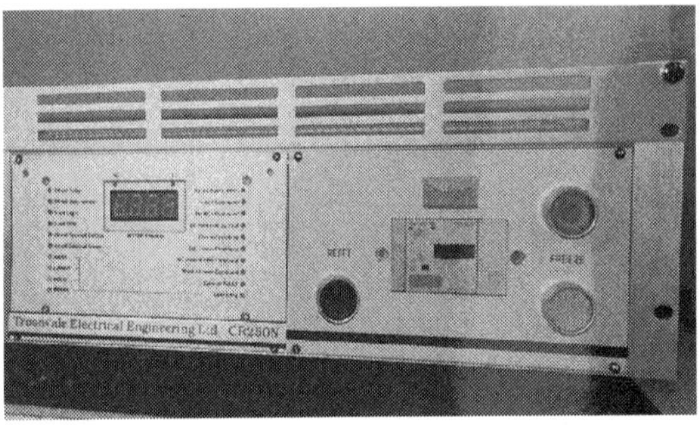

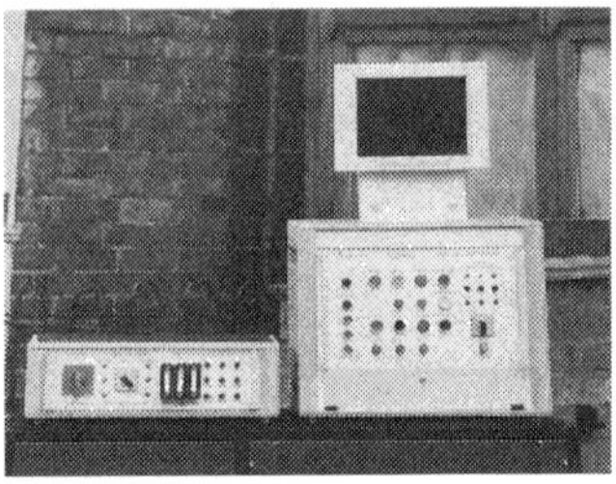

Mobile test control system, Nuclear Power stations, Hartlepool and Heysham

Nuclear control rod cooling system

Following a few years of intense hard work, the business was doing well again so I put an advert in the Financial Times looking for people to come and join the business. It was then that I was approached by a consortium of three men with a proposition to take over the business with me remaining in a managerial capacity. One of these people was the manager of the United Arab Bank, another was a big insurance broker, and the other was the accountant for ABTA. They were really pleasant people, but I was soon to discover that they had no patience for this new company and had unrealistic aspirations, being eager for it to make far more profit in a short space of time than was humanly possible. I believe that sometimes people have unrealistic ideas of the time and effort it takes to build a solid client base and the ensuing commissions to result in higher profits.

They very soon gave up on the business and did not continue to pay the rent to the farmer, whose premises I was using, and he put all my equipment in a wagon for collection. I had to arrange to get all that into storage quickly, before it was destroyed by the weather, whilst I sought an office space to work out of.

Here we go again!

I was now set up to work from home, on my own, to make a living and support my family. Fortuitously, I managed to get the Nuclear Power Stations I had worked with in the past to give me ALL their service and repair work due to my good reputation with them over the many years where I had designed and provided most of their control systems.

In the course of this work from home I met a Scottish gentleman called Bill Harris, who had just finished working for a very large electrical company in Peebles. We found we got along very well, so jointly set up a company called 'Troonvale' that led me to obtain business from a Scottish Company making various products for the Commercial Automotive market.

I went on to design various safety products for them and other similar companies in this field.

I eventually found office space in Wellingborough. I needed an office because I was doing work for the nuclear power people and repairs and designs for several power stations. I was also working with water companies on their dosing pumps and with Pilkington's Glass creating control systems to create self-cleaning glass. I was very busy with work at that time and fortunately had my son, John, on board working with me.

At the back of the office was a workshop that an ex-colleague rented and there was room in which I could store the larger equipment. The man, Mr. G, was now doing some of the design work for my projects, designing circuit boards, but he was not always very reliable and he didn't seem to get on very well with John.

It didn't really work out working with Mr G, yet again, as he messed up a large contract I was working on at Dungeness Power Station. At this time my son, John, was working with me taking out the old systems at Dungeness and designing and installing new control systems. All was going well when Mr. G started to try to take over the installation and began creating problems and delays in his design work resulting in me not being able to deliver a project on time. He had apparently been colluding with a guy who ran a printed circuit company to try to take over my business with Nuclear Power. He went to Dungeness to the EDF head office to present himself, bragging that he was the one doing all the designs and requested that all the nuclear business be given over to him. Fortunately the energy company were fairly clued in as to who had completed most of the project and were loyal to me. This created some ill feeling between Mr. G and me at the time, and, to make matters worse, someone tried to commit an act of arson on my company premises whilst I was there, pouring petrol in through the letterbox and endangering the factory premises, equipment and myself whist at work late one evening. Fortunately the fire did not catch on, petering out before it could do too much damage.

I always had my suspicions but the perpetrator was never found. Mr. G was able to design circuit boards but he wasn't a 'Nuclear Engineer' which is how he was selling himself to Nuclear Power. All this had created delays to the project and I had to go to Dungeness, cap in hand saying that I couldn't promise to compete the project on time.

The directors at the power station were very upset by this, as they had booked my time to commission the units a year in advance. I was not going to be ready in time due to Gordon's interference. They would have to now wait another year to book a slot of time for the new equipment to be installed, and so my contract with them was not going to be renewed. I was very sorry to have let them down – this had not ever happened to me in all the contracts I had completed in my working lifetime. I was extremely disappointed. Mr. G and I parted company and I closed that office down, operating out of my home again in Cold Higham, Northamptonshire instead. and my reputation with the nuclear power companies took a plummet drastically.

I continued to work from home from then onwards, doing the design work and then putting the individual work out to be put together, such as the making of the PCBs and the housing units. My son, John, was a great help in the business, putting it all together and then it was returned to me and shipped out to the customers.

In the meantime, John had set up his own small electronics business and was beginning to do well for himself.

36. Troonvale

The "Troonvale" business was now up and running. In the early 2000's I had a lot of work on. I had also been involved with Pilkington's Glass, making a control unit for them for the making of a new type of glass which was self-cleaning. (Pilkington discovered the ability to make this glass in 2001). Alongside this we were continuing to work on water pumps for local authorities.

In 2008 I had received a contract to supply a programmed system for making the punched and shaped steel floors for a new model of Van to be manufactured by the LDV Vans Company in Wolverhampton. The design, using PLC controllers, was very successful and we manufactured and installed it in their factory. As a consequence of so much time spent by me at this Company, I came to know the Directors and top engineers there. I also came to know the Manager of a top Arab Bank who was financing a large deal for the purchase of fleets of vans for two Middle Eastern companies. These companies were interested in LDV Vans as they were fitted with Peugeot engines. LDV were also trying to sell their vans to the British Government and I had heard that the Home Office was looking for replacement vans for the Police and Prison service.

Through another of my contacts, who was a leading Conservative in the London area, I managed to get a dining appointment with the then Home Secretary, Michael Howard, at the House of Commons. The Directors of LDV came to pick me up at my Factory in Daventry and we journeyed down to Westminster together. We were eventually shown up to Michael Howard's Office. My Banker friend was also there, and we had a good meeting discussing the matters relating to these sales and the future for the Van Company with some Government backing. The Home Secretary agreed to put forward his backing for the deal as this was the only British owned Commercial vehicle maker. A further deal was made regarding the Arab requirement, so the directors of the LDV Company were delighted. Following this long meeting we all went into another room, as it was after six o'clock and dinner was served. The dinner was excellent. I was sitting opposite Michael Howard so had a lengthy conversation with him about my business and my part in this business affair. I got on very well with him and he liked my jokes! I thought he was a very pleasant person, totally different to how he was portrayed by the press. He later became leader of the Conservative party.

I have always been sorry that I did not follow up with other meetings with him. Although these deals were worth many millions to those concerned, I did not personally gain, but I did get more business and respect from the people concerned.

Two years or so later LDV went into liquidation. I heard that the Directors came out of it well financially but 3,000 people lost their jobs. A pity.

Consultancy for EDF Energy 2013

In 2013 I received a telephone call from EDF Energy and, after a lengthy conversation, we arranged that they would come and visit me to talk about a proposition. I had been doing work for them over a 40-year period; it seemed I was being head-hunted! It transpired that they wanted me to be a consultant for them, a paid role where I would be required to attend a few meetings a year. They also wanted to purchase from me all my designs, drawings and intellectual property of everything I had made for all the nuclear power stations. Following negotiations, I received a large sum of money for the designs and equipment. It was good timing on their part as I was 89 and therefore would probably not be able to fulfil any large contracts for them in the future - for me too. The designs, test gear, sample units of the control modules, and other machinery were handed over to a company they contracted to make all their machinery. This company did a lot of work on nuclear submarines and had agreed to take on all this work for the power stations. John and I went to Bristol to visit the company and to discuss with the directors and engineers any issues that might arise from the designs and the machinery. I had a few phone calls from them regarding a few follow-up issues, and then I heard no more.

I remained a consultant with EDF for about a year. Job done!

Troonvale Scientific continued designing and manufacturing safety equipment and control systems for the next few years. We supplied many industries, including process production, aircraft, and transport. Our current range includes equipment available for additional safety when using the tail lift on heavy goods vehicles. Equipment could be designed and manufactured to individual specifications for any purpose.

In 2020 I decided to retire. Finally, as covid hit the world, it was difficult to market and negotiate the selling of a business where sales had stagnated, like so many businesses during this time. Business has now started to pick up in 2022, and there are a few interested parties keen to purchase.

I have always loved telling stories to children, be it my own, my grandchildren, or my great-grandchildren. In the last few years, I have written four children's books. They are all about the adventures of a character named 'Dusty', who is a teddy bear. 'Dusty's Troubles' was the first and 'Dusty and Spot Go Home' the second in the series of adventures that Dusty and his friends go on. As I became involved with The Shuttleworth Collection and heard about some of the ideas that they were planning for raising funds I offered to write one of Dusty's adventures around a visit to Shuttleworth and Dusty flying in one of the planes, which has now been printed. The last one written in the series was "Dusty & Old Harry', about Dusty visiting an old teddy bear, Harry, who was a mascot for a photo reconnaissance pilot.

Three of the four children's books written by George Pritchard

37. The BBMF at RAF Coningsby

It was on my 95th birthday that my daughter announced to me that they had a surprise for me as I was to be a special guest at the BBMF – Battle of Britain Memorial Flight, based at RAF Coningsby, Lincolnshire. Her nephew-in-law, Douglas, who was at the time in the RAF himself, helped to organise the visit with the staff at Coningsby. Many, many thanks to him.

RAF Coningsby is a Typhoon base and has a few large hangars where priceless artefacts of the RAF National Heritage are maintained in airworthy condition in order to commemorate those who have fallen in the service of this country, promote the modern-day Air Force, and inspire future generations. The flight operates six Spitfires, two Hurricanes, a Lancaster, a C47 Dakota, and two Chipmunk aircraft, and all of these are flown by regular RAF aircrew.

I have occasionally spotted these aircraft in the skies when they are flown to celebrate and commemorate public and military events. It was exciting to think that I could go and visit these beautiful aircraft in their hangars and hopefully meet some of the people who are tasked with their preservation and operation. So it was that on the morning of March 25th, 2019, we set out to Lincolnshire to see this amazing collection of aircraft, wondering if any of them were ones that I had personally flown in the 1940's.

We were greeted by Diane, the Administration Executive, who then proceeded to collect together a group of people to meet and escort us around the aircraft. The general public are generally cordoned off behind a barrier from where they can view, from a distance, the aircraft and the engineers and maintenance crew going about their business. I was most fortunate to be allowed to get 'up close and personal' with each and every aircraft, chatting to the maintenance crew and staff responsible for the smooth running and conservation of these precious aircraft. It was at this time I was to meet Commanding Officer Mark Discombe (Disco) and Squadron Leader, Executive Officer Mark Sugden (Sugsy) who were to become good friends and regular visitors from then onwards, along with Diane.

The aircraft we saw took me right back to that place in time during the 1940s when I was maintaining planes, then flying such planes firstly in the ADLS (Air Letter Delivery Service), where I got to deliver post, parts, and people to most of the aerodromes throughout the British Isles, and secondly flying in the PRU – Photo Reconnaissance Unit, where I was to take photographs across enemy territory for intelligence purposes according to my brief. These aircraft at Coningsby were amazing! They were so well maintained whilst trying to keep them as original as possible. I truly felt like royalty as all who greeted me wanted to ask questions about my life and experiences during WW2. As if touring the hangar with the WW2 planes was not enough, we then were introduced to a modern-day fighter pilot of one of the Typhoons, FLt. Tori Turner. She was a most interesting person to chat to and we discussed at length the trials and tribulations of the modern-day cockpit controls compared with the Mosquito used in the PRU during WW2. Not many of us get to view the workings of a modern-day fighter jet! But give me a Mozzi any day!

They had a blackboard at Coningsby signed by many veterans, including some very famous ones, like Johnny Johnson. I felt privileged to be asked to sign my name there.

George Pritchard

Writing on the veteran 'board of remembrance' at RAF Coningsby

That was a brilliant day and, a little hoarse from over-use of my voice in the many conversations we'd had, we headed home, vowing to visit again soon. This day had been the start of many new friendships and experiences to come in the not-too-distant future.

5th October 2019 – End of Season RAF Veterans Dinner at the Petwood Hotel

Our next trip to RAF Coningsby occurred a few months later following a special invitation to the annual End of Season Dinner, where war veterans like myself, and many RAF personnel linked to RAF Coningsby were invited. The dinner was to be held at the Petwood Hotel, home to the famous 'Dambusters' from 617 squadron, where the 'bouncing bomb' was designed by Barnes-Wallace and dam-busting raids were planned. We booked an overnight stay at the Petwood Hotel, where we met Emma Brierley, the lovely manager of the Petwood, who was charming and specifically sought me out for a chat, showing her deep interest in the historical aspects of Petwood's contribution to WW2.

Walking into the grand dining room, all beautifully laid out and decorated, we were stunned to find that our table for ten diners was named "Pritchard" table; indeed, all the other 12-15 tables were each named after a WW2 invited veteran, with many RAF personnel linked to the BBMF seated at each table, all keen to listen to the many anecdotes and tales told by the invited veterans. One of the most famous veterans was Johnny Johnson, the last surviving "Dambuster", aged 98 at the time. During the speeches, each of the veterans was presented with a fabulous book containing art linked to RAF aircraft. This book was published to honour the 75th anniversary of WW2 victory.

Following the dinner and speeches, we enjoyed many long conversations with both veterans and RAF personnel, finally retiring for the night at 1 am, very tired but very uplifted following the evening's events.

At breakfast, our conversations with other veterans continued until it was sadly time to head home following a lovely weekend. But not before we had walked around part of the extensive grounds of The Petwood Hotel and seen the actual prototype 'bouncing bomb' designed by Barnes-Wallace and used as a memorial to the man and group of men from 617 squadron.

Soon after this dinner, in the following March 2020, the whole country was to go into lockdown following a Covid19 pandemic, so the 2020 veteran dinner had to be cancelled.

It was a hard time for me (and for many people) because I was truly locked in, as much of my family was not allowed to visit, coming from afar. However, I do have two sons and some grandchildren who live nearby, plus many lovely neighbours and friends who were able to ensure that I had everything that I needed. During this time, I was often contacted by Disco, Sugs, and Diane, who even sent me packages of homemade cakes and jams to enjoy.

21st Sept 2020 – The Shuttleworth Collection, Bedfordshire

Our next encounter with Disco, Sugs, and Diane was when we were collected by them from my home and taken to the Shuttleworth Museum in Bedfordshire, to see an Avro Anson aircraft (configured as a passenger aircraft) plus the collection of other aircraft at the museum. They had laid on an outdoor lunch for us, outdoor because it was during the first summer of the covid outbreak when we were beginning to gain some freedom from lockdown, but most indoor restaurants were not open at that time. It was great to have time with these friends and to see the lovely aircraft again on this lovely sunny day, especially after being locked into my home for months on end.

24th August 2021 - Tea party at the BBMF, RAF Coningsby

An invitation came my way, inviting me and my daughter, Penny, to a tea party beneath the wings of the Lancaster Bomber at RAF Coningsby. Penny and I decided that it was a long way to drive in one day, so we would treat ourselves to a stay over at the Petwood Hotel, hopefully seeing the manager, Emma, again whilst there.

As it happened, the Lancaster had been flown to The IWM Duxford (Imperial War Museum, Duxford) for some repair work and could not get back in time for the party, due to the combination of the runway being short and the wind being in the wrong direction for a successful take-off. However, we were not disappointed as the party was surrounded by Spitfires and other WW2 planes within the hangar.

As we, the veterans, amassed in readiness for our afternoon tea, I found myself in conversation with two particular veterans who I found out I had actually known during my time in the RAF in the 1940s. I was astounded to meet them as I had believed that I was the only one left from the many squadrons I had been affiliated to. One of these people was a Mr Brown, from 217 squadron and the other was Malcolm Glede, Operational Training Unit. It was great to finally find some people I knew back then and to reminisce, sharing stories and anecdotes of our own histories.

The afternoon tea was fabulous, of course, with some very delicious home-made cakes and sandwiches prepared by a local catering company and some of the RAF personnel. 'Disco' gave a short speech and there was a special celebration iced cake to be shared. A truly wonderful afternoon.

16th October 2021 – End of season RAF veterans Dinner at The Petwood Hotel

We had received another invite for the End of Season Dinner and were crossing our fingers that it would not have to be cancelled for another lockdown due to the ongoing Covid19 pandemic. Fortunately, it went ahead. This time we were most honoured to be a part of the top table, again named "Pritchard", with the outgoing C.O. Mark Discombe and the incoming C.O. Mark Sugden and other RAF personnel. By now, we are getting to know a lot of the people at the dinner, both veterans and RAF persons alike. I had brought along a vintage champagne to give to Disco as a thank you and in recognition of his moving on to 29 squadron. We gathered together a small group of friends, including Sugs, Disco, Diane, Mandy, Penny, myself, and a few others and, with glasses at the ready, opened the bottle. Unfortunately, it was a very flat, musty liquid that escaped rather than the fresh, fruity bubbles that we expected. How disappointing! Still, another fresh bottle of champagne was purchased, and we could then toast the 'new beginnings' of our friends as they set forth in their new roles. We did get to have a chat with Johnny Johnson, who was soon to celebrate his 100th birthday on 25th November 2021. He was looking good and, though tied to a wheelchair, was able to thoroughly enjoy the evening, being a bit tipsy by the end of the evening. Bless him! Having enjoyed the love, laughter, and camaraderie, and after a stay overnight at the Petwood, we headed home again, having thoroughly enjoyed our weekend.

38. War Memorial to Photo Reconnaissance Unit

In December 2021, a Scottish friend of mine, Ian Menzies, was reading his local newspaper, whereupon he came across an article written by his local MP, Andrew Bowie, who was searching for any veterans from the Photo Reconnaissance Unit during the war. My friend then telephoned his MP, giving my name and contact details, which led to Andrew Bowie telephoning and informing me that he was just about to go into a debate in the House of Commons regarding the initiative to build a memorial to the PRU to commemorate those PRU officers killed, shot, or injured during the war who otherwise had no known grave. He then proceeded to relate my story and the story of other, less fortunate members of the PRU, to the MPs in the House during the debate. In the course of the debate, he was supported by my local MP for Northampton, Andrew Lewer. Andrew Bowie MP subsequently sent me a video link to the item in the debate and a written copy of the discussions.

They had begun to start the ball rolling on getting government approval for a special monument to be erected on behalf of all the pilots lost from the PRU during World War two. Apparently, the PRU saw the second greatest loss of life from any of the forces. This was mostly due to the fact that they were flying unarmed planes over enemy territory, and, if they were shot down and the pilot survived, they were caught and then killed on Hitler's orders, many being buried in unmarked graves. It is for these brave men from this little-known unit that the memorial is to be built, to commemorate their bravery and service to our country in the winning of the war.

On Wednesday 19th January 2022 the issue of the PRU monument was brought up as question 9 on 'Prime Minister's Question Time' in which my name was mentioned regarding my service in the Reconnaissance Unit (PRU) and the proposed monument to this Unit of brave men. The House supported the proposal.

It seems that there are still four of us left from the PRU.

Through the mechanism of the media, I was contacted by a gentleman named Anthony Hoskins, who is spearheading a charity called "SPITFIREAA810". Antony has located and recovered a WW2 Spitfire from a mountainside in Norway. It transpires that this was the plane of Sandy Gunn, a pilot shot down as he was undergoing photo reconnaissance duties. Although the pilot survived and was imprisoned, he escaped only to be shot and killed just a short distance from a safe border. The charity was set up to honour pilots such as Sandy Gunn, for whom, as yet, there is no recognition by way of a memorial, for the efforts and sacrifices they made during WW2. It is the purpose of this charity to seek recognition for these pilots, many of whom "never made it back for the last drink". 500 men would become casualties, and 144 of those lost have no known grave.

In 2019 the SPITFIREAA810 project began to gain momentum in requesting a national monument to the Photo

Reconnaissance Unit (PRU) be built by directly challenging the UK government to at last commemorate the role this unit played in securing an Allied victory. Things then slowed down for two years due to the Covid pandemic. Since this motion for a memorial was passed in 2022, it is hoped that a National Monument will be designed, built, and unveiled in 2024. I felt privileged to be invited to help with fundraising and supporting the Spitfire project for the charity.

The latest of four children's books to support the charity

I have completed a few tasks in order to start the ball rolling on raising funds. The first is a children's book, the third in my "Dusty" series called "Dusty and Old Harry", the proceeds from this one being dedicated to the SPITFIREAA810 charity. This story of Dusty the teddy bear tells of Dusty meeting another, much older bear called Harry, who was a mascot for his owner, a PRU pilot, and the stories this bear tells of his exciting missions with his owner.

A second task was to support the manufacture of thousands of beer mats that would have details of the SPITFIREAA810 charity in order that people may donate to the charity. It is hoped that breweries and public houses would support the charity by purchasing and using the beermats on their premises.

Beermat to support the charity

Thus began a series of articles in local and national news involving me, the MPs and the charity.

39. Article in the Northampton on-line news

World War Two pilot backs campaign to honour photographic unit

By Craig Lewis

BBC News Online (Northampton)

Published

5 December 2021

George Pritchard, second right, flew de Havilland Mosquitos on missions to capture vital images of enemy territory

During World War Two, the RAF's Photographic Reconnaissance Unit (PRU) produced more than 20 million images providing vital intelligence for the allied war effort. What were their missions like?

"When I look back, I think, 'why wasn't I scared out of my mind'?" says 97-year-old George Pritchard, a former PRU pilot. "But I wasn't scared at all."

By all accounts, he should have been scared.

Their planes were unarmed and stripped down, which, while helping them outpace the enemy, left them more vulnerable to attack.

The survival rate in the unit was proportionally the second lowest of any Allied aerial unit during the entire war.

George Pritchard

George Pritchard is one of a handful of Photographic Reconnaissance Unit pilots and crew still alive

In a recent House of Commons debate, MP Andrew Bowie said of the 1,287 men who flew in the PRU, 378 were killed.

Many were shot down over France, with 145 of those who died buried in unmarked graves.

The images made by the unit flying in a variety of aircraft, including Mosquitos and Spitfires, helped in the planning of major milestones of the war, including the D-Day landings and the Dambusters raid.

The unit also first spotted the German V1 and V2 missiles.

Mr Pritchard, believed to be one of just four PRU pilots still alive, has vivid memories of life in the unit.

"At three o'clock in the morning, we woke up with a cup of tea," he says.

"We would dive straight into our flying suits. It would be a miserable morning with thick mists and rain, and dense cloud.

"We'd head down the runway, taxi round the perimeter, and take off hell for leather completely blind.

"You could just about make out the runway between the lights."

Once the planes took off, Mr Pritchard says, they would reach 21,000ft (6,400m) before dropping to around 3,000ft (914m) to take pictures.

With one eye on fuel, the pilots would return to base after their mission was completed.

"When we landed, the cameras would be taken off and we'd have egg and bacon," Mr Pritchard says. "You'd get two hours sleep and report back for the next operation."

Mr Pritchard's desire to serve as a pilot was sparked one day in August 1940.

Then aged just 16, he had a job making ammunition boxes for the Acme Corrugated Cardboard Company, based on the edge of Croydon Airfield.

He remembers begging his then foreman for overtime but was told he was too young and instead had to head home.

Once there, he joined his mother and father in their garden, overlooking the airport.

Mr Pritchard remembers seeing planes overhead and what his father thought were parachutes coming out of them.

George Pritchard

George Pritchard, far left, decided to join the RAF after his workmates were killed in a German bombing raid

"A matter of seconds" later, he says, explosions rang out. The parachutes had been bombs.

"Hurricanes came and chased them off or shot them down as I understand it," he says.

"I rode back to work, and there was a policeman there. I said, 'I work at Acme', he said 'you used to, you don't any longer, it's no longer there'."

All of his friends and workmates had been killed in the bombing.

"I stood there as a 16-year-old, and I cried," he says.

"I made my mind up, absolutely definitely, that I was going to join the RAF and get my own back."

If his foreman had bent the rules and allowed him to continue working, he would have died along with everyone else.

By 17, Mr Pritchard had joined the RAF, and eventually, he became a pilot in the PRU.

Of his 22-strong joining cohort, only Mr Pritchard would survive the war. Those lost included his best friend.

The sacrifices of those who served in the PRU are now the subject of a campaign to build a monument in their memory.

It is spearheaded by the Spitfire AA810 Project, which is currently also rebuilding the Spitfire of PRU pilot Sandy Gunn, who was killed after being shot down over Norway.

MP for Aberdeenshire Mr Bowie received cross-party support when he brought the idea to Parliament, including from Northampton South MP Andrew Lewer.

These days Mr Pritchard lives in Duston, Northampton, making Mr Lewer his constituency MP.

The Conservative politician said the "lively and active" Mr Pritchard is "living tribute to the outstanding work he and his fellow PRU personnel undertook in defence of our freedoms".

Mr Pritchard, however, says his proudest moments came after the war when making medical electronics.

His achievements in a life less ordinary include working on the first cardiac pacemaker and designing control panels for nuclear power stations.

In more recent years he has written children's books, illustrated by his daughter, Vicki. The proceeds go to Great Ormond Street Hospital.

As for his wartime efforts, he says PRU pilots constantly lived in the shadow of death.

"You were young, and you thought it would happen to everyone else but not you," he says.

"You have to have that, otherwise, you would run away.

"I didn't think I was going to live. I thought I would catch it sooner or later. You would have guys there one morning, and then you didn't.

"You got the feeling if your number is up, you will get it either that day or at some time, so why worry in the meanwhile."

The war left harsh memories though.

Mr Pritchard remembers one occasion when he was gripped with fear while walking through Notting Hill Gate underground station.

"I ran up 300 steps and collapsed on the pavement," he says. "I went to the doctor, and he said it was a build-up of stress over time.

"A vast number of pilots were murdered on the orders of Hitler. They were either hanged or shot.

"Nobody remembers them, how could they? With a monument with their names on, they'd always be remembered.

"It's a very good thing to do in remembrance of people who gave their lives up. I was just one of the lucky ones."

40. Article in the Daily Express – 9th December 2021

Calls for a monument to unknown World War 2 pilots who 'turned the tide of war'

THE DOWNING of a Spitfire aircraft over Norway during World War 2 led to the capture of one of Britain's most significant prison camp escapees.

Scot Alastair "Sandy" Gunn was piloting the AA810 when it was shot down on a mission to photograph the German battleship, Tirpitz, in March 1942. Its remains were left strewn across the side of a mountain - and Fl Lt Gunn was taken to Stalag Luft III, where he played a key role in The Great Escape.

The breakout of 76 men from the POW camp in Poland is the storyline of the iconic 1963 blockbuster of the same name, featuring Steve McQueen.

Gunn, from Auchterarder in Perthshire, would go on to tunnel his way out of the camp - only to be captured and murdered by the Gestapo.

And he has now inspired another campaign - after remnants of the Spitfire were discovered on the Norwegian mountainside in 2018.

The plane's discovery led to an outpouring of dozens of unknown tales of World War 2 bravery, honouring his involvement in the Photo Reconnaissance Unit (PRU).

Tony Hoskins, who discovered AA810, said: "The stories of the men who flew these planes are absolutely incredible."

The remains of Sandy's Spitfire laid out in Surnadal town hall, Norway (Image: Tony Hoskins)

The remains of Sandy's Spitfire laid out in Surnadal town hall, Norway (Image: Tony Hoskins)

Reports of the discovery led to families of veterans coming forward to tell more stories of unknown heroism.

This triggered a campaign for national recognition for members of the Photo Reconnaissance Unit (PRU) - as part of Project AA810 - which raises awareness of the unit through school talks.

George Pritchard, 97, is one of four known surviving veterans.

He joined the RAF in April 1941, completing about 20 operational photo reconnaissance flights during the war.

He signed up after the Luftwaffe bombed RAF Croydon, where he worked in a cardboard factory as a boy.

It was a lucky escape for the then 16-year-old - who watched in horror from his parents' back garden as bombs rained down.

On his way to the site afterwards, fearing for his colleagues, he was stopped by a policeman and told: "You have no more friends. There are none left."

After training, Mr Pritchard flew "Wooden Wonder" Mosquitoes from RAF Wyton over France and Germany, searching for U-Boat activity and carrying out D-Day reconnaissance.

Taking off in the early morning, he recalled rising to 20,000 feet before descending to 3,000 feet, maintaining a steady speed, so the cameras captured the target, then heading home.

Fraught with danger, a German Focke-Wulf FW 190 appeared out of the blue on one mission.

Mr Pritchard said: "I saw it just in the nick of time. I shot off before he got the chance to fire at me."

Asked if he feared for his life, he said: "When you're 20 years old, you don't look at it that way.

"We had a fatalistic attitude. I don't know whether I was frightened or not. We didn't think of ourselves as heroes.

"I don't consider myself to be particularly brave. I just did what I was told."

Andrew Bowie, who represents West Aberdeenshire and Kincardine, is spearheading efforts in Parliament to secure Government support for the monument.

In a Westminster Hall debate in November, Mr. Bowie and Northampton South MP Andrew Lewer hailed the campaign.

Mr Bowie, who served with the Royal Navy, told Express.co.uk: "It is not an understatement to say these guys turned the tide of the war. They were incredibly brave.

"There are three or four [PRU veterans] left. It is surely the right thing to do while these men are still with us. Let's get it done."

Mr Hoskins said: "It is recognition of the sacrifice and efforts made by a group of people that has gone totally unnoticed for 80 years.

"These guys helped win the war. They should be recognised. They did this with no way of defending or protecting themselves, and that takes balls."

He added just 29 percent of those who flew survived, with the bodies of many casualties missing even today.

Campaigners hope the monument will get the go-ahead and for it to be positioned in a prominent location linked to the PRU's history.

Photo reconnaissance proved useful in World War 1 too - but interest in developing it waned.

Prior to the outbreak of World War 2, a group of people, including James Bond author Ian Fleming, flew clandestine operations over countries including Germany, France, and Belgium to photograph what was happening.

Mr Hoskins said: "This unit was mightily valuable. Before the British Expeditionary Force went to France, we could see what [armaments] Germany was amassing."

After Britain declared war, the group was formalised. By 1940, the No. 1 Photographic Reconnaissance Unit was under RAF control and based at RAF Benson in Oxfordshire.

Pilots flew aircraft including Supermarine Spitfires and de Havilland Mosquitos, modified to reach higher altitudes and to travel further.

But with a majority of the unit's planes unarmed to make them lighter and faster, those inside were vulnerable.

Almost 26 million photos were taken during the war with the majority now kept at the National Collection of Aerial Photography in Edinburgh.

The unit's advantage was the speed with which information could be passed to the Government and military top brass.

A plane could fly over enemy territory, take up to 1,500 photos and return to base.

Interpreters scoured the images before passing any intelligence on within hours of the aircraft landing.

One air photographic interpreter tasked with studying prints was screen legend Dirk Bogarde, who selected ground targets for RAF Bomber Command.

Mr Hoskins said: “Without [photo reconnaissance], we would really have struggled.”

The method was used in the D-Day landings, which led to the discovery of V1 rocket launch sites and the bombing of V2 factories.

A total of 1,300 men were in the unit - which in 1942 was split into five squadrons - alongside 700 women, including Winston Churchill’s daughter Sarah.

Mr Pritchard, from Duston, Northampton, left the RAF in 1947 and went on to become an engineer, helping to design the internal pacemaker.

On what a monument would mean to him, the veteran said: “Like all monuments, it is something for people later on to realise what went on and what those guys did. This warrants a memorial to those poor fellas who are buried somewhere in Europe.”

41. Report in the Chronicle and Echo, 2022

By Max Pearson

MP Andrew Lewer campaigns for London memorial to RAF reconnaissance unit and its 98-year-old Northampton survivor

The memorial is hoped to be built in London to memorialise the hundreds who died in the unit's service

Image – Andrew Lewer/Chronicle & Echo

A Northampton-based war veteran's campaign to memorialise a lesser-known RAF unit from the Second World War has been backed by Andrew Lewer, the MP for Northampton South.

The National PRU Monument campaign, spearheaded in 2019 by the Spitfire AA810 project, hopes to build the memorial in honour of the Photo Reconnaissance Unit (PRU), who flew unarmed 'Mosquito' aircraft over enemy territory to feed vital intelligence back to Allied command.

The unit would capture more than 20 million images of enemy operations during the war, all while flying completely unarmed. Sadly, more than 500 of those servicemen became casualties, with 144 lost with no known grave.

George Pritchard, who has lived in Northampton for many years now, joined the RAF at just 17 and is one of the only surviving veterans of the PRU. He said that he was glad of the support offered by not one, but two MPs.

The now 98-year-old veteran said: "I have a list of 3,148 men that were in it, like me, up to 1945. Now I'm one of only four men left.

"I think it's great to have Andrew on board. We get on famously. To have both Andrew Lewer and Andrew Bowie helping to get this made is a great help."

MP Andrew Lewer gave his support to the campaign after being introduced to George by Conservative MP for West Aberdeenshire and Kincardine, Andrew Bowie, who had picked up the campaign once his predecessor had lost his seat.

The MP said he respected the tough work and sacrifice of the servicemen and that he wanted them to be suitably remembered for it.

Mr Lewer said: "There are only four living airmen from the PRU. I am proud to say that my Northampton South constituent George, now entering his 99th year, is one of them.

“My support for this memorial draws back to the conversations I had with George about his comrades who lost their lives in service to their country in a time of war, undertaking extraordinary and dangerous missions in extraordinary and dangerous times.

"Quite a few of those who lost their lives were never buried. It is fitting that we remember them by name. George is passionate about having their names remembered, and it is the least I can do to help him realise this goal.

"This is why I am campaigning with George for a national memorial, to set in stone the names of those brave airmen who, to paraphrase John Maxwell Edmonds, gave their today for our tomorrow in a unit that helped change the course of the war."

Anyone who is interested in the campaign can visit the SpitfireAA810 website.

42. ....And Finally

Sitting here with not quite so much to do now, I can get on and finish the task of completing this autobiography of my life's adventures.

These are what I feel are the most important thoughts to finish on.....

Now that I have reached my 99th year, I look back at my past history quite often and realise that through working and trying as hard as I could, I did achieve the very peak of my career, but along the way, there were learning opportunities by the dozen and quite a few lucky breaks too.

I did get to the top of my tree in my profession, becoming an Electrical Engineer Consultant; you can't get much better than that in my trade, being head-hunted and consulting with a Nuclear Power Group. I came with a vast plethora of experiences, from making electrical fires, to making machines to create turbine blades from crystals, making one of the first pacemakers and heart-lung machines to being head-hunted by EDF energy as a nuclear power consultant. There are probably not many people who have the range of experiences that I have accrued throughout my lifetime. And I'm still working on the list!

I am still working, running my own business, and probably will till my dying day. I am currently working on various articles to sell in large quantities to raise funds for the PRU Memorial Project. I have also written four children's books around a teddy bear character called Dusty. The last of these story books incorporates a theme where Dusty is with a pilot in the Photo Reconnaissance Unit, and these will be sold in order to raise further funds for the PRU memorial.

This whole career had started with a 14-year-old working in an electrical shop!

Some of my happiest moments in life were all down to having a wonderful wife and family. We had some lovely, happy times away on holiday in Cornwall, chasing into the sea and running up and down on the sandy beaches. It was great having children, and we were lucky enough to have had four! Some of the happiest moments in my memories were those from our Sunday mornings, where the children would all wake up, some earlier than others, and they would all pile onto our bed where we would drink tea, dunk biscuits, and tell stories and chat whilst the younger ones would romp about on the bed. Even the cat joined in! It was a lovely way to spend an hour or two (sometimes three) on a Sunday morning, and thinking about it always brings back a big smile. It seems that it has become quite a tradition that some of our children, and grandchildren, have continued. You couldn't get any happier than that. Simple pleasures!

There are two events (apart from family events) that stand out in my life that I am most proud of. The first and most important was my role in the development of the pacemaker in helping to save so many lives, my own included. The second is that moment standing on the parade ground with the other 20 or so RAF trainees receiving our 'wings'; we had finally made it.

Although the metal 'gold' was elusive in great quantity, my real 'gold' I found in my beautiful wife Florence, with her copper gold tresses down to her waist, when she was young. She was the real 'gold' in my life, and I now know how extremely lucky I was to have found such a truly great lady in my life. We went through such tremendous and tremulous times together. She was faultless, never told a lie in her life, was always right in her judgements, and had a wonderful nature. The best wife and mother ever possible.

After the 74 wonderful years we spent together, I still suffer the pain of missing her every single day of the last decade since she passed, but I have very many fond memories of our time together to hold on to.

What a life!

Printed in Great Britain
by Amazon

12080028R00205